THE LESBIAN BAR *Chronicles*

THE LESBIAN BAR *Chronicles*

THE LIVING HISTORY AND HOPEFUL FUTURE OF AMERICA'S DYKE DIVES AND SAPPHIC SPACES

RACHEL KARP

COCREATOR OF *Cruising*

Interviews and Reporting by Sarah Gabrielli

HOST AND COCREATOR OF *Cruising*

BEACON PRESS, BOSTON

BEACON PRESS
24 Farnsworth Street
Boston, Massachusetts
www.beacon.org

Beacon Press books
are published under the auspices of
the Unitarian Universalist Association of Congregations.

Printed in the United States of America

29 28 27 26 8 7 6 5 4 3 2

This book is printed on acid-free paper that meets the uncoated paper
ANSI/NISO specifications for permanence as revised in 1992.

Text design and composition by Kim Arney

The names of some people mentioned in this book
have been changed to protect their privacy.

*Library of Congress Cataloguing-in-Publication
Data is available for this title.*
Hardcover ISBN: 978-0-8070-2344-0
E-book ISBN: 978-0-8070-2345-7
Audiobook: 978-0-8070-2336-5

The authorized representative in the EU for product safety and
compliance is Easy Access System Europe 16879218, Mustamäe tee 50,
10621 Tallinn, Estonia: https://beacon.org/eu-contact.

For Eve Adams, Nancy Valverde, Alice Brady,
Charlene Schneider, Leslie Martinez,
Mona Nystrom-Hood, Rikki Streicher,
Shelley Brothers, Pat Ramseyer, Vicky Hester,
and Dianté Spring.

You made space for us.

And for everyone who has shared their stories,
without whom this book would not exist.

CONTENTS

PREFACE

On New Year's Eve heading into 2021, I turned to my friend, Sarah, and my then girlfriend—now wife—Jen, and said: "Want to road-trip to every lesbian bar in the country?" I wasn't chasing a spot in *The Guinness Book of World Records* for longest bar crawl ever. It was stories that I was after. I wanted to uncover the histories of these spaces, which have offered sanctuary when safety for the queer community was otherwise elusive. I wanted to collect the stories of the people who run these bars and the people who've come to call them home.

I knew how much our own local New York lesbian bars meant to the three of us: the ways our stories had unfolded within them, and the queer history that was practically etched into their walls. I had a theory that the rest of the country's lesbian bars would be the same.

Sarah, Jen, and I had been dreaming of creating a podcast together, and this felt like the idea we'd been waiting for. We would call it *Cruising*. Armed with a microphone and a recorder, we would sit down with bar owners, staff members, and regulars in queer bars around the country, inviting them to talk about their first loves, secrets, sacrifices, losses, and dreams.

Lesbian bars had suddenly become a hot topic around this time. Mainstream media had grown interested in the idea that they were disappearing. "Where Did All the Lesbian Bars Go?" read one May 2020 *New York Times* headline.[1] "21 lesbian bars remain in America," stated a PBS News feature the following summer.[2] It was a sharp decline from the approximately 200 lesbian bars that existed in the 1980s. Closures were attributed to a constellation of factors: gentrification, the rise of dating apps, and an increased social acceptance of LGBTQ+ folks, which diminished the need for explicitly queer spaces. Still, gay male-centric bars continued to flourish, leading many to point to the gendered wealth gap and to gendered stereotypes—that women don't drink as much, or that women are more likely to enter monogamous relationships and stop going out. While many mourned the shuttering of these gathering places, we looked to an unlikely upside: it seemed physically possible to drive to all the remaining lesbian bars in a reasonable amount of time.

The three of us would make the perfect team. Jen, who is sixteen years my senior, started exploring New York City's lesbian bars in 1998 at the age of eighteen. As a first-year at Staten Island's Wagner College, she rode the ferry to Manhattan, accompanied by more than enough upperclassmen for her to slip into the bars along with them and avoid being carded. Jen was accustomed to bars, having spent much of her childhood trailing family members to long-standing Rhode Island establishments. But these places had always been straight. In New York, she was astonished to find a different kind of bar scene: vibrant and unapologetically queer, this world would hold her throughout her two-plus decades in the city. Jen also loves to drive—a helpful asset for a cross-country road trip. Plus, she's the type of lesbian who can change a flat tire, walk into any room and make friends, and keep everyone around her fed and caffeinated.

As for Sarah, I've known her since middle school. We grew up in the same Boston suburb in the 2000s and 2010s. Being gay was not going to get you beat up or kicked out of school, but it felt severely uncool. Back then, same-sex marriage had yet to be legalized on the federal level. In our public high school social studies class, it was somehow deemed appropriate for the teacher to poll students on whether we thought gay people should be allowed to wed. Most raised their hands to vote yes, but some—including many of the "popular kids" whose opinions shaped the social hierarchy of the school—voted no. Sarah and I came out to each other before we told anyone else.

We drifted apart in college but reconnected over two-dollar margaritas at the Manhattan lesbian bar Cubbyhole during a summer that we both happened to be working internships in the city. Sarah is the question asker, the reporter, and the audio technician of our group. She has no qualms about walking into a bar, asking a stranger for an interview, and then pulling their entire life story out of them. The stories you'll read in this book are largely thanks to Sarah.

As for me, I am the dreamer, the planner, and the listener. I was constantly revising our route to incorporate the new spaces I kept discovering online that met our criteria: bars run by queer women or nonbinary folks that intentionally centered the queer women and nonbinary community. While Jen drove, I was in the passenger seat, figuring out where we would be sleeping each night. I booked motels, Airbnbs, and—much to everyone's chagrin—the occasional campsite. While Sarah asked questions, I sat beside her, quietly listening, absorbing story after story.

At first, we thought that in collecting these stories, we might find answers to the question everyone seemed to be asking: Why were lesbian bars disappearing? Yet, we didn't find lesbian bars that were dying. Instead, we found them thriving. Through the stories we uncovered, we began to understand it wasn't a *why* that we were after, but a *how*: How do these spaces survive? How are they built? How do they support us? How do we support them? How are they intertwined with our community, our history, our fight for liberation, and our chosen families?

After twenty bars and thirty days on the road, we returned to Brooklyn on October 13, 2021, thinking that we'd answered our questions and concluded our journey. What we didn't know was that the country was on the cusp of a lesbian bar resurgence. With LGBTQ+ rights under attack across the country and transphobia rearing its ugly head, the need for a new kind of lesbian bar—one that centers radical inclusion and collective resistance—has become increasingly urgent. As people step up to fill that need, new bars have continued to open, calling us back to the road. At the same time, a nationwide renewed interest in lesbian culture has sent us on a deep dive into historic spaces that no longer exist but have left their mark.

As our podcast began showing up in queer studies classes, and as listeners, researchers, and followers started requesting transcripts and asking about a book, we set our sights on synthesizing the stories we've gathered over the years into physical pages they could turn to.

This book follows a path much like our 2021 road trip, though with a bit of time travel, moving counterclockwise around the country. Each region reveals something new about what defines a lesbian bar and what helps it endure. We begin in 1925 New York City, with what some consider the first lesbian bar. From there, we visit today's bars of the Northeast: neighborhood institutions that raised us, and community-driven spaces built to survive. In the Midwest, we explore the central rule of the modern lesbian bar: be nice or leave. Then we head west, following in the footsteps of so many queers before us, who made the same pilgrimage in pursuit of freedom and community. Finally, we return home through the South, where we witness how lesbian bars—and the communities around them—offer safety and sanctuary in the face of bigotry and discrimination.

So many queer stories are lost. Or rather, they were never told in the first place. For centuries, queerness was often a secret taken to the grave. This is why so much of queer history is found not in books, but in bars. These pages are an attempt to capture as many of our stories as possible—an unofficial history of lesbian life in America.

Part One

THE NORTHEAST

LESBIAN BARS ARE NEIGHBORHOOD BARS

Chapter One

EVE'S HANGOUT

THE FIRST LESBIAN BAR?

NEW YORK, NY

In 1999, Nina Alvarez spotted an unusual book on the mantle of an old fireplace in the lobby of her Albany apartment building, where a small free library had emerged. A self-identified bisexual bibliophile, Nina was drawn to the book for two reasons. One, it looked handmade; it was a plain hardcover green book with an off-white cloth label pasted on the front cover.[1] And two, the book was titled *Lesbian Love* by Evelyn Adams.[2]

Inside *Lesbian Love*, Nina discovered erotic illustrations of women alongside seemingly fictitious short stories about lesbian relationships, all carefully typeset and professionally printed. Nina and her friends puzzled over the book. The hairstyles and outfits of the women in the pictures appeared to be straight out of the 1920s, and the book itself seemed to be from the early twentieth century. But the stories felt strikingly modern. One mentions a gay dinner party. Another describes two women who "talk of getting married to each other," and who "really believe they can have a baby." A third introduces Jimmie, a young person who "felt far more comfortable in boyish clothes."[3]

Nina kept the book tucked away on a shelf. More than a decade later, she began sorting through her book collection, looking up the resale values of some of the older titles. "I looked up *Lesbian Love* by Evelyn Adams and I couldn't find anything about it. [. . .] It wasn't available for sale anywhere. It certainly was not on Amazon," she recalls during our interview.

Finally, she came across a blog post on an early twentieth-century woman by the name of Eve Adams. It mentioned the lesbian tearoom that she'd run in Manhattan's Greenwich Village in 1925—as well as her book, *Lesbian Love*, which she'd published that same year. "My jaw started to drop," Nina tells us. "I had never even thought to look it up before. I'd been carrying it around since 1999."

Nina took the book to a local antiquarian fair to consult an expert on its value. After examining it and doing some research, he declined to offer a valuation. "It's sort of priceless," he told Nina. Up until this point, *Lesbian Love* had all but vanished from existence. Yale's Sterling Library had once held a single copy, but in 2005 it had mysteriously gone missing.[4] Nina's was now the only known copy.

"That began my real journey of learning about Eve," Nina says. She finally grasped the rarity of the book, but it would take time before she came to understand the importance of it: the role it had played in Eve's life, and the deadly consequences it would have for her, sparking her deportation to Europe at precisely the worst time to be a queer Jewish woman there.

Eve's story is one of a gender-nonconforming lesbian anarchist immigrant. It's one that historians, librarians, playwrights, and Eve's surviving relatives have pieced together over the past few decades. Each of them has had their own unique journey to Eve. There's Nina, of course, who found Eve on a bookshelf in Albany. There's the playwright Barbara Kahn, who discovered Eve while scouring the internet in the early 2000s for stories of—as she puts it—"the forgotten women." There's historian Jonathan Ned Katz, who came across Eve's name in a *New York Times* article and, shocked that he had never heard of her, went on to write her only biography.

I first stumbled upon Eve while trying to answer a seemingly simple question: Where was America's first lesbian bar? There's a lot of debate as to which establishment might claim this title, and some do cite Eve's tearoom—or Eve's Hangout, as it was called. But the question is more complicated than it seems. How are we defining a lesbian bar? How are we defining a lesbian, for that matter? Well, the common definition of a lesbian is a woman who is attracted to other women—and yes, this includes trans women, seeing as trans women are women. But I've also met nonbinary lesbians, as well as trans men who still identify with the lesbian community, and I'm certainly not in the business of policing who can and cannot be a lesbian. If you say you're a lesbian—and not in the joking way that cis men sometimes do—then in my eyes, you're a lesbian. For the purposes of this book, then, let's say a lesbian bar is a) a bar that is b) owned or operated by lesbians, LGBTQ+ women, or nonbinary folks, and c) intentionally welcomes lesbians, LGBTQ+ women, and nonbinary folks.

Eve Adams identified as a lesbian. Her book, *Lesbian Love*, clearly declares as much. As Jonathan Ned Katz asserts: "To name the book *Lesbian Love*, to say those words publicly, she was coming out. [. . .] 'There is such a thing as lesbian love,' she was saying."

Eve describes queer women's spaces multiple times throughout her book, and they often resemble her own tearoom. In one short story, she writes of two women, Sammie and Dottie, who "rented a basement" in "a famous neighborhood of the metropolis" and opened a spot called the "Flowery Tea Pot."[5] Sammie is masculine while Dottie is feminine, and Eve writes that the pair are often referred to as husband and wife. Their fictitious tearoom sounds a lot like the real Eve's Hangout, which also operated in a basement at 129 MacDougal Street, just south of Washington Square Park in Greenwich Village.[6] Eve goes on to describe the Flowery Tea Pot as "a very popular and interesting rendezvous for loving couples of the same sex, mostly the fair sex . . . where over a cup of tea lovers meet and wistfully look into each other's eyes."[7]

Sammie attracts attention for the way she dresses, with strangers doubting she is a woman—she often wears a "tightly fitting tailored suit, and the inevitable attached collar and tie, which means so much in the life of a Lesbian,"[8] Eve writes. In the few existing photos of Eve, she too sports collared shirts, ties, suit jackets, and pants. She has a short crop of curly hair and stands formidably at five feet fall. Eve's very presence in her tearoom signaled a safe environment for other lesbians.

Yet, both Jonathan Ned Katz and Barbara Kahn, experts on Eve's life story, are quick to emphasize that Eve's Hangout was by no means exclusively for women. "She welcomed all kinds of people," Jonathan stresses.

"It was a very welcoming place for lesbians. And lesbians knew that, and they congregated there," Barbara says, "but [Eve] also was very much a supporter of the arts, particularly of local Greenwich Village writers at the beginnings of their careers. And she would have salon evenings that would target a particular poet who could present his or her work for that evening."

Eve's Hangout clearly meets two of the criteria we've set for lesbian bars; Eve was an LGBTQ+ woman who ran a space that welcomed LGBTQ+ women and people of all kinds. But was Eve's Hangout a bar?

This question is made complicated by the fact that the tearoom operated during Prohibition. From 1920 to 1933, the sale of alcohol was illegal in the United States. Forget lesbian bars—there were no public bars at all during those thirteen years. There were, however, plenty of underground speakeasies. Jonathan points out that "tearoom" was often "a euphemism for a place [where] liquor was served."

Barbara, though, is doubtful that Eve was secretly slinging drinks. "I went to the municipal archives, and I pulled up [Eve's] arrest records," she says. "They threw everything at her that they could, but nowhere was it mentioned during this time of Prohibition that she was charged with running a speakeasy. [Or] that she was arrested for selling alcohol. [. . .] And my feeling was if they had found a drop there in this public facility, they would've included that."

Whether or not we can call Eve's Hangout a true bar remains up for debate. In my opinion, however, it is the first documented lesbian bar. Whatever folks were drinking, the energy of the space matched the ethos of contemporary lesbian bars. It was a place that welcomed everyone so long as they were respectful and tolerant. It was a safe haven for lesbians, queer women, and all sorts of people who didn't fit the norms and binaries of sexuality and gender. And, like at today's lesbian bars, even if alcohol was served, it wasn't the main event. Eve helped build a model for queer and lesbian bars that still endures today.

Eve's own story begins in Poland, in 1891, where she was born Chawa Zloczewer.[9] At twenty years old, she immigrated alone to New York City in June of 1912.[10] We don't know why she chose to come to the US when she did, but one can imagine she was chasing some semblance of the "American Dream": freedom and economic opportunity.

In New York, Eve quickly fell in with the bohemians and radical free thinkers of Greenwich Village. She began working for *Mother Earth*, an anarchist journal[11] founded by Emma Goldman in 1906.[12] At the time of Eve's arrival, the journal was being edited by Alexander Berkman, Goldman's fellow anarchist, longtime friend, and sometimes lover.[13] *Mother Earth* published articles critiquing capitalism, government, military, war, and policing. Its pages advocated for workers' rights and sex education, and it discussed the efficacy of unions, protest, and direct action.[14] Through her work distributing and supporting *Mother Earth*, Eve met her lifelong friend, Ben Reitman, the publication's business manager and a radical doctor and staunch reproductive rights advocate. The publication disbanded in 1917 following the arrests of Emma Goldman and Alexander Berkman, who were charged with anti-war and anti-draft activity. After serving two years in prison, they were deported to Soviet Russia in 1919.[15]

Eve, however, remained dedicated to their causes. By 1919, she was spending most of her time on the road selling radical leftist publications and going by her chosen name, Eve Adams.[16] This job is how she initially attracted the attention of the Bureau of Investigation—the predecessor agency to the FBI. For years, agents kept tabs on Eve, following her from Connecticut and Los Angeles to San Francisco and St. Louis. They labeled her an "agitator,"[17] but they couldn't seem to find enough evidence to actually charge her with anything. Until she wrote *Lesbian Love.*

When she returned to New York City in early 1925, Eve opened her tearoom and had 150 copies of *Lesbian Love* printed. Perhaps knowing the danger such a book could put her in, she declared her intent to distribute copies only to friends. The phrase "for private circulation" is printed in the book's front matter.[18]

For many months, Eve avoided trouble, sharing her book with trusted friends and running her tearoom. Patrons would descend the stairs from street level and step into a room with brick walls, a fireplace, and low ceilings, giving it a cozy and intimate feel. Its small, high windows offered only glimpses of the outside world—feet passing by on the sidewalk. On a typical evening, you would have found gender benders and queer folks like Eve mingling with bohemians, intellectuals, and theatergoers. They gathered for art showings or poetry readings—which, depending on the crowd, could get raucous.

As the charismatic proprietress of this refuge, Eve perhaps felt untouchable. In the spring of 1925, likely missing home, she began making plans to visit Poland—not knowing the profound consequences this trip would have. Two years prior, Eve had signed a declaration of intent to become a US citizen, but she didn't yet have official citizenship.[19] Since this was before the time of green cards or permanent resident statuses, Eve needed a permit to be guaranteed reentry to the US. The following fall, after her permit application was approved, she set off to visit family. She returned to New York in December.[20]

About six months later, a young woman started frequenting Eve's Hangout. She befriended Eve, and they began to spend more time together:

dinner, dancing, a Broadway show. Eve entrusted her with a copy of *Lesbian Love*. Then, in June of 1926, the New York City police burst into Eve's Hangout. It's a scene that would become sadly familiar in gay and lesbian bars for decades to come: authorities shattering the safety of a queer space and finding reasons to make arrests. As for Eve's new companion? She was the arresting officer,[21] Margaret Leanord, sent by the NYPD to entrap her.

Eve was charged with publishing an obscene book under New York Penal Law section 1141,[22] which criminalized the sale of or intent to sell an "obscene, lewd, lascivious, filthy, indecent, sadistic, masochistic or disgusting book."[23] While some such obscenity laws are still on the books at both the federal and state levels today, the accepted definition of *obscenity* has shifted. In Eve's day, the state considered homosexual content to be obscene. Eve also faced a disorderly conduct charge, which stemmed from Margaret's allegation that Eve had attempted to have sex with her—a claim that Eve would firmly deny in court.[24]

That summer, Eve stood trial for both charges. The press quickly picked up the story, and rumors about Eve swirled. Robert Edwards, a local Greenwich Village figure and editor of a publication called *The Quill*, published a nasty satirical listing for Eve's Hangout: "Where ladies prefer each other. Not very healthy for she adolescents, nor comfortable for he-men."[25] Robert had a history of clashing with Eve, and in general had a distaste for radicals, queer people, and women—particularly women who didn't want to sleep with him. A few years prior, he had published a poem in *The Quill* titled "I Hate 'Em." Each of its five stanzas began with the line "I hate women."[26]

Variety covered the story of Eve's arrest in a series of increasingly wild articles. One called attention to Eve's "mannish clothes" and labeled her a "man-hater."[27] Another alleged that Eve was being financed by a "ring of wealthy women cultists" as a "procuress"[28]—a pimp.

Eve was found guilty of both the obscenity and disorderly conduct charges. For the obscenity charge, she was given the maximum sentence of one year in prison. It is likely no coincidence that this was also the minimum amount of jail time required for her to be deported—something the court recommended that the Office of Immigration pursue.[29]

Eve's recent trip back to Poland was awfully convenient for the immigration prosecutors. According to the Immigration Act of 1917, an alien could be deported if they had been sentenced to one or more years in prison for a crime of "moral turpitude" committed within five years of entering the

US.[30] Jonathan Ned Katz, in his biography of Eve, wonders: "Did immigration officials issue Eve a permit to leave so that they could prosecute her on her return?" He points to evidence that suggests officials had initially intended to deny her the permit but then changed their minds.[31]

Eve was brought back into court for a series of deportation hearings. Unlike with her previous criminal trials, complete transcripts of these hearings exist.[32] They reveal Eve's painstaking defense of her identity, her work, and her right to remain in the US.

As she sat in a room filled with powerful men who had already made up their minds, Eve calmly fielded ridiculous questions from the prosecution, deftly denying and deflecting.

"Had you been in the habit of picking up young girls on the street or elsewhere, taking them to your room and having intimate or immoral relations with them?"

"No, I don't know what you are talking about, sir," Eve replied.

"Did anybody ever accuse you of practicing Sapphism?"

"What is that?" Eve asked, though she knew perfectly well what Sapphism was, having included an excerpt of Swinburne's poem "Sapphics" at the start of her book.[33]

"Were you ever afflicted with a venereal disease?"

"No," Eve replied.

"Are you a drug addict?"

"No, I don't even drink liquor," she answered.

When it came time to speak about her so-called "obscene" book, she said:

"I admit having written a book entitled *Lesbian Love*, based on true facts and living characters of today. [. . .] There is not one word in the whole book that is vulgar."[34]

Throughout the hearings, Eve was steadfast in her desire to remain in the US. When asked if she had anything further to say about why she should not be deported, Eve declared: "I love this country with my whole heart and soul. [. . .] I want to become a citizen."[35]

In December of 1927, Eve was deported back to Poland.[36] Letters from her time there detail the bitter cold, the lack of economic opportunity, and the isolation and loneliness she felt.[37] In 1930, Eve made her way to Paris, where she earned a living selling "dirty books" to American tourists. In 1933, as Hitler and the Nazi party rose to power in Germany, Eve met Hella Olstein, a cabaret singer with whom she would spend the final decade of her life. "My dearest friend, most beloved girl, a German refugee, a marvelous artist and singer and the most beautiful thing to look at," Eve wrote of her new companion in a 1934 letter to Ben Reitman.[38] As the Nazis took over France, Eve's letters to Reitman grew more anguished. "I need not tell you what life has become here in Europe," she wrote again to Reitman in 1941.[39] Perhaps he could somehow help her acquire a US visa. "I want to desperately come back to the States. I must!"

Eve and Hella managed to evade capture until December of 1943, when, within a week of one another, they were each detained by Nazi forces and taken to the Drancy internment camp, northeast of Paris.[40] Records show that Eve and Hella were placed on Transport 63 to Auschwitz.[41] When Auschwitz was liberated in January of 1945, Eve and Hella were not listed among the survivors.[42]

While I would like to imagine that they escaped somehow—living out the rest of their days in a cottage somewhere in the countryside, off the grid and unable to be reached by their searching family members—I know that this is likely not the truth.

Still, the work that Eve did during her fifty-something years on this earth, both in documenting and creating queer community, would ripple through the generations to come. I have to wonder what a visionary like Eve would think of our world today. What would she think of the one hundred years of lesbian bars and history that have unfolded in America since Eve's Hangout shut its doors for the last time?

Would she be overjoyed to learn that same-sex couples can not only hold hands and dance in public but also (at least, at the time of this writing) legally marry? Or would she scoff at the idea of participating in the patriarchal institution of marriage? Would she embrace contemporary terms like *nonbinary* or *genderqueer* or *transmasc*, excited to find new language that might better fit her gender identity and expression? Would she be impressed by the few dozen lesbian bars that exist today, or would she be surprised that there are so few?

Would she be appalled that gender and sexuality are still policed? That the government cares about what bathroom you use? That hundreds of new bills threatening the safety of the LGBTQ+ community continue to be introduced each year? That America continues to turn its back on immigrants seeking safety?

It's impossible to say for certain what Eve would think of our world—so different, yet in so many ways unchanged, from the one in which she lived. But I think she would agree with me on this: making space is important. So is telling our stories—writing them down so that others can see: lesbian love exists.

The stories in this book—of lesbian and queer love, and also of queer joy, queer grief, queer friendship, queer community, queer chosen family, and queer solidarity—they're for Eve. And they're for all of us.

Chapter Two

HENRIETTA HUDSON

LESBIAN BARS ARE EVOLVING

NEW YORK, NY

A mere thousand feet east of where Eve's Hangout once sat, you'll find one of Manhattan's two open and operating lesbian bars. Henrietta Hudson—often abbreviated to Henrietta's, or just Hen's—occupies the bottom floor of a brick building on the corner of Hudson and Morton Streets in the West Village.

Sarah, Jen, and I have each spent our fair share of blurry nights at Henrietta's: playing pool—though the pool table is no longer—and sweating on the dance floor. As iconic as Hen's itself, and our many nights spent in it, is the bar's owner: local legend Lisa Cannistraci.

Lisa first opened Henrietta's in 1991 with her business partner Minnie Rivera. Today, it's a vibrant, thriving, queer space. On weekend nights, you'll find a packed dance floor beneath a sparkling disco ball, the DJ pumping out music until 4 a.m., and a crowd gathered around the horseshoe-shaped bar. A second room houses a more laid-back, lounge space, a (usually long) line for the bathroom, and a window into the kitchen. In the warmer months, cabanas line the street outside, with cozy seating for those who desire a quieter experience.

Lisa got her start in the bar business on Wall Street in the early 1980s. "It was *The Wolf of Wall Street* days. The movie was not exaggerated at all," Lisa proclaims in her distinctive, raspy voice. As depicted in the aforementioned film starring Leonardo DiCaprio, Wall Street was characterized by greed and financial crime. The 1980s were "the decade of excess, and money was thrown around like water," Lisa says matter-of-factly.

Behind the bar, some of that money landed in Lisa's hands. "I hung out with those guys. I partied with them. Heavy, heavy, heavy duty," she reveals. At first, Lisa was afraid to come out of the closet in this hypermasculine, heteronormative environment. Allyship to the queer community wasn't exactly high on the list of priorities for the Wall Street crowd. "And then I realized the guys were kind of hitting on me, and the women were getting annoyed," Lisa recounts. So, thinking it would diffuse the situation, she decided to tell her customers she was gay. While she didn't get the homophobic response she initially feared, her sexuality didn't help her predicament. Instead, the guys were only further taken with her, and the women started hitting on her too!

Lisa didn't have any complaints. "I was the token lesbian," she says wryly, "and [I] did not care because it was a ride. It was a wild ride." But after a handful of years, Lisa was ready to get off the roller coaster. "I can cut to the chase. I'm sober today. [. . .] I'm the bar owner who doesn't drink," Lisa confesses. She is one of many lesbian bar owners we have met across the country who don't drink themselves. It's not as nonsensical as you might think; many bar owners appreciate a bit of distance from the job, and in general, alcohol is not centric to lesbian bars in the way it is for, say, Wall Street bars.

In 1985, Lisa began searching for another bartending gig. One afternoon, after being rejected on the spot for a job at an upscale restaurant in the West Village because she "looked too young," Lisa set off down Hudson Street to catch the F train back home to Brooklyn. On her way, it started to rain. "I'm not kidding, the sky opened up," she recalls. To escape the downpour, she ducked into a bar on the corner of Hudson and Morton Streets. Though she didn't know it yet, she was dripping rainwater on the future floor of Henrietta Hudson.

Back then, the bar Lisa entered was another lesbian spot called Cubby Hole—not to be confused with the current Cubbyhole on West Twelfth Street. Lisa was hired to bartend there that very day.

The world Lisa came crashing into in the West Village was the stark antithesis of the one she'd left behind on Wall Street. There was a "real queer culture embedded in the West Village," Lisa says with a smile. The neighborhood had long been a gathering place for the queer community: from the bohemian speakeasies of Eve's time to the Mafia-run bars and clubs of the mid-century, to the gay and lesbian–owned spaces of the '70s and beyond.

By the mid-'80s, "[straight] people didn't come and try to hang out," Lisa emphatically states. At least not until the late 1990s, when the neighborhood began to shift—a change Lisa attributes to two factors. First, an increasing number of mainstream shops, restaurants, and nightclubs began to open in the meatpacking district. And second, "*Sex and the City* came [out]. [. . .] That's when everything changed," Lisa tells us with a laugh.

But back in the 1980s, before those shifts took hold, "the West Village was a real activist community. It was very rough and rugged. It was edgy [. . .] and it was radical. It was a time that you can never, ever redo," Lisa asserts. When she recounts this period, it's not all wistful nostalgia and longing. The 1980s were an incredibly painful decade for the queer community around the world. More than one hundred thousand HIV/AIDS-related deaths were reported in the US between 1981 and 1990.[1] There's an edge to Lisa's voice as she explains: "The AIDS epidemic ravaged New York City."

For Lisa, these cases weren't just numbers: "My friends were dying. They would get diagnosed and be dead in ten days. That's how quickly they died. My friends who were lesbians and the [other] gay women in the city, we went to St. Vincent's Hospital to take care of our guy friends because the guys were terrified to go in. They didn't know how [AIDS] was transmitted back then, [. . .] if it was saliva, if it was through the air. There was no research."

It wasn't just Lisa's community of queer women in New York who were showing up for their gay friends. It was women across the country. In Salt Lake City, lesbian doctor Kristen Ries was one of the only medical professionals in the area willing to provide care to AIDS patients.[2] When Cape Cod Hospital couldn't meet the needs of HIV+ people, lesbians in Provincetown volunteered to drive them to Boston to receive care.[3] In California, the predominantly lesbian group "San Diego Blood Sisters" organized blood drives to keep pace with the needs of local HIV and AIDS patients, in the wake of the FDA's ban on gay men donating blood.[4]

Women took on more than just caregiving. "Activism was a big thing," Lisa explains, "because essentially the US government wouldn't even say the word *AIDS* or *HIV*. We had to take to the streets, and we were radical." President Ronald Reagan publicly uttered the word *AIDS* for the first time during a press conference in September of 1985, more than four years after the first cases were reported.[5] In the years to follow, government action and major research into HIV/AIDS remained insufficient. So, in March of 1987, ACT UP, the AIDS Coalition to Unleash Power, was founded in New York City. The group's mission was to use direct-action tactics to force government agencies; healthcare, insurance, and pharmaceutical companies; and religious institutions to act in the fight against HIV/AIDS.[6] Their first action protested some of the very people to whom Lisa used to serve drinks. On March 24, 1987, ACT UP members took to Wall Street to protest pharmaceutical companies who were exploiting the epidemic in pursuit of profits.[7]

Lisa herself participated in various ACT UP actions throughout the city. "We stormed St. Patrick's Cathedral on Sunday, and we took over Grand Central Station," she details. Storming St. Patrick's Cathedral was part of the December 10, 1989, action known as "Stop the Church." More than seven thousand protestors gathered outside, and hundreds managed to peacefully enter, Lisa among them. "The service was going on. We opened the front doors, and we walked right through," she recounts. They staged a "die-in," lying down in the aisles of the church during Sunday Mass to symbolize those dying of AIDS and to implicate the Catholic Church in their deaths.

Amid all her activism, opening a bar of her own was the last thing on Lisa's mind. But, in 1990, the original Cubby Hole where Lisa had been bartending, closed. The owner, Elaine Romagnoli, moved a block east and opened another lesbian bar called Crazy Nanny's. Most of the staff followed, Lisa included. She also started bartending at a spot across the street called Kelly's. "When I went to Kelly's, everybody came and followed me," Lisa says, as if still surprised all these decades later that she had such loyal customers.

At Kelly's, Lisa began dipping her toes into the world of lesbian events. "I started doing Sunday night parties there," she tells us. Back then, hosting a weekly party wasn't as simple as creating a Facebook event or posting on Instagram. "You took people's names and put them on index cards and that's how you developed your mailing list. And it was literally a *mailing* list," Lisa clarifies. "You printed out flyers [. . .] and you put them in an envelope with a stamp and mailed them to the person's house. I know it sounds crazy. And it was so much work because everything was so *heavy*, right? The printed cards were heavy. The envelopes. You got paper cuts. You had to pay hundreds of dollars in postage. And you couldn't put a return address on it, because a lot of people were in the closet."

Pre–social media, this was what had to be done to create queer community, and Lisa was happy to do it. Still, she drew the line at running her own bar. "It was not in the cards. [. . .] I never wanted to own a bar. [. . .] I loved bartending. I took the money. I went home," Lisa says adamantly. "My customers were begging me to open the old Cubby Hole," she continues, "and I said, 'Oh hell no!'"

But then, a woman named Minnie Rivera walked into Crazy Nanny's during one of Lisa's shifts. She was on her way to pick up a friend from the airport and had a few hours to kill. "[She] never made it to the airport," Lisa says with a smile. Not because Lisa had done anything nefarious. Minnie was just having such a great time at the bar with Lisa, so she never left.

Minnie was already well known in the West Village and beyond. She had been working in queer events and nightlife since the 1970s. "She owned a couple of night clubs which were pretty infamous, like this place called Network on Sixteenth and Sixth. Madonna used to go there and Jellybean would DJ there. She owned a place in Tribeca, when Tribeca was desolate in the '80s, called Garbo's," Lisa details. Minnie also ran a pseudo lesbian-travel company. Before there were the Olivia Cruises of today, there was Minnie Rivera. "She would lease out entire airplanes and take lesbians to the Bahamas," Lisa says, her voice tinged with respect.

Lisa made quite the impression on Minnie that night at Crazy Nanny's. Shortly thereafter, Minnie tracked Lisa down and asked her to dinner. "The next thing I knew we were opening this place. It just was kind of in a whirlwind," Lisa adds.

During Pride of 1991, Lisa and Minnie opened Henrietta Hudson in the space where the old Cubby Hole used to be.[8] Before long, the new bar was a success. "We were the hottest ticket in town. And the way that you know that is, back then, taxis lined up in front of your bar to pick people up. Because that's how busy you are," Lisa recalls with satisfaction.

Today, more than thirty years later, Henrietta's is still going strong. The space has evolved in many ways over the past three decades. Lisa always knows when it's time for a change. But "it's not methodical. And it's not sought after," she clarifies. "This business to me has a heartbeat of its own. Like it's a live organism, Henrietta Hudson. It's got a soul. So, it speaks to me. I know that might sound weird, but the space, the energy, the vibe of the people. I always know when it's time to pivot. Because I'm listening. I'm watching. I'm feeling."

In 2013, Lisa rebranded Hen's as "a lesbian-centric queer human bar," rather than simply a "lesbian bar." This shift in language was accompanied by what Lisa calls a "brand refresh." Like all the changes Lisa makes at Hen's, this one was prompted by various observations and conversations. "I saw the community changing and I was so happy. I saw all these young, queer kids becoming. Just becoming. [. . .] And I realized [. . .] they weren't coming here," Lisa recalls. So, she asked some of them directly: Would they ever go to Henrietta's?

"Oh no, that place is so old," they told her.

"That's all I needed to hear," Lisa says.

Lisa began making a series of small adjustments to the bar, though she won't say precisely what she changed aside from their updated, inclusive tagline. "I can't really give all my secrets away. [. . .] But I know exactly what I did," she declares elusively. However, she did tell us this: "It fucking worked. [. . .] The floodgates opened. In a good way." Suddenly, Henrietta's was the place to be for this young, queer, more gender-expansive crowd.

During the fifteen months that the bar was shuttered due to COVID, Henrietta's underwent a series of renovations and Lisa rebranded yet again, reopening in 2021 with yet another new tagline: "a queer human bar built by lesbians." Lisa felt this messaging was a more authentic representation of Hen's. She wanted to, in her words, "really embrace and rubber-stamp the fact that we're all-inclusive. [. . .] There's no gray area there. I don't want anybody to be confused."

They did get some pushback on social media for this new tagline. "Sad to lose yet another lesbian bar as the global list continues shrinking," one user commented on Instagram. "THERE GOES ANOTHER ONE, LADIES," said another.[9] But Lisa doesn't think anything has been lost at her bar. She is putting words to what has always been the reality of the Henrietta Hudson community, and she has a message for her critics:

"It's been that bar for the past ten years; we just didn't put it in a tagline. It's been like that. There's been trans people among you. There's been queer people among you. There's been nonbinary people among you. They've been here, so shame on you for wanting to exclude them when you didn't even realize they were in the fucking room the whole time."

Chapter Three

CUBBYHOLE

IN TIMES OF CRISIS WHERE DO YOU GO?

NEW YORK, NY

While the first Cubby Hole where Lisa Canistracci once bartended never reopened, today, there is another Cubbyhole in town, an ode to the original beloved bar. This newer Cubbyhole was the first lesbian bar Sarah and I ever visited, back in 2017. Even now, walking through its doors brings back that magical feeling of what it was like to be surrounded by people like me for the very first time.

We missed Cubbyhole dearly while it was closed due to the pandemic, so Sarah and I eagerly showed up at their reopening on April 8, 2021. As if a second Cubbyhole isn't confusing enough, it is also run by a second Lisa: Lisa Menichino, who inherited the bar from its original owner Tanya Saunders. The reopening was an emotional day for Lisa, who, seated inside the bar's newly constructed sidewalk cabana, tells us that, until the pandemic, Cubbyhole had not closed its doors for a single day in its twenty-seven-year history.

Aside from the new outdoor seating, Cubbyhole looks exactly as it did pre-pandemic: Perched on the corner of West Twelfth and West Fourth Streets, its large windows are covered with rainbow daisies, and a rainbow flag hangs from the green awning. Articles featuring the bar are displayed proudly in the windows as well, including two pages from *GO Magazine*'s piece memorializing Tanya Saunders, published after she passed in 2018 at eighty-two years old. Photos beam out from the pages: an older Tanya sitting at the bar, grinning in a black fedora, a young Tanya in black and white gazing sultrily into the camera, wrapped in a feathery boa and sporting a chic, Liza Minnelli-esque haircut.

In 1987, having recently been laid off from her job in advertising, Tanya spotted a sign in this very window on West Twelfth Street: bar for sale. She had long harbored a secret fantasy of bar ownership, so she stepped inside. Later that year, she bought the bar and opened DT's Fat Cat, in partnership with her friend Debbie Fierro; the D stood for Debbie and the T stood for Tanya.

DT's Fat Cat had a vastly different aesthetic from the Cubbyhole of today. "It was very dark. [. . .] The walls were black," notes Lisa. "It actually had a piano player, if you can imagine, in that little space."

The bar began to change in 1993, when Tanya bought out Debbie. The pair had realized their visions didn't align, so Debbie moved on to open another Manhattan lesbian bar, Rubyfruit, while Tanya stayed and revamped the existing space. The first thing she had to change was the bar's name; "T's Fat Cat" didn't quite have the same ring to it. Elaine Romagnoli had recently closed the original Cubby Hole, and Tanya thought the name would be a good fit for her quaint, narrow space. With Elaine's blessing, Tanya rebranded the bar as "Cubbyhole," putting a bit of her own spin on it by making it one word.

Tanya swapped the bar's black walls for green and began an eclectic art installation on the ceiling. She was inspired by a restaurant she visited in New Orleans that had a canopy of plants overhead and wanted to recreate that kind of fun and welcoming aesthetic in Cubbyhole. Instead of plants, she used a multicolored array of decorative objects: paper lanterns, kites, umbrellas, wind spinners, and more. To this day, Cubbyhole's ceiling is its most notable feature.

Under Tanya's ownership, Cubbyhole quickly became a neighborhood bar. Tanya "wanted everyone who walked around the corner of West Twelfth and West Fourth, no matter who they were [. . .] to feel welcome," says Deb Greenberg, who bartended at Cubbyhole from 2010 to 2023. These days, this inclusive messaging is common practice for all lesbian bars, but in the '90s, it caused a bit of a stir. "There were dykes marching in front of the bar. [. . .] The dykes were mad because they didn't want it to be inclusive," Deb exclaims.

For Tanya, inclusivity wasn't a threat to her gay identity. In the company of trusted friends, she had been out for a long time. In 1963, Tanya met her first girlfriend, Geri, and they soon moved in together. "Both of their families were going to disown them if they found out that they were together," Lisa tells us. So, Tanya and Geri came up with the perfect cover; they married the two gay men who lived upstairs. Both were businessmen who risked being fired if they were outed at work, and as they got older, their bachelorhood drew increasing suspicion. So, in what is known as a "lavender marriage," the two men married the two women—in a double ceremony, no less. There is an incredible photo of Geri and Tanya standing side by side in their wedding gowns and veils, almost as if they were marrying each other.

Tanya and Geri were together for about ten years before ending things romantically. In 1974, Tanya met Nancy, whom Lisa calls "the love of [Tanya's] life." Tanya and Geri remained close friends, though this is not to say that they always got along. They argued frequently. Yet their disagreements never lasted. "Geri was her best friend. So even if they had these crazy fights, they always made up within a day or two," Lisa recalls.

Tanya had a temper, but it stemmed from her passion: her love for her community, her friends, her family, and her bar. "When she felt she was being disrespected in any way, or anybody said anything bad about the bar, she would go off," Lisa says with a small laugh. Tanya was fiercely protective.

As Deb puts it: "She was so kind and her heart was big, but you didn't fuck with Tanya either." Deb remembers seeing this side of Tanya in action. One day, while Deb was bartending, a woman walked into the bar, dressed to the nines, nails done, Louis Vuitton bag in hand. She sat down and began chatting with another customer. At some point, Deb chimed in, as bartenders often do.

"Excuse me. I wasn't talking to you. I don't think I was talking to the bartender," the woman snapped at Deb.

Tanya, from her seat at the other end of the bar, sprang into action. "Can you come here?" she asked the woman. "Did I just hear you talk to my bartender like that? What did you say? Get the hell out of my bar!" See, Tanya's inclusivity did *not* apply to rude, disrespectful, or hateful individuals. This is how she maintained Cubbyhole as a safe space.

Tanya's protective nature extended to all living things. She once insisted that the rats in the bar's basement not be killed. "She was driving the exterminator crazy," Lisa remembers.

"I heard that you could just put a noise that they don't like, or a smell," Tanya suggested.

"No, you can't, that's not gonna work," replied the exterminator. Tanya remained steadfast. "They're rats!" the exterminator argued.

"They don't *know* they're rats!" Tanya shot back.

Lisa attributes Tanya's compassion and protectiveness to her general love of life. "Her mother always instilled in her that [you should] enjoy, because anything could be taken away by the drop of a dime. You could lose it all," Lisa explains. Tanya's mother escaped Nazi Germany in 1939, a recently widowed Jewish refugee with a three-year-old Tanya in tow.

Throughout her life, Tanya derived much of her joy from Cubbyhole itself. "She loved talking to people and she loved just being around that bar. That bar was like a living, breathing thing for her," says Lisa.

Tanya would often order pizza for the whole bar. And if Tanya wasn't there to do it herself, Deb remembers her calling the bar phone to ask: "Honey, did you order pizza?" Cubbyhole's "pizza nights" have endured; often, during happy hour, you can still grab a free slice.

Tanya was never particularly concerned with how much money Cubbyhole was making. She just wanted to be able to stay open. In fact, Tanya was the one who made sure that Cubbyhole was *always* open. "Even through all the hurricanes and nor'easters and Sandy and 9/11 and blizzards and blackouts and everything. [Tanya] kept her doors open, even if it was just for a couple of hours, because she knew people were anxious about the environment," Lisa tells us.

In times of crisis, Cubbyhole's patrons showed up for the bar, and its staff too. Lisa, whose stepmother was killed in 9/11, was behind the bar that day. "I got a message from my dad, frantic that he couldn't get in touch with his wife," she says. Of course, she wanted to be with him, but the entire city was shut down. The subways and buses weren't running. The bridges and tunnels out of the city were closed. And besides, Lisa didn't have a car. "One of the regular customers actually gave me the keys to her car. [. . .] She knew the one route where you [could] get out through Queens. And said just go. And I was able to get home to my father," Lisa recalls, still grateful all these years later.

Tanya understood the power of community during frightening times. "She felt like the Cubbyhole was a beacon. Not just for the LGBTQ+ [community] but for the neighborhood people that would come in," Lisa says. Yet there was another reason Tanya strived to always keep the bar open: superstition. "She felt like you could never, ever close. That's bad luck."

Tanya inherited her deeply superstitious nature from her mother. "Her mother had told her that it's bad luck to look back. You never look back. You don't celebrate anniversaries, you don't do any of that," Lisa details.

Today, Lisa laughs recalling Tanya's obstinance. Yet, when it comes to Cubbyhole, Lisa is inclined to follow Tanya's example, keeping her eyes on the future. "[Tanya] always said this, and it's true, you have to reinvent yourself to some degree as things change, as people change, as new generations come in," Lisa explains.

Of course, Lisa allows herself the occasional glance back at Tanya. "Whatever I do, I try and keep her in mind," she remarks. "If I was half as good as Tanya was, that would be a success for me. She was truly an amazing, special person."

Chapter Four

GINGER'S

WHERE EVERYBODY KNOWS RUTHIE'S NAME

BROOKLYN, NY

One evening in 1990, Sheila Frayne and her cousin approached Julie's, a lesbian bar on East Fifty-Eighth in Manhattan, excited for a night out among queer community. When they reached the door, Sheila's cousin was denied entry; men weren't allowed inside.

"But he's gay!" Sheila protested. Still, the bouncer wouldn't budge. Perhaps this was to be expected of a bar like Julie's. It operated through the early 2000s and in various online listings would later be described as "upscale and apparently uptight," a place where you could "expect power couples and lots of Prada suits."[1]

Seemingly, Sheila and her cousin wouldn't have enjoyed the crowd at Julie's anyway. But the whole experience did not sit well with them. "I have to open up a bar where we're all accepted," Sheila thought to herself.

Today, Sheila owns that bar: Ginger's, a Park Slope mainstay. Park Slope spans about thirty blocks of Brooklyn, gently sloping down from Prospect Park on its eastern border, to Fourth Avenue to its west. Think brownstones, row houses, and tree-lined streets bustling with young families and queer folks.

To this day, the incident with Sheila's cousin more than thirty-five years ago shapes the way Sheila runs her business. While she identifies as a lesbian, and the bar is often filled with crowds of queer women, Sheila says they "don't discriminate against anybody." She goes on to add, "I just want everybody to feel comfortable. I'm the youngest of seven siblings. I want *them* to come and feel comfortable. I want *you* to bring your mother there and feel comfortable."

Sheila is an expert at making people feel comfortable. For our interview, she invites us out to what she jokingly calls her "little fucking cabin," and we settle in the sunroom, a spread of snacks laid out on the table. The cabin is nestled beside a small lake in New Jersey, which has become a lesbian micro-community itself; Sheila rattles off the names of all the other queer women whose properties dot the shoreline.

She speaks with a lilting Irish accent and has a head of red curls: "I *am* Ginger," she declares with a smile. People often think Ginger is her name—she'll even respond to it around the bar. Sheila was born into a large family in Wexford, Ireland, a rural town southeast of Dublin. "We were poor as poor," she states bluntly.

Throughout Sheila's teenage years, the gay rights movement was unfolding in Ireland's larger cities, but homosexuality was never talked about in her small community. Sheila first realized she was gay at about thirteen, on a school trip to France. She was at a disco, sitting on the bathroom counter, and smoking a cigarette. "This woman came in and walked right up to me and kissed me," Sheila exclaims, "and then just looked at me and left." Sheila never saw the woman again. But in that moment, she knew.

Nearly a decade later, in 1989, Sheila and her first girlfriend bought one-way tickets to the US and settled in New York. Back then, Sheila was fearless. "What are you afraid of when you're twenty-two? Jesus, help me," Sheila remarks.

After that fateful incident at Julie's, over a decade would pass before Sheila was able to open a bar of her own. In 2000, she founded Ginger's on Fifth Avenue between Fifth and Sixth Streets in Park Slope. The neighborhood looked different back then. Gentrification was underway, but it was only beginning to creep down the slope from the more commercial, busier Seventh Avenue. Fifth Avenue was known then for its low rents and ample square footage. It was lined with local bars and pubs, storefront churches, barber shops, the occasional mom-and-pop restaurant, and many boarded-up buildings. Absent were the gourmet grocery stores and acclaimed dining spots of today.

Yet, Park Slope already had a reputation as a lesbian neighborhood. Since the 1970s, lesbians have been flocking there. Jack Jen Gieseking, environmental psychologist and queer theorist, traces this phenomenon to the nearby Prospect Park and its softball fields. "Brooklyn lesbians are playing sports in this park, so people are migrating in and out of the park weekly," he tells us. Soon, an influx of queer- and lesbian-owned businesses and institutions popped up around the park. La Papaya—a feminist vegetarian restaurant with a feminist bookstore upstairs—opened in 1980.[2] The Lesbian Herstory Archives moved into a Park Slope brownstone in 1991.[3] Rising Café, a queer Irish pub not unlike Ginger's, opened on Fifth Avenue in 1996.[4]

Still, when Ginger's opened, not everyone welcomed their presence. The pay phone on the wall used to ring multiple times a week with someone on the other end making their disapproval known. Sheila recalls answering and hearing: "We're gonna come and kill all you fucking faggots and we're gonna shoot you all." She went to the police, who tapped the phone but never caught anybody.

More so than by the cops, Sheila felt protected by her new neighbors. One of the first things Sheila did when Ginger's opened was head over to Jackie's Fifth Amendment, a bar a few blocks south. "Jackie's was very [. . .] Mafia," Sheila explains. She figured: "If I get on their side, they'll be nice to me. [. . .] And if Ginger's was a target back in the day, because Fifth Avenue was kind of dodgy, [. . .] they would look out for me."

She was quick to win over the Jackie's crowd. "They liked me too, because [. . .] what you see is what you get. I don't lie," Sheila says. "If you have a problem, you come talk to me about it," she would tell the folks at Jackie's, "because I'm here, I'm human, I'm normal. We're fucking queer but that's who we are." Eventually, likely because of Sheila's new friends in the neighborhood, the threatening phone calls to the bar stopped. "They always looked out for me," Sheila reflects with a mixture of disbelief and pride that her plan had worked.

Jackie's closed in 2013, but Ginger's remains a neighborhood staple. Today, it's our own neighborhood bar. My wife Jen and I live a fifteen-minute walk away, in the still fairly lesbian neighborhood of Park Slope, and for Sarah, it's about a fifteen-minute bike ride. We've spent many a night at Ginger's celebrating after one of Jen's Prospect Park softball games or gathered around a table in the backyard talking.

However, in September of 2021, when we set out on our initial road trip to lesbian bars around the country, Ginger's sat shuttered. For a while, no one was sure whether they would ever reopen after the pandemic. Then, shortly after we returned to Brooklyn from our cross-country travels, the news broke: Ginger's was coming back.

The next month, Ginger's reopened. Sheila had brought in a new partner, and they made a few upgrades. The bar now smells less like Bud Light than it used to, but Ginger's is largely still the same Ginger's. Its bright blue exterior with golden-yellow lettering and rainbow flags still catches the attention of passersby on Fifth Avenue. The pay phone that used to ring with threatening calls still hangs on the wall next to the bar, now silent. The pool table still sits in the back room. And by the pool table is Ruthie.

Ruthie Boirie is a Ginger's regular. She stands about five feet tall and is often dressed in a T-shirt layered under a vest, a pair of jeans with her keys clipped to a belt loop, and a baseball hat over a bandana. Ginger's is Ruthie's home. She is there every night, playing pool, chatting with the young folks, and sipping her seltzer water with lemon *and* lime (she doesn't drink alcohol). Sarah and I have known Ruthie for about five years, and Jen has for probably a decade. Seeing her at the pool table after Ginger's reopened, it dawned on me: we had asked regulars in lesbian bars across the country for their stories, but we didn't know Ruthie's. So, one evening, we asked her.

Outside the bar, Ruthie sits in the passenger seat of her maroon minivan, dangling her feet out the open door. Sarah, Jen, and I clamor around her on the sidewalk eager to listen. "I think I was gay from the age of two years old," Ruthie offers with a smile. She was born in the Bronx and remembers having a crush on a little girl who lived in her family's apartment building. She would sit on the building stoop, looking at the other toddler and playing a toy guitar. "She was so pretty," Ruthie details. "I didn't know how to explain it yet—because I didn't talk—but I knew that she was pretty and that whatever the hell I was playing on the damn [guitar], I was looking at her."

At four years old, Ruthie still wasn't talking, and her mother had begun to worry. At five, when it came time to start kindergarten, Ruthie was placed into what was called a CRMD class, which stood for "children with retarded mental development."

By the time Ruthie was six, her family had moved to Brooklyn, into an apartment complex filled with other children. Every day, all the kids would wait for the building super, Mr. Roberts, to finish cleaning and play games with them. But Mr. Roberts would never let Ruthie join. "No, not you because you are a dummy," Ruthie remembers him telling her. One day, Ruthie's desperation to participate and connect with the other kids grew too much for her to contain. She took a deep breath, looked up at Mr. Roberts, opened her mouth, and said, "Oh, *no*!"

Mr. Roberts peered down at little Ruthie with a smile on his face. "*Vente*," he said to her in Spanish, stretching out his hand—*come.* Looking back, Ruthie thinks Mr. Roberts knew exactly what he was doing. It might not have been the kindest approach, but he had been trying to get her to speak. And it worked. From then on, Ruthie could talk.

But as far as schooling went, it was too late. As a Black girl in the NYC public school system in 1952, Ruthie had just about everything stacked against her. As early as the 1940s, Black parents in NYC were criticizing the public school system's racist practices that placed more children of color into CRMD classes, arguing that this was effectively segregation, and that it prevented Black children from preparing for better jobs.[5] While Ruthie's mother managed to convince the school to have her retested, the school refused to share the results. "But I think I passed," Ruthie murmurs. Ruthie was kept in CRMD classes for the entirety of her schooling. As she moved on to high school, she learned how cruel other children could be. In the lunchroom, they mocked and ridiculed Ruthie and the other students in her class, calling them slow. "I felt like I wanted to jump over the table and whoop their ass," she exclaims, "but, you know, I had to be cool."

At sixteen, fed up with being treated this way, Ruthie dropped out. That same year, her parents discovered she was gay. She came home from playing basketball one evening to find them holding a letter. "Read this," they told her. It was addressed to Ruthie's parents, purportedly from a local mother, accusing Ruthie of messing around with her daughter. Ruthie, however, knew immediately that the letter was forged. In reality, it had been written by the daughter herself, who liked Ruthie and was jealous that Ruthie liked someone else. "She told my mother and father what I was, just to be spiteful and whatnot," Ruthie remarks.

Ruthie had read only about two lines into the letter before she looked up at her parents with defiance and said: "Yes I am, and I'm not changing for nobody."

In response to this news, Ruthie's parents took her to see a psychiatrist. "I don't know why I'm here, because I'm not changing for nobody. I like girls," Ruthie told the doctor.

The next year, at seventeen, Ruthie informed her mother she was leaving home. "You sure you want to go out there in that world?" her mother asked.

"Yeah, I'm leaving. I want to go," Ruthie answered.

When she told her father, his only response was: "Don't make that mistake to come back."

"That's always stayed in my head," Ruthie muses. She never did return home. At least, not in her father's lifetime. "I was homeless for a while," she explains. "I can tell you the places that I look at today where I slept. [. . .] There's a house that was really nice on the stoop, [. . .] the Hoyt-Schermerhorn [subway] station, [. . .] and then I rode the trains back and forward, the G train all the way up, all the way back down." Sometimes she stayed with friends. Sometimes she would be able to rent a room or a studio somewhere.

Ruthie worked odd jobs, factory jobs, anything that didn't require a high school diploma. Eventually, she landed a steady gig as a nurse's aide at a hospital in East Flatbush. She worked there for fourteen years, until she abruptly quit in 1992. A nurse had spoken rudely to Ruthie, repeatedly calling her "you." When Ruthie stood up for herself, asking to be called by her name, the nurse reported her. The hospital administration called Ruthie into a meeting to tell her she was being written up, so she walked out. *Did I just leave my fourteen-year job? My pension, my social security, all that?* she thought at the time, tears of anger streaming down her face.

But the next morning, she got herself out of bed and went for a walk through her Brooklyn neighborhood. Behind the glass of one of the storefronts, something caught her eye: "these lady barbers working in this barber shop," Ruthie remembers. "Something told me to go inside and get a haircut."

During Ruthie's haircut, she learned that the owner of the shop, Bill, taught aspiring barbers how to cut. So, Ruthie got in touch with him. "He taught me everything that he could possibly teach me. And he said that I was going to become an artist in hair," Ruthie marvels.

In 1996, she opened Ruthie's Neighborhood Barber Shop on St. Mark's between Fifth and Sixth Avenues in Brooklyn. Ruthie cuts hair there to this day.

Soon after Ginger's opened in 2000, just fifteen blocks south of Ruthie's shop, clients started telling Ruthie she had to visit. One Sunday, she decided to finally give Ginger's a chance. "I sat right there in the front. And I just watched everybody," Ruthie recalls. From that first visit, she was hooked: "When I started coming here, I never stopped."

As Ruthie continued coming to Ginger's, she ventured further into the bar. She discovered the pool table and the backyard. And she began to meet more people. "I just started introducing myself. You know, I'm real deep, but I'm not much of a talker. [. . .] I'm very quiet," she explains.

Soon, Ginger's was part of Ruthie's daily routine. Every day after work, she would make her way over to the bar, although she's never been interested in drinking or in picking up women. "I'm just a plain old square," Ruthie tells us with a laugh. So, what keeps her coming back after all these years? "Oh, well, because I have nothing else to do," she says, matter-of-factly. "This is a warm place to me. You know what I mean? It's very warm. And I meet a lot of different people. [. . .] I love Ginger's."

I think what Ruthie loves so much about Ginger's is that she gets to be herself and be among people who see her and love her and respect her for who she is. There's no Mr. Roberts guarding the pool table and telling her she can't play, no jeering cafeteria kids calling her slow, no psychiatrist trying to fix her simply for liking women. And at Ginger's, everyone knows Ruthie's name.

When we finish our sidewalk interview with her and walk back into the bar, everybody cheers—and they're certainly not cheering for us. They're cheering for Ruthie. Of course, if you ask Ruthie about her celebrity status, she'll brush it off. "What do I do? Do I ever talk a lot? You know that I don't talk a lot," she exclaims softly. Though with a little more prodding, she admits: "I give all my love and hugs to everybody. [. . .] If they're going through something, I listen and I say, 'Come on, everything's gonna be good. Stop it. Get out of that. Let's move forward. Come on. Let's go play some pool.'"

Chapter Five

THE BUSH

A NEW DYKE BAR IN TOWN

BROOKLYN, NY

In Brooklyn, there's a new dyke bar in town: The Bush, located in Bushwick, nearly on the border of Queens. Historically, Bushwick is a working-class, largely Hispanic and Latinx neighborhood, though the past few decades have seen rapid gentrification. Today, it's also known as a hipster haven, attracting artists, musicians, and theater makers, while still hanging on to its immigrant roots. It's a more industrial part of the borough, known for the vibrant murals that cover the exteriors of old factories and warehouses, many of which have since been converted into lofts, nightclubs, restaurants, and music venues.

If you're familiar with Brooklyn geography, you know that a trip from Bushwick down to Park Slope, where Ginger's is located, usually requires you to ride the subway *into* Manhattan and then back out again. Suffice to say, North Brooklyn was thrilled to get a lesbian bar of their own when Nikke Alleyne and Justine LaViolette opened The Bush in April of 2023. People were lined up on the sidewalk for the bar's debut before they even opened the doors.

You can tell by the way the two cut each other off with jokes and clarifying details—and sometimes actually finish each other's sentences—that Nikke and Justine are not only business partners, but best friends. It's early evening and we are seated around a small table at the front of The Bush. Nikke wears a chunky pair of glasses and her bleached-blonde eyebrows stand out against her otherwise more conventional aesthetic. Justine's hair is cropped into a bob and dyed a similar shade of bleached blonde to Nikke's eyebrows, plus a pink streak in the front. Daylight floods in through the floor-to-ceiling windows, as well as the skylight overhead, when the pair begin to share the origin story of their friendship. They met through a serendipitous, though complicated, series of New York lesbian nightlife connections. They eventually wound up being introduced by a mutual friend at a sapphic party held every Wednesday at The Woods, another Brooklyn bar, and immediately hit it off.

"So, we had this little clique of lesbians," Nikke starts, adding in more details.

"—very big," Justine cuts in.

"Big clique, I guess, of lesbians," Nikke continues, "that we hung out with in our twenties."

Both had moved to NYC after college in the mid-2010s and were experiencing an expansive queer community for the first time. Nikke was born in Trinidad and moved to New Jersey at age seven. "In Trinidad, it is predominantly Black and Indian. [. . .] My own family is like a modge-podge of ethnicities and races, [. . .] so it was a huge cultural shock," she says of the move. By the time she reached high school, Nikke was dating women, and while she had some queer friends, it couldn't compare to the community she later found in NYC.

Justine grew up in a white family in the upper peninsula of rural Michigan. They describe the community in their small town as one "that had a lot of homophobia and racism [. . .] but also had the people resisting that," like the gay man who participated in the annual Rocky Horror Picture Show each Halloween. "It felt very formative for me as a young queer person [. . .] like, I'm agender and I've never identified as a lesbian. I'm just an agender slut, essentially," Justine explains. Seeing this person perform each year showed Justine that there was something beyond the heteronormative gender binary by which they were otherwise surrounded. "It's really brave and really resistant to be who you are in a community that's not necessarily always safe. When I was little somebody got killed for being gay in my hometown. That, I think, has an effect on your psyche," Justine adds.

Nikke, too, reflects on the impact of coming from a place where being gay isn't widely accepted. While her family members still living in Trinidad know she is gay and are supportive, larger cultural attitudes toward queer people in the country are mixed, and as of 2025, same-sex intimacy remains against the law.[1]

Coming from places where there was an underlying message that queerness wasn't okay is part of what compelled both Justine and Nikke to open The Bush—where queerness isn't just accepted but celebrated.

Nikke and Justine's vision for The Bush was also shaped by their years spent immersed in queer nightlife in NYC. "We did a lot of silly things in our twenties," Nikke reminisces. "We would go out and come home at 5:00 AM. And then I would get dressed and go back to work." They often spent nights at familiar lesbian bars, Cubbyhole, Henrietta Hudson, and Ginger's, as well as at various queer and lesbian pop-up parties throughout the city, like Wednesdays at The Woods and Hot Rabbit events. They loved their community, and they had a lot of fun. But eventually, it started to feel like something was lacking.

"None of the lesbian bars here had a cocktail program," Justine points out. As they got older, they started to crave more curated drink experiences, beyond the vodka sodas and basic margaritas you could find at most lesbian bars at the time.

"They also didn't have, like, a place to sit," Nikke says, "or a big enough dance floor." These features could be found at various queer and lesbian nights throughout the city, but none of the bars and clubs in which they were held "were owned and operated by dykes."

"We were going to a lot of parties in spaces made for gay men, or straight spaces, and we wanted to have our own space," adds Justine.

"I guess if we want these things, we're just going to have to do them ourselves," they began thinking, but weren't seriously considering opening a bar. At least not yet. "It was kind of a joke that got out of control," Justine says, to emphatic agreement from Nikke.

Despite their many nights spent partying among queer friends, Nikke and Justine's twenties were marked with a cultural narrative that lesbian bars were disappearing. Crazy Nanny's—where Henrietta's Lisa Canistracci used to bartend—closed in 2004, as did beloved lesbian bar Meow Mix. So did Rubyfruit, four years later in 2008. The following year, Park Slope's Cattyshack shut its doors for good, leaving Ginger's as the sole lesbian bar in Brooklyn. These closures weren't just happening in New York. San Francisco's iconic dyke bar The Lex closed in 2015. DC lesbian mainstay Phase 1 closed in 2016. In 2017, LA's only remaining lesbian bar Oxwood Inn shut its doors as well. The closures were often attributed to two leading causes: the queer community felt increasingly comfortable spending time in non-LGBTQ+ specific spaces, and rising rents driven by rapid gentrification made it hard for lesbian bars to survive.

"There was a lot of art happening that was memorializing lesbian bars, [. . .] talking about these spaces as though they were things of the past," Justine reflects. In the fall of 2015, Justine and Nikke attended Macon Reed's Brooklyn art installation titled *Eulogy for the Dyke Bar*. Macon had built a life-size, interactive dyke bar out of papier-mâché and cardboard in a Bushwick space called Wayfarer's Gallery. Archival images of lesbian bars from the 1930s through the present day were displayed on the walls, alongside letters and printed-out Facebook posts from bar owners explaining why they were closing.

The project was born out of Macon's own disillusionment with the spaces available to them. "I couldn't find a queer space that felt like it centered me and the people that I wanted to make out with. [. . .] I was really frustrated, and I felt lonely," Macon confesses. As Macon began talking casually with friends and acquaintances about the reason for these closures, they noticed a common stereotype: "Dyke and dyke-adjacent people don't like to cruise or have sex as much and just want to hang out at home and drink tea with their cats," Macon summarizes with bemusement. "There's nothing wrong with hanging out at home and drinking tea with your cats, but I was like, is that really true?"

So, Macon began interviewing queer elders and long-standing community members to parse through "the conversations and stereotypes and assumptions around why [dyke bars] weren't thriving."

They soon discovered that the factors dictating the creation and survival of dyke spaces go far beyond individual preferences within the community. There is a set of distinct socioeconomic factors that, as Macon puts it, "specifically cis, white, gay men don't experience in the same way that all other queer people do."

"[If] you go back in history, [. . .] women weren't allowed to even order a drink by themselves. [. . .] They had to have a man with them to get a drink," Macon explains. "Women weren't allowed to have credit cards until the 1970s [. . .] and women were paid so much less for their salaries in general because it was assumed that if a woman was working, it was supplementary to a husband."

Historically, these socioeconomic conditions impacted the health and longevity of queer women's spaces in two ways: "When you don't have as much money to go out, you're less likely to party. But also [. . .] you're less likely to have resources to [stay] open if you're running a bar."

Today, women can get credit cards and take out loans. We're allowed to buy a drink without a man present. And, in recent years, great strides have been made toward closing the gender pay gap. But in many ways, we are still feeling the ripple effects from decades of inequity.

Reflecting on the many dyke bars memorialized in the exhibit, Justine and Nikke had a realization: "We don't want it to be a thing of the past," Justine says.

"Looking back, I would not do it again," Nikke exclaims, as she and Justine burst into laughter. They're extremely proud of the space they've created, but they have no qualms about admitting that opening a bar has been a challenging journey.

In 2020, after a few years of research and planning, Nikke and Justine thought they had found their space. They were in lease negotiations when in March, with COVID-19 cases popping up across the country, they decided to back out. In retrospect, Justine says: "I'm very glad we did because we would have been screwed. [. . .] We would have shot our shot too early. [. . .] [The Bush] wouldn't have gotten off the ground if we had to close for COVID."

Then, in early 2022, they were in contentious lease negotiations for a spot on Wyckoff Avenue. The landlord there was "really Christian and worried about us being too political," Justine details, "and we're like, well, what do you mean by that?"

He told them he didn't want them to "put stuff in the windows."

Justine and Nikke were somewhat baffled by this. They hadn't even shared their plans for the space with him yet. "Is being gay political to you? [. . .] What about us and what we've presented to you, which is a pitch deck for a cocktail bar, makes you feel like you need to put something in our lease about us being political?" Justine questioned. "I was shocked by how conservative a lot of the landlords in New York are."

Soon after that lease fell through, The Bush finally found a home on the corner of Troutman and Irving. A deep and somewhat narrow space, it had room for everything they were envisioning: a large dance floor in the back, a long bar—with an extensive craft cocktail menu—and plenty of places to install seating.

"We opened this bar on credit cards and a little bit of hope and gumption," remarks Justine. "It makes sense to me now, after doing it [. . .] why there's so few spaces. Because it's made to be a very difficult thing to do."

Nonetheless, on April 14, 2023, Nikke and Justine officially opened "The Bush: A Dyke Bar for Queers." Their tagline is designed to signal who is welcome in the space—all queers—while proudly advertising its identity as a "dyke bar."

Dyke is a term with a thorny history. It was originally a slur used to describe masculine-presenting lesbians. As early as the 1970s, though, some lesbians sought to reclaim the term. Dykes on Bikes is a lesbian motorcycling group founded in 1972 in San Francisco. Alison Bechdel penned the famous weekly comic strip *Dykes to Watch Out For* from 1983 to 2008.[2] In the 1990s, Dyke Marches began popping up in cities across the country during Pride.

Today, many Gen Zers and millennials like me feel attracted to the word as well. Macon chose to use the word in the title of their art installation *Eulogy for the Dyke Bar*, which has since had six iterations around the world. "Dyke felt like the most open version of what I was trying to say," Macon explains. "If you've ever, or think you might ever, identify with dykeness or dyke culture [. . .] then this is a place for you." Macon feels the word *dyke* is "less attached to a specific gender or sexuality" and more attached to "an ethos of mutual aid and fuck you to fucked up systems."

Dyke Beer, a Brooklyn-based craft beer company whose beverages can be found at The Bush, selected the word for their name as well. Cofounder Sarah Hallonquist remarks: "We're trying to reclaim the word *dyke* like the word *queer* was reclaimed." Like Macon, Sarah appreciates the gender inclusiveness of dyke. "There's a lot of folks who fall underneath the term *dyke*. I feel like *dyke* is this little umbrella term underneath *queer*."

Of course, *dyke* isn't the only word in The Bush's full title that turns some heads. *Bush* is a double entendre. "Queer bars have this long history of naughty names. They're always something like the Pink Pussycat or like The Ramrod. I think The Ramrod is actually a real bar," Justine says. They're correct: The Ramrod was a gay leather bar in the West Village that catered primarily to men and ran from around 1973 until 1980.[3]

Justine and Nikke wanted the name of their bar to be "naughty," but they also wanted it to be inclusive. They wanted a name that reflects what it means "to be a dyke bar in 2024," Nikke declares. They settled on The Bush, because, as Nikke aptly explains, "most people can have a bush." Bushwick, of course, seemed the natural neighborhood choice.

They've gotten a lot of positive feedback on the name. "Everyone loves it," Nikke affirms.

"I mean, well, a lot of our vendors are old guys," Justine follows up. "They never say anything though. Everyone's always very discreet. Sometimes they'll turn red and [. . .] you can see them clock it."

"We also coincidentally love pubic hair," adds Justine.

To which Nikke replies: "Exactly. Long live the bush."

Chapter Six

A LEAGUE OF HER OWN AND AS YOU ARE

SURVIVAL READY

WASHINGTON, DC

Over the course of one single day in 2018, Rach "Coach" Pike shaved their head, met their future wife, Jo, and set into motion a series of events that would lead to the creation of a new, radically inclusive queer space in Washington, DC.

The week prior, Coach and a friend wandered into Pitchers, a bar in Adams Morgan that caters to gay men. As Coach recalls, a security guard clocked them and said, "Queer women, come take the tour, look what we're building!" Pitchers' ownership was opening a lesbian bar in the basement of their ten-thousand-plus-square-foot venue. Coach descended the stairs, spotting Jo McDaniel, general manager of the soon-to-open A League of Her Own, or ALOHO as it's known. The two said a brief hello before Jo hastily returned to working on renovations.

Excited by the prospect of a lesbian bar in town for the first time since Phase 1 had closed after forty-five years of business, Coach decided to apply for a security position at ALOHO.[1] When Coach returned for their interview, Jo—expecting the long-haired, "dapper to the nines" individual she had spotted the weekend before—almost didn't recognize them.

"I had literally shaved my head thirty minutes before I showed up," Coach shares, "which was liberating and I'd wanted to do [it] my whole life. And then I looked in the mirror and was like, 'Ohh I'm pretty white, this looks terrible.' So, I wore a lot of hats."

Jo must not have thought the cut looked too bad. "The moment we met, we fell into step," she remarks. "Our missions align. And we yin and yang so well." For one, they share the same values surrounding what a queer space should be, and who it should be for. "I like to say I'm queering the gay agenda," explains Jo. "And by that, I mean [making] it more inclusive and [. . .] anti-oppressive and a little bit less capitalistic."

Jo herself has a long history of working in the DC LGBTQ+ nightlife scene. Before ALOHO, she worked at Apex, Cobalt, Freddy's Beach Bar and Grill, Phase 1, and Phase 1 of Dupont. "I think in gay bars historically, and I know this because I worked there, there is cattiness, there is misogyny, there is racism, there is white supremacy, there's rape culture. These things that we think we're not capable of because we're a queer community or a marginalized community are absolutely possible," Jo says emphatically.

A key part of "queering the gay agenda" is thinking about intersectionality. As Coach says, the queer community is "a marginalized community that touches all other marginalized communities. [. . .] There are queer people that are not able-bodied, there are queer people that are POC, Black, Deaf and hard of hearing." According to Coach, a queer space is "more than a bar or a restaurant, [it's] a community post." And it has the responsibility to take care of all the humans within that community.

In August of 2018, A League of Her Own opened its doors to the public. Being connected to Pitchers offers financial stability that some lesbian bars struggle to find. While both bars are owned by Dave Perruzza, a cis gay man, ALOHO has always been predominantly run by queer women.

During their time at ALOHO, Jo and Coach were able to make significant strides toward taking care of the entire community. Jo, for example, introduced what she calls the "enthusiastic model of consent" for ordering drinks. This policy means that you can only order as many drinks as there are people in front of the bartender. And everyone must confirm that they want one. "If five people ask for shots, five people have to say, 'Hell yes,' or at least raise their hands. You can't buy a drink for someone without asking them," Jo explains. "Yeah, I know it's less romantic to go introduce yourself, and—" Jo continues, but Coach cuts her off:

"I dunno. I think it's sexier," they tease, exchanging a knowing smile with Jo.

Coach also developed a comprehensive safety management program for the bar. "We wanted to shift from just being a responsive or reactive security staff to being a preventative security staff," they assert. Coach is clear: this does *not* mean policing who is and is not allowed inside the bar. "I'm a big advocate for not profiling anyone at the door," Coach says bluntly. Historically, many lesbian bars would turn away men and straight folks in an attempt to maintain safety. Today with "recognition of gender expression and gender identity [. . .] that's a really terrible thing to do to people, because they are part of your community and they might not read as your stereotypical gay person," Coach explains. "If you are coming in here, you are welcome to come in here, and so long as your behavior celebrates and appreciates and is loving toward our culture, whether you're queer or not, you can stay."

This inclusivity simply requires more communication to keep everyone safe and comfortable. "It doesn't take ego and aggressive[ness] and this kind of toxic masculine presence to be a good security guard. It just takes honest, impeccable conversation to find out what people are doing and let them know what's acceptable," says Coach.

Still, some of Jo and Coach's ideas were out of reach at ALOHO. "When you're not the owner, your mission only goes so far, because ultimately you're going to come up against the person who is actually in charge," Jo emphasizes. She and Coach wanted to install a wheelchair lift to make the upstairs dance floor that they shared with Pitchers accessible. They wanted to include young people by offering some events open to folks under twenty-one. They were interested in creating more options for non-drinkers. If you're thinking of a bar as a strictly capitalist business, these ideas might not make a lot of sense. But Jo and Coach are invested in people more than profit.

At the beginning of 2021, the pair left ALOHO. One, because they were starting to make plans for opening a business of their own, and two, because ALOHO had a strict no fraternization policy for its staff. "And we were in *love*," Coach croons.

The two had always had palpable chemistry. As Coach says, "Everybody in that place thought we were already dating." But it wasn't until the first COVID-19 lockdown that they acknowledged their feelings for one another. In November of 2020, they made their relationship official. A year later, they were signing a commercial lease in DC's Capitol Hill, with plans to open As You Are. Coach came up with the name. "It's as simple as that," they explain. "I just want to be able to come as I am, I want to use the restroom as I am, I want to see my friends come in as they are."

We meet Coach and Jo for the first time in DC in the summer of 2021 before the official opening of As You Are. They are both wearing the upcoming bar's merch: Coach in a backwards black baseball cap and Jo in a T-shirt cut into a tank top. Their teen kid, Jo's from a previous relationship, joins us for brunch and it strikes me that the pair gives off impeccably cool, young queer mom and dad vibes. Certainly, this stems from their deep commitment to caregiving—for the queer community and its most vulnerable members. When we connect again, two years into running As You Are, it does not surprise me in the slightest to hear that many of the younger regulars actually call them Mom and Dad.

But Coach and Jo detail the struggles of getting their business off the ground before this success. Securing their space was only the beginning of a fairly grueling process. "Opening was uh . . . tough," Coach tells us.

"Yeah, *challenging*," chimes in Jo with a wry smile.

"That's putting it lightly, I think," Coach follows up. "Between DC agencies and then the neighbors. They really didn't want us here. They have a very different opinion now. They love us. But they were worried about sound. They had very strong preconceived notions about what the queer community is like," Coach continues.

In DC, a community's opinion of an incoming bar or restaurant matters more than it does in most cities. "You essentially have to get the permission of the neighborhood in order to apply for a liquor license," Jo explains. Because DC's municipal government is uniquely defined by federal law, every ward has an Advisory Neighborhood Commission (ANC), designed to give citizens a greater voice in their community. ANCs have the power to protest a liquor license, and the Alcohol Beverage Control board is required by law to give great weight to the ANC's recommendations.[2]

"We sat [in] on roughly sixteen hours' worth of meetings with the neighborhood," Jo recounts, during which she and Coach painstakingly argued their case as the neighbors aired their concerns.

"They thought [that] we were just gonna be like 'pouring onto the street drunk.' They didn't want our 'love affairs in their front yards,' these are direct quotes," Coach says.

One neighborhood resident, Pope Barrow, went so far as to send a letter to the ANC ahead of a meeting, expressing his concerns.[3] In it, he questioned: "What kind of business plan proposes to start a business in a totally hostile neighborhood, knowing ahead of time that ALL nearby neighbors are in adamant opposition?" He went on to explain his support for other types of businesses in the neighborhood, even "the Popeyes with its rats" and the former "porno studio on 8th between E and G" but expressed that As You Are was "a step too far."

The afternoon before the meeting, a copy of Barrow's letter was tweeted by @thehillishome, an account that shares news and info for the DC Capitol Hill neighborhood, drumming up both support for and opposition to As You Are, and bolstering attendance at the meeting.[4] Pope Barrow himself was of course present, and accusations of homophobia and racism flew in the chat as other neighbors sided with him. Reporter Laura Hayes covered the meeting in an article for *Washington City Paper* titled "Meeting About As You Are Bar's Liquor License Lasts Three Ugly Hours." Hayes wrote, "It will be hard to forget how tense the meeting became at times. The chat read like trolls subtweeting each other; at one point, Barrow guaranteed that the business would fail."

Jo and Coach learned a key lesson from that contentious meeting. "The people that typically come to ANC meetings, they work one job, nine to five, they're usually monied, they're often white, they're often older, and they often come because they want to make sure that their complaints get heard," Coach describes. Whereas many of the people who would support a business like As You Are don't even know to show up. So, Jo and Coach put out a call to the community.

"It's two of us versus like thirty of them. And they are wrong about who we are and how we behave and what the benefits of a space like this [are]," Coach remembers telling friends. A few weeks later, Jo and Coach shared a post on As You Are's Instagram page inviting supporters to attend the final meeting during which the ANC would vote on the bar's liquor license.

It worked. Community members flooded the meeting to support As You Are, with many volunteering to share what the bar would mean to them personally. ANC commissioner Robb Dooling, who is a Deaf, queer person, spoke and signed, acknowledging As You Are's commitment to provide ASL interpretation for all their events with spoken elements. "I wanted to [. . .] emphasize how much this space means to not only the LGBTQ+ community but also the Deaf community,"[5] he said.

Mike Silverstein, an older community member, discussed being twenty years old at the time of the 1969 Stonewall Riots. "I was transfixed by it, but deeply in the closet, and I knew that if I would ever say anything, I would probably lose many of my friends, my hopes of ever being a broadcast journalist would be gone, I'd probably be kicked out of my fraternity," he recounted. "Over my life, I've seen other people work to make it possible for me to be myself, and I've seen things that I never would have dreamed up, and tonight was one of those," he said, referring to the outpouring of love and support he witnessed for Jo, Coach, and As You Are.[6]

By the end of the meeting, "there wasn't much they could argue with," Coach reasons. "What are you going to say? We don't care about these communities?" The commission voted unanimously in support of As You Are's liquor license. In March of 2022, the bar finally opened. While As You Are is branded as a "safe and celebratory space for the LGBTQIA+ community," they don't shy away from the lesbian bar label, either. Coach asserts that we don't have to stop calling our spaces lesbian bars; we simply need to "define them in such a way that people recognize this isn't your typical, historical lesbian [bar. . . .] However you show up, however you live, however you identify, you can sit with me."

"Your best friend that you sit at the bar with for twenty years, [whom] you thought was a lesbian—a cisgendered, female lesbian—might have all along been genderqueer or trans or nonbinary, and just never had the space or the language," Coach continues. And a lesbian bar should continue to be a safe space for that person once they do find that language.

Today, As You Are's two-level space allows them to meet the needs of a great portion of the LGBTQ+ community. Downstairs is a cozy coffee shop. It's open to people of all ages until 9 p.m., providing an after-school and weekend hangout for LGBTQ+ youth. Upstairs is the dance floor. Historically, gay and queer bars have revolved around the dark dance floor experience, where drinks flow, music booms, and sweaty make-outs abound. While you can certainly find that upstairs on a weekend night, Jo and Coach want to offer their community more. "A huge component of our mission [is] that we are decentering booze and sex," Coach stresses.

Despite the positive reception from the community, and ultimately from the neighborhood, As You Are's path forward has been far from obstacle-free. First, early 2024 financial struggles threatened to shutter the bar. So, they launched a GoFundMe, raising $150,000 in eighty-seven hours—more than enough to keep them afloat. Then, the following summer, heavy rains and flooding forced them to close during a lengthy period of repairs. They were able to reopen, but these financial and logistical setbacks have stood in the way of some of Jo and Coach's accessibility goals. As of early 2025, they haven't yet been able to install a lift for wheelchair users to access the upstairs dance floor.

"I think owning the building before we invest [the] kind of money it would take to put a lift in is a priority," Jo explains to us. Owning the building is an ultimate dream of Jo and Coach's because "we know that's how queer spaces stay."

Perhaps the most frightening challenge they face currently is the onslaught of anti-LGBTQ+ legislation passing through the US Capitol, just blocks away. There are bills and executive orders blocking trans folks from using their bathrooms of choice, playing sports, accessing gender-affirming care, or getting the correct gender markers on their passports. Budgets for key LGBTQ+ support programs have been slashed, like the 988 suicide lifeline for LGBTQ+ youth. DC, it feels, has become the epicenter of attacks on the queer community in the US, and Jo and Coach worry both about the direct effects of anti-LGBTQ+ policy on their community members and about the generally hostile environment being cultivated in their city.

"We think that the frequency in which we need to act in a protective way is going to be higher," Coach says, speaking to the logistics of running their security team. But Coach and Jo are clear: the queer community isn't going anywhere. "We've fought through these things. We are survival ready. We're going to find each other, stick together, and make it. And it might be ugly, and it might be hard, but we're gonna survive it," Coach reflects.

Part Two

THE MIDWEST

BE NICE OR LEAVE

Chapter Seven

LOST & FOUND AND EXECUTIVE SWEET

A HISTORY OF RESPECT AND RESISTANCE

CHICAGO, IL

It's 3 p.m. in Chicago on Sunday, November 13, 2022, and Lizard's Liquid Lounge is packed. Old-timers sip Coronas and snack off paper plates. Two folding tables line the walls, loaded with food, including a chocolate cake scrawled with the words "Happy 80th Birthday Linda!"

The bar in which we've all gathered to celebrate Linda Barsaloux is not just any old pub. Previously, it was Chicago's oldest, continuously operating lesbian bar: Lost & Found.

Lost & Found, or L&F as it's lovingly called, opened in 1965 and ran until 2008 when former owner Ava Allen sold the bar to Liz Kavanagh, who created Chicago's friendly neighborhood bar Lizard's Liquid Lounge. Still, the space remains a hangout spot for former L&F regulars like Linda who celebrates her eightieth birthday dressed in a brightly colored, festive Hawaiian shirt and spends the afternoon beaming at her surrounding friends and family.

Short, round faced, and kind eyed, Linda walked into L&F for the first time on Saint Patrick's Day of—she thinks—1985, at age forty-two. It was a laid-back spot that attracted a predominantly working-class crowd and was filled with sports paraphernalia, including items from the bar's own softball team. Former owner Ava herself could usually be found behind the bar, charming patrons with her Southern accent and her dance moves.

"She was [a] pretty wild woman. She used to dance on the bar," Linda tells us, the slightest hint of a lisp evident in her words.

Ava was "the main attraction," recalls another former L&F regular, Barbara, now in her seventies, with a shock of short, white hair and a pair of black, bedazzled glasses. Barbara stepped into L&F for the first time in the fall of 1973. Back then, she had long, red hair and was "very thin and very young," she tells us over the phone with a laugh. She had recently turned twenty-five, had an infant at home, and was in the midst of a contentious divorce from her first husband. She worked at her mother's beauty shop—a gig she despised—and one of her customers invited her out for drinks. Barbara agreed, and the customer took her to L&F.

That same year, Ava started working for L&F after getting together with the original owner, Shirley Christensen. Shirley "was the boss. But she felt very comfortable putting Ava up front," remarks Barbara. When Shirley passed away from cancer in 1986, Ava inherited the space, running the bar for another twenty-two years.

"I always got the feeling that she kind of felt trapped, like she had to stay there," reflects Linda, "but she also loved it." Beyond this, Linda won't reveal much of Ava's story. "She's a very private person," Linda explains. "Only certain people were allowed to be in her world, and luckily, I was one of them, so I don't wanna say too much. I don't wanna jeopardize my seat."

When Linda first started frequenting L&F, she was on the younger side of the crowd. "It used to be called Menopause Manor," she recalls with a laugh, "because it's where all the old ladies went." She notes that L&F had a plethora of unspoken rules: "You didn't sit in certain seats." Many of the regulars had particular bar stools where they always sat. Wally, for example, was "considered the mayor of lesbian land," Linda says, though she can't remember how Wally earned this title. She would "just sit there and everybody would cater to her. She was very manly. She drove a taxicab."

Another rule at L&F: the front door was always locked. For the forty-three years that the bar was in business, you had to knock or ring and get buzzed in by security—a process first implemented for safety purposes and later kept for the sake of tradition. Chicago LGBTQ+ journalist Tracy Baim remembers approaching the corner building, climbing the two steps to the door, and nervously pressing the buzzer. She would glance up at the door's darkened glass panel: "They could see out, but I couldn't see in," she recalls. "My heart would beat. Are they gonna let me in? And what am I gonna say?"

Tracy's nerves were heightened by the fact that often, she was there not only as a customer, but as a reporter, hoping to take photographs for *Windy City Times*, the local gay newspaper she'd cofounded. Many of the patrons did not take kindly to the sight of a camera in their place of sanctuary. "It was hard to ask people to take their photos, especially older, closeted women, or women who just didn't want to be in the limelight," Tracy reflects. Whatever their reasoning, Tracy always respected it. She understood the consequences a photo could hold. "This was before the internet, but even just being in a gay paper could have repercussions," she explains. "I got a lot of nos there, and I just really stopped asking a lot of the old timers."

There was a social code of privacy and respectability at L&F, particularly among the older generation. The idea of being "out," of claiming one's sexual orientation as an identity, wasn't a part of the culture. Linda, when speaking of the women she has been with throughout her life, proclaims: "None of my lovers have been gay except for one." Today, this statement might sound laughable. Wouldn't the very act of being Linda's lover make a woman at least a little gay? But for many women of Linda's generation, and those before, identity and sexuality existed in a hazy, undefined space.

"[For] many people in our community back then, everything was hush-hush," reflects Barbara, who perfectly exemplifies how one can move through life in this gray area. When Barbara first walked into L&F, she "didn't realize that [L&F was] different than a regular bar." But then she looked more closely at the couples all around her: "It dawned on me that some of these guys were girls!" Barbara exclaims with a giggle.

The "guys" that Barbara thought she saw when she first stepped into L&F, were, of course, all butch women. Barbara was not perturbed and remembers being embraced and respected by the butches and femmes alike. "And when I was invited back again, I came back again," she says. She had no inclination of being attracted to women herself, at least not yet, but she was curious about the community. "I had never seen anything like this," Barbara explains, "and I wanted to see more."

Through L&F, Barbara befriended a woman named Kay Price. Neither woman had a partner, and both were living with their mothers. Kay soon found an apartment and suggested she and Barbara split the expenses and cohabitate, along with Barbara's young son, Anthony. Barbara said yes, and so began a lengthy and nuanced partnership.

"Out of the fourteen years [we were together] . . . " Barbara trails off. "I'll bet you half of that [time we were] intimate." It didn't start out that way, though. When they moved into the shared apartment, they were truly just close friends, with Kay in one bedroom and Barbara and Anthony sharing the other.

One night, Kay invited Barbara into her room. "And then it was touchy-feely, and it just went from there," Barbara describes.

Barbara and Kay clearly meant a great deal to each other, yet they never defined or labeled their relationship. "There was never any commitment of any kind," Barbara explains. "[Kay] was fourteen, almost fifteen years older than me, and she always said, 'You are your own person, you do what you want. [. . .] You're young. Go.'"

Despite the ambiguity of their relationship, Barbara never hid her feelings for Kay from her son or her mother. When Anthony was about ten, Barbara sat him down. "You know Mom's friends and everybody, they're a little different . . . " Barbara began, but Anthony didn't need any sort of an explanation. A smart and perceptive kid, he'd heard Barbara and Kay refer to their friends as gay many times, and he understood what it meant. Still, Barbara continued: "There's different kinds of love. [. . .] Even though Kay and I are both women, we love each other like we're married."

Anthony, of course, had already put two and two together. "Oh, I know all about that, Mom!" he exclaimed with a grin, rolling his eyes. And that was that. Anthony embraced his mother and her partner fully.

Barbara's mother, Arlene, was equally accepting. She even began tagging along with Barbara to the gay bars, beginning with a visit to L&F during one of Ava's notorious annual costume parties.

"Well, can't I come to the party?" Arlene asked.

"It's a public place and you're a woman, why not?" Barbara answered.

So, Arlene went. "She had a ball," Barbara says. Every so often, Arlene would continue to join Barbara for a night out. "She became good friends with some of these girls, but they looked at her like a mom."

In the early 1990s, Barbara and Kay split. Barbara had a few brief flings with other women, but Kay was her only serious queer relationship. Today, Barbara is married to a man named Jim. "I think every one of us is born with the capability of being with a man or a woman," she muses. "Living this life for as long as I did, [. . .] certain women, their ways, their actions, their mannerisms, you become attracted to them. Once you're attracted to somebody, you're curious as to their personal life. What is it like to have dinner with them? What is it like to cuddle with them?"

She's never shared this side of herself with Jim, although she doesn't shy away from discussing her time at L&F and the many L&F women with whom she maintains friendships. "He knows that they are my friends, I am their friend, and I won't give up my friendship with my gay friends for any other community. They helped me through life," she reflects.

From talking to both Barbara and Linda, it is clear that the L&F community has long outlived the bar itself. In fact, a good percentage of guests at Linda's eightieth birthday were former L&F regulars. "And there was fifty people that didn't come," Linda exclaims. "I'm not kidding you, I got a whole list of these people."

At Linda's party, we meet Michelle—tall, energetic, and boldly unfiltered. She's of a younger L&F generation than Barbara and Linda, and she's more outspoken about her identity. Within minutes of meeting us, she's telling us how she joined the military at seventeen when she realized she was gay. "I'm like, well, if gays can't join the military, I should join the military. I won't run into any gay people, and I'll be fine," Michelle says, laughing incredulously at just how wrong her younger self was.

When Michelle first started frequenting L&F in the mid 1990s, she wasn't exactly embraced. "The patrons were very off-putting and cold," she describes, "and I could never figure out if it was because I'm African American or because I'm not a sports enthusiast."

Most of the lesbian bars in Chicago in the 1990s were predominantly white. Journalist Tracy Baim estimates the crowd at L&F was at least 95 percent white. To our knowledge, people of color were never explicitly turned away there but they were not made to feel particularly welcome. L&F was not unique in this regard, and certainly at other lesbian bars in Chicago and beyond, women of color faced more explicit discrimination.

We cannot talk about lesbian bar history, L&F included, without also addressing the racial context in which it unfolded. Historically, white lesbians had greater access to both financial and social capital, meaning they could more easily open and sustain bars of their own. Plus, white women seemed a more lucrative customer base for outsiders—from gay men to Mafia members—who sought a profit in the lesbian bar business. Particularly in Chicago, one of the most racially segregated cities in the country,[1] Black lesbians often had to make a choice: challenge racism at the predominantly white bars or carve out queer space of their own by way of house parties and pop-up events.

Patricia McCombs, a lesbian organizer in every sense of the word, did both—planning protests and parties. Sarah and I meet her in her apartment on the South Side of Chicago, where she begins to tell us her story. In 1974, Pat noticed that Black women like herself were being discriminated against at CK's, another lesbian bar on Chicago's North Side. The bouncer would often ask women of color to present multiple forms of ID at the door, turning them away if they couldn't. It was a clear racial tactic to prevent women of color from entering the space—who carries multiple forms of ID for a night out?

This was not the first time that Pat experienced prejudice in the Chicago lesbian bar scene, which she'd been frequenting since she was in college. "Mind you, I didn't have any trouble getting in bars when [I was] around a bunch of white girls," she recalls. "It's when we come by [ourselves] that I noticed we had certain problems. It's like they didn't want a lot of us in the place at one time."

In 1975, having had enough, Pat organized a protest outside CK's and got together a group of fellow activists to form the Black Lesbian Discrimination Investigation Committee. They reported CK's to the state liquor commission.[2] So as not to lose their liquor license, CK's conceded to publicly post a list of accepted forms of ID at the door, ensuring that everyone was held to the same standards.[3]

But Pat was reluctant to continue patronizing CK's. "Why go to them [if] they don't want you there? [. . .] That's what made me really want to just organize my own parties," Pat reflects. "Black people have a different kind of community. See, you've been with the white girls," Pat tells us, referring to the historic brick-and-mortar spaces we've been covering, like L&F. "They had the bars. We didn't. We had parties. [In] people's homes and stuff." Pat does recall a few Black gay bars on the South Side of Chicago, but they were predominantly for men and would often get raided.

Pat soon joined Executive Sweet, a women-of-color-centered group creating LGBTQ+ events in the city, and by 1982, she was leading it alongside her friend Vera Washington. "We'd walk around and find different bars that weren't doing very well on the weekends," Pat explains. Pat and Vera would approach the owners of these bars with discretion surrounding the exact nature of Executive Sweet's events. "[We] didn't really say we were lesbians 'cause a lot of 'em would have discriminated against us. We told them we were a sorority, and we were having a meeting, and so it would be mostly all women," Pat recounts. She and Vera would dress the part too: "One thing about white people, they're very visual. So, you walk in, you look very businesslike, and they assume."

"We just traveled around all over the city of Chicago. [. . .] I always liked to rent real fabulous [places] 'cause I liked for people to dress up. [Guests] had to dress up when they came [to our events]," Pat details, reflecting on the decades of parties she threw with Executive Sweet.

Part of the mission of Executive Sweet was to create a safe space for queer women who, as Pat says, had to be "undercover." Pat would refrain from putting the words *lesbian* or *gay* on the flyers she distributed to advertise for her parties, despite that being the target audience. "Professional Black women who have certain jobs, they just can't go out to certain places 'cause they don't want to be seen," Pat explains. "If you['re] Doctor such-and-such, you don't want to go to a certain bar and then [the police] come and raid the bar and here you are, the doctor sitting up in there," she adds, noting the constant risk of being outed.

Pat herself had to be cautious due to her own employment; she worked as a special education teacher in the Chicago Public Schools for four decades. "I was undercover for years," she tells us. "Tracy Baim always tried to take pictures," Pat remarks, and for years, she would have to tell Tracy no.

In 2000, Pat was inducted into the Chicago LGBT Hall of Fame, stepping out of the closet publicly. "They had the highlights from the Gay and Lesbian Hall of Fame on Channel 11 and one of my students saw it," she recalls.

"Miss McCombs, I saw you on TV!" exclaimed the student in class the next day.

"Oh, really darling?" Pat answered, but on the inside, she remembers thinking, *Oh, fuck.* She kept her cool. "Oh, honey, did I look good?" she asked the student.

"Yeah, Miss McCombs, you was looking nice," he replied.

"Oh, thank you, baby. [Now] turn to page two hundred in your math book," Pat remembers saying.

And the lesson continued. "I acted like it was no big thing; he acted like it was no big thing," Pat reflects. Times had changed since Pat first started teaching. Her sexuality was no longer a threat to her job.

Pat and Vera continued to host Executive Sweet parties through the early 2000s,[4] and in more recent years they've hosted reunion events.[5] Eventually, Pat even let Tracy take her picture. In one of Tracy's photos from a 2013 reunion, Pat looks straight into the camera, a wide smile on her face.[6] "You [could] always depend on Tracy Baim gonna be there if nothing else. That was one white girl that was coming," Pat asserts.

"I always felt welcome as a white woman, even if I was in the 1 percent at some of the events," notes Tracy. "[Executive Sweet] was always welcom[ing] to all. And women of color, not just Black women, but Latina women, Asian women, et cetera, were always welcome."

"We had all races because I didn't discriminate against who was coming. I just wanted to give a good party," Pat says. "Our main emphasis was women of color. Cause we were the ones being discriminated against. But *we* didn't discriminate. [. . .] All they had to do was be on good behavior and want to have a good time. That was our emphasis, just to have a good time [in] a safe environment for all women."

Chapter Eight

NOBODY'S DARLING

FOR THE OUTCASTS

CHICAGO, IL

At Nobody's Darling, Chicago's Black, queer, women-owned cocktail bar, you can often find Shirley J seated at a high-top table, her spot marked with a custom-made RESERVED sign. We immediately hear tales of Shirley J when we visit the bar for the first time in 2021. Now in her eighties, Shirley has been lovingly dubbed "the mayor of Nobody's Darling." She's well known around the bar for her generosity and her strong presence, often buying drinks for the younger crowd. Her VIP status stems not only from her effervescent personality and marked altruism but also from her legacy in Chicago LGBTQ+ nightlife.

Shirley first stepped onto the scene in the early 1970s, at thirty years old. One night, a friend took her to a gay bar, where she unexpectedly found her brother and learned he was gay. Looking around, she quickly realized she was gay too. "You have these feelings, you know, for women. Back in the day, you couldn't just act on them," Shirley explains. She remembers walking into that gay bar and being hit with the revelation that all these other people felt the same way she did.

Shirley quickly became ingrained in the Chicago queer community. Soon, she and a group of her friends began venturing to New York to explore the nightlife scene there. They would often attend The Loft, the famous weekly dance party hosted by David Mancuso in his downtown Manhattan loft apartment. The party "would start [at] midnight and last [until] seven in the morning," Shirley recalls. The crowd at The Loft was diverse in every sense of the word. Folks were of all races, genders, sexualities, and ages,[1] and the music ranged from disco to jazz to R&B.[2]

In 1977, Shirley and her friends brought this type of party to Chicago. "We just started with a house party, and it was big, huge, okay? And after that, we had parties every [. . .] Saturday night. That was it," Shirley states. When they outgrew their house party model, they rented a warehouse space in what's now the West Loop. "We turned it into a club, you know? It was just beautiful, with the disco ball and balloons," describes Shirley. The party was aptly dubbed "The Warehouse."

Like The Loft, The Warehouse operated on a model of exclusivity. You had to be invited to attend The Loft in New York. In Chicago, Shirley and her friends came up with a membership system. "You had to come to a party three times in a row to become a member, so we would get to know you," she says. Existing members could bring guests, and guests could then become members.

Unlike The Loft, The Warehouse was a predominantly Black and gay crowd, though membership was open to everyone. Being "men and women, boys and girls," as Shirley puts it, offered some cover by way of the illusion of heteronormativity. But members still had to be cautious of attracting too much attention. Shirley remembers some of her male friends renting lockers nearby to change clothes "because they didn't want to travel on public transportation looking gay."

At The Warehouse, a new genre of music was born: house music. "That's why house music now is called house, because when we opened up The Warehouse, people would say 'Are you going to the House tonight?'" explains Shirley. Eventually, *house* would come to be used as a descriptor for the kind of music played there, "because it was a different type of music. It wasn't the disco music anymore. It was a house sound. If you know anything about house music, you understand what I'm saying."

House music, as it first came to be in Chicago, blended disco with soul, R&B, funk, and new electronic music. The Warehouse's resident DJ was the iconic Frankie Knuckles, and the music he played was expansive, rhythmic, and deeply danceable. He layered steady, electronic beats with warm bass lines, soaring vocals, melodic riffs, and sweeping synths. The result? A transcendent dance floor experience unlike anything anyone had ever known before.[3]

Shirley and her friends would also frequent the city's other gay and lesbian bars. Like Pat McCombs, who had protested CKs just two years before The Warehouse opened, Shirley experienced racial discrimination at many of these institutions. "For Black gay women or lesbian women, it was harder to get in as a group to some of the bars that were open. If it was more than two of you, and you were Black, they wouldn't let you in," she recalls. "That was the '70s," she continues matter-of-factly.

Today, Shirley has a lesbian bar where she knows she's always welcome: Nobody's Darling, which was cofounded by Angela Barnes and Renauda Riddle in 2021. During our visit, the two are holding court at a high-top table in the front corner of the bar. They're effortlessly comfortable, chatting with friends and patrons and overseeing their space.

Angela has always been drawn to the bar business. "As I grew up, I was very much into making drinks for friends. And I thought 'Oh my God, I can totally bartend,'" she reflects. However, life initially took her in another direction. She went off to college, then law school. Today, she also balances a career in corporate law. Before cofounding Nobody's Darling, she would often ask her childhood friend, whose family owned a bar business, for a chance behind the bar.

"You're a lawyer, you can't bartend!" her friend would tell her.

"I sort of secretly harbored this desire to figure out how I could bartend," Angela confesses. Then, she met Renauda Riddle. They crossed paths at Chicago's LGBTQ+ community center: the Center on Halsted. Renauda led the Women's Action Committee there, often programming events for the center, outside of which she had also built a career in queer nightlife. Renauda grew up a Jehovah's Witness in Huntsville, Alabama, without any semblance of a queer community. "I didn't realize I was gay until fifteen or sixteen. And didn't know what that really was until I got to college and got around other people that were gay," she explains.

Angela and Renauda first bonded over their common interests. "We figured out we both like to golf and drink," Angela remarks. It was on the golf course that Renauda eventually floated the idea of opening a bar together. A local lesbian-owned wine bar called Joie De Vine was closing, and the owners had approached Renauda about taking over the space.

And Angela? "She finally said yes, after a few asks," Renauda shares.

In March of 2021, they got to work flipping the old Joie De Vine space in Chicago's Andersonville neighborhood. Both were a bit nervous about "being two Black women opening a bar in a predominantly white neighborhood," Angela reflects. Much to their relief, the community embraced them. Before they even opened, the neighbors stopped by to welcome them.

In May of 2021, Nobody's Darling officially opened. Angela was especially excited; she would finally get the chance to step behind the bar. However, she quickly realized that bartending was harder than she thought it would be. "I panicked and I started making shots," she recounts. Now, Angela mostly leaves the bartending to the professionals. We get a taste of Angela's version of bartending when we visit; she insists we all do a shot of Malört together, a Chicago tradition. We toast and Jen, Sarah, and I swallow down the brown liquid—bitter and with a hint of gasoline—beneath the chalkboard scrawled with the text of the poem "Be Nobody's Darling," for which the bar is named.

It was Angela who came up with the name, sending the idea to Renauda along with the poem by outspoken queer, Black writer Alice Walker. "Be Nobody's Darling" encourages the reader to be an outcast, to belong only to themself, and to find community among other outsiders, both living and dead. Instantly, Renauda knew that's what their bar would be called: "the poem itself, being an outcast, all those things just speak to who we are and what we wanted to bring to the bar and the space."

Chapter Nine

DOROTHY

WHERE ANY FRIEND OF DOROTHY IS WELCOME

CHICAGO, IL

Zoe Schor and Whitney LaMora fell in love while opening the Chicago lesbian bar Dorothy. "You also like to tell people that we met on Craigslist," Whitney teases Zoe, going on to clarify that she had been on the website searching for a job, not a partner. It's early afternoon and we're seated in the empty, subterranean bar, many hours before opening. Both Zoe and Whitney have short brown haircuts and tattoos that reflect their passions; on Zoe's arms, a carrot and a martini hint at her love of cooking and crafting cocktails, while Whitney's sleeves of intricate, colorful designs speak to her love of art. They met back in 2018. Zoe was working as a chef, serving comfort food and craft cocktails at her restaurant Split Rail when Whitney came in for a job interview. Whitney had been working in corporate sales but had dreams of opening a gallery and event venue. "I left the nine-to-five world and ended up applying for restaurant work so I could open up space in my day in order to pursue [my dreams]," Whitney explains.

Meanwhile, Zoe was already making plans for her next business endeavor: opening a bar beneath Split Rail. Despite already having the basement under contract, Zoe hadn't yet shared her plans publicly. One night after a long shift at the restaurant, Zoe told Whitney her idea.

"Do you want to come see it?" Zoe asked.

"*Obviously*," Whitney responded.

So, the two headed over and descended the stairs under Split Rail. The space was raw; it had recently been gutted. "It was like wires from the ceiling," Whitney describes. There was a large horseshoe bar in the center of the room and a baby grand piano in one corner. Aside from that, "it was just dust, construction, horror, terror," Whitney says.

At that moment, Whitney knew there was something between her and Zoe. "I'm in this basement with this one other person. And it is feeling like a thing," Whitney remembers.

"We should probably go!" Whitney exclaimed to Zoe in a panic.

It wasn't just the shock of falling for her boss that had Whitney looking for an exit. "Up until that point, I had identified strictly as a straight person," she reveals to Jen, Sarah, and me. "I had never dated a woman. I had never really entertained the thought." In the end, Whitney embraced the truth: "I was like, nah girl, you're falling for this woman. Like real hard."

The two eventually admitted their feelings for one another, and in addition to becoming romantic partners, became business partners. Together, Zoe and Whitney transformed the basement, modeling the bar after a speakeasy. Patrons would have to know what they were looking for to find it, with the bar marked only by a single red door bearing the word *lounge* in yellow lettering. Behind the door, a staircase would lead guests down into a lush, timeless establishment, the aesthetic a combination of 1920s Prohibition, 1940s Hollywood, and 1970s disco. Zoe and Whitney installed glimmering disco balls, collected an eclectic mix of vintage art and furniture, and outfitted a corner of the main room with custom-built, plush, red, deep couches, creating an area they call "the bed lounge." In what would have otherwise been an utterly romantic gesture, a milestone in both their personal and professional relationships, they opened Dorothy on Valentine's Day—February 14, 2020. But the timing could not have been worse. A month later, the COVID-19 pandemic forced them to close.

After sixteen long months, pandemic restrictions were finally lifted throughout the city of Chicago. Folks started venturing out of their homes in search of community, and while Split Rail began welcoming dine-in customers again, the future of Dorothy still remained uncertain.

That is, until Rainn Thomas started Fruit Salad, a monthly queer open-mic night.

Rainn grew up in Milwaukee and made the move to Chicago in 2019, prompted by a lack of Black queer community and Black art community in their hometown. Shortly after their arrival, they were hired as an event assistant at Whitney's newly opened gallery the Martin. Rainn also became involved in the DIY Chicago scene, often attending house shows, open-mic nights, and small concerts for independent artists throughout the city.

Yet, they found the DIY music and art community to be "mostly cis, straight, white men," and felt somewhat alienated as a Black lesbian. "I don't want to walk in a room at an art event and know every person of color there. That has never been my goal. It is not a compliment to me to be in a space with other queer Black people [where] there's like two or three of us. It's insulting and really weird," they remarks. In large part, this lack of diversity was the impetus for Fruit Salad, which Rainn launched in October of 2021 as curator and emcee in Whitney's gallery space, located next to Split Rail and above the shuttered Dorothy. While anyone was welcome to attend and participate in the open mic, Rainn wanted to make a specific effort to platform individuals who might not have the opportunity to perform in many of Chicago's other venues.

Rainn is passionate about creating space for queer folks, particularly "people who are new on their queer journey," and who are embracing their identity later in life. This stems from "good old religious trauma," as Rainn puts it, and a desire for the type of community they wished they had earlier. Rainn calls themself a "late-in-life lesbian." They grew up in an extremely religious, evangelical family. "Do you know what evangelical is?" they ask us, and not waiting for an answer, continue: "It's the shouting and screaming and fainting version, [. . .] late night televangelists telling you that Pokémon cards are evil and the demons will jump out of the card and into your body."

It was Rainn's mom who drove their family's participation in evangelicalism. "My mom, I love you, but girl you be saying some stuff," Rainn exclaims. "My mom believes that gay people caused the pandemic by being allowed to be married. So that's the type of Christianity I'm talking about." Rainn's mom had homeschooled them and their ten siblings through middle school, so that prayer and religion could be integrated into their curriculum. "We would read the Bible every day. I think I've read the Bible three times in my lifetime," Rainn says.

In their young adulthood, with increasing awareness of their own queerness, Rainn had a lot of internalized homophobia to process. For a while, they embraced their desire "to sleep with women and people who aren't cis men," as they put it, but they couldn't get themself to see these individuals as romantic partners. Rainn was patient with themself through this chapter of their life, waiting to date anyone of any gender until it eventually felt right.

"I had this super cute neighbor," Rainn shares. "She had this scratchy voice, and she was this artist and immediately it was like, I wanna hold her hand and bake her some brownies." Something had clicked. "I felt I had the permission now to start dating as a queer person because I addressed that part in my brain that was equating queer people to just how I feel about them sexually, instead of seeing queer people as people," Rainn reflects.

Having fully come out to themself, Rainn felt it was time to come out to their mom. "As any fire sign would do, I sent my mom my poetry book, and in the front, I was like, 'By the way, I'm gay.' And just mailed it to her," Rainn recounts. Rainn did not get the reaction they hoped for, but they did get the one they expected.

"I'll pray for you," Rainn's mom told them over the phone.

"Okay, Mom. Don't call me until you're okay with me being a lesbian," Rainn answered, and hung up.

Still, Rainn holds an admirable amount of empathy for their mother. Speaking to their mom's commitment to evangelicalism, Rainn explains: "I believe it's truly what they felt was right, as a way to address trauma and as a way to keep a community [. . . and] her family together." Rainn traces the roots of Christianity in the Black community within the US: "Going all the way back to enslavement days, [. . .] a lot of the reasoning behind slavery was to 'save African people from themselves,' and a huge reason was because [white people] thought we were too amorous, like naturally sexually deviant. And then some enslaved [people's] owners started having church for these enslaved folks."

Rainn continues: "[In the] Jim Crow era, church still became a really great way for Black people to gather and find safety. And as time progressed on, white Christianity still became a way to become acceptable. [. . .] Respectability politics has a lot to do with that. To be seen as a person, you kind of have to play the same game." Today, Rainn believes that "a lot of Black people continue on with Christianity as a cultural expectation, never really questioning the why."

Over the years, Rainn themself has sought fellowship outside of the church, carving out a community that is more reflective of their own identity. "I cannot tell you what it's like to grow up thinking you're the only Black queer person and then you walk into a room with like three hundred people who are all Black and gay and they're all dancing with each other."

By January of 2022, Fruit Salad was soaring in popularity. "We had sold fifty tickets, but we were still allowing people in for the night, and people just kept coming and coming. And I had to cut it off at seventy-five. There's just not room," Whitney recalls.

Following that evening, Rainn, Whitney, and Zoe realized they needed a much bigger space for the event. Dorothy sat right below them, empty. So, for one night a month, Dorothy became home to Fruit Salad. In February, they allowed in one hundred guests. In March, they welcomed one hundred twenty. Whitney remembers seeing "the desire for the show explode" and "the queer community explode around it."

In July of 2022, Dorothy reopened fully. The success of the Fruit Salad events pushed Zoe to embrace the lesbian label for the bar. "Fruit Salad was [. . .] the biggest reason why [Zoe] felt comfortable finally saying 'I can open a lesbian place, and the queer community will show up because they're already here. And they're already loving it and they're already seeing it as a queer space,'" Whitney reflects.

Today, Dorothy's tagline is "a neighborhood lesbian cocktail lounge for every friend of Dorothy." Even before the rebrand as a lesbian bar, Zoe and Whitney say the name Dorothy was a nod to the legacy of the phrase *friend of Dorothy*. Historically, the saying was used as a coded way of identifying yourself as gay to other queer folks without outing yourself to straight folks. You could ask someone, "Are you a friend of Dorothy?" and if they said yes, you would know they were gay. If they said no, or looked confused, you could simply walk away.

There are a few competing theories as to the origin of the phrase. The leading theory is that it is a reference to *The Wizard of Oz*, and that it was popularized after the 1939 movie due to the gay community's love of the film. But there is some evidence of the phrase's use before the film's release, in the 1920s and early 1930s. One possibility is that it was a reference to the Wizard of Oz books by Frank L Baum. Another is that the phrase originally referred to a real woman named Dorothy: Dorothy Parker. Parker was a writer and critic based in New York who had large circles of gay friends. She was known to host opulent parties during Prohibition, and supposedly, gay folks would use the code "friend of Dorothy" to gain admission.[1]

Whatever the true origin of the phrase, by the mid-twentieth century it had become a beacon of safety and acceptance for queer folks throughout the country. Today, it signals Dorothy's inclusive nature. Yes, it's a lesbian bar. But all "friends of Dorothy"—all queer folks and all allies to the community—are welcome.

Zoe and Whitney shut down Split Rail and the Martin in December of 2023, and Fruit Salad ended in October of 2024 after three wildly successful years. But Dorothy lives on, challenging the notion that the lesbian bar is no longer a viable business model.

"Dorothy has saved us all," reflects Whitney.

Chapter Ten

SLAMMERS

A FAMILY AFFAIR

COLUMBUS, OH

Marcia Riley is shy. That's the first thing we learn about the founder of Slammers—Columbus, Ohio's lesbian bar since 1993. Deb Gordon tells us this when she greets us at the door during our visit in 2021. Deb is quite the opposite of shy. She's Marcia's best friend, and though the duo spent decades running Slammers together, Deb never had an official job title. "I don't like titles. I don't want a title," Deb explains to us. "I just tell people I'm Marcia's wingman."

Deb has been by Marcia's side since the bar's inception. In the early days of Slammers, Deb would meet Marcia at the front door each evening. It was always packed, and Marcia would be too nervous to make her way through the crowd alone. "Marcia's quiet," Deb tells us, "but she is the trailblazer." Of course, we were desperate to meet Marcia ourselves. Deb had told her we were coming, but it seemed unlikely she would make it out to the bar that evening.

Deb escorts us through Slammers, much as she used to do for Marcia. We walk past the lengthy bar in the front room, past the kitchen, where they make their famous pizzas, and into the back room, where we post up at a high-top table. Afternoon light streams through huge, glass garage doors that overlook Slammers' outdoor patio. The doors are a remnant of the space's previous business: an auto repair shop.

About an hour and a half into our time at Slammers, a small woman with a dark brown pixie cut quietly slips into the back room. It's Marcia herself. She tells us that she'd been making her partner drive around in circles as she wavered on whether she wanted to come talk with us.

"I don't speak. I always make them do it," Marcia insists, gesturing to Deb and the rest of her team. This will be the first of many times throughout the evening that she tells us she does not do interviews. Still, she sits down and—after a few shots of Patron—begins to share her story.

"I knew from a very young age that I was different," Marcia tells us. But it wasn't until she was in her thirties that she tumbled out of the closet. She had a husband of fourteen years and two young daughters. "It wasn't that I had a terrible marriage, because I did not. But I wasn't happy," Marcia says.

A friendship with a woman at work finally sparked Marcia's gay awakening. "I never felt that way around anybody. And I knew there was something going on," she recalls. The two became close friends but never dated. Still, the feelings this woman had inspired in Marcia made her marriage altogether untenable.

"I decided that I wanted [to get] divorced," Marcia explains, "and that was a hard thing to do. Because he didn't understand why." She wasn't ready to tell her soon-to-be ex-husband that she was gay. Marcia's mom was the first family member she came out to. It was shortly after she had shared her intent to file for divorce, and her mom wanted to know why.

"Is it another man?" Marcia's mom questioned.

"No," Marcia responded.

Finally, after a long list of other possible reasons for divorce, Marcia's mom asked: "Is it another woman?"

"Yes," Marcia muttered.

"Okay, that's fine," her mom said, "but we need to tell your dad."

Marcia's father was not nearly as supportive as her mother. "We had a long time, maybe two years, where we hardly talk[ed]," Marcia admits. Soon, Marcia's nine siblings found out too; "Some of them accepted it. And most of them did not."

The divorce and Marcia's coming out was particularly hard on her two daughters. "My ex-husband went to the school and told the principal why we got divorced. That started the whole ball rolling about all the kids teasing my daughters, and it was a bad scene," Marcia recounts.

Slammers itself played a significant role in helping Marcia's less-understanding family members learn to accept her. Deb says that "seeing how successful Marcia has been, and how she is such a rock star in this community, [. . .] how many people adore her and follow her" has inspired them to set aside their homophobia and embrace her.

The bar was initially the dream of Marcia's then-girlfriend, Brenda. "I did not want to do the bar," Marcia reflects on her early feelings about the business. "I had two children, I worked, and I drove back and forth to Columbus from Newark," she adds. Brenda was in the bar business and planned to open Slammers on her own after selling her previous spot to her business partner. But when her former business partner caught wind of her plans, he sued her for violating a non-compete clause that prohibited her from opening another bar in the area.

Brenda begged Marcia to open Slammers in her name instead. "We talked for a long time, and I ended up doing it. And I'm glad I did. I had a lot of ups and downs, but I'm glad I hung in there and stuck with it," Marcia tells us.

In the process of opening Slammers, Marcia moved to Columbus, where she and Brenda had bought a house together. One afternoon, the two were picking out wallpaper when Marcia started talking with the store manager: Deb Gordon.

"She said she knew we were gay the minute we walked in. I don't know why. I don't know how. But she said she did," says Marcia with bewilderment.

Deb says it was obvious. "Marcia walked in there with her partner of that particular time, Brenda, and the gaydar just went *nee-nah-nee-nah-nee*," Deb mimics, grinning. Marcia told Deb about the bar she was opening downtown, inviting her to come by and see it, and as Deb likes to say, "the rest is history."

Deb began to spend all her free time at the bar, helping Marcia with painting and renovations. To Marcia's surprise, her mom showed up to lend a hand too. "She helped me do remodeling on the inside. She did a lot," Marcia recalls fondly.

On August 31, 1993, Slammers finally opened to the public. "The bar was packed from the minute we opened until 2:30 [a.m.], every day, every night," Marcia recalls. "There's many times I hid in the closet back there crying because I was so overwhelmed." The transition from being a closeted suburban mom of two to being the owner and face of a successful lesbian bar was not easy. "I'm a little farm girl. I don't do too bad now. But it was hard for me."

Deb says that initially, the crowd at the bar was almost entirely women. "Back in the day, there was a lot of women that didn't *want* men in here," she adds. That was never how Marcia and Deb felt, though. "We just wanted people to know, yeah, it's a lesbian bar, but anyone is welcome," Deb clarifies.

This was an invitation that extended to Marcia's family too; over the years, they have all spent time at Slammers, and some have even worked there. Her mom spent many evenings at the bar well into her nineties, sipping a glass of Moscato and eating a pizza. Marcia's two daughters, now grown, have both bartended at Slammers, as have Marcia's two nieces, Carly and Kez. "I always knew there was something different about Kez," Marcia says. "She finally told me that she was gay. And I said, 'Well, come on. I have a job for you.'" Some of Marcia's siblings have even filled in as bartenders during her employee Christmas parties. So, when Marcia decided it was time for her to retire from bar ownership, after nearly thirty years in the business, she made sure to keep Slammers in the family. In 2022, she sold the bar to her nephew, Carson Nethers, who is also gay.

Neither Deb nor Marcia is particularly active in the day-to-day operations of the bar these days, but one thing hasn't changed. After all these years, Deb is undeniably still Marcia's wingman. Not only that: she's part of Marcia's family. "I'm like the eleventh kid," Deb tells us. "They take me on vacation. I go to all their parties. They're my family now."

"No matter what, I've always included [Deb] in my family. Easter, Christmas, everything, because she had no family here," Marcia adds. As Marcia's mom got older, Deb even took on caregiving responsibilities with the rest of the siblings. "We told [Deb], if she's gonna be in this family, she has to take a turn," Marcia says.

For Deb, Slammers gave her a family in Ohio that she didn't have. For Marcia, Slammers allowed her to show her existing family who she was and to finally be met with open arms. Today, when Marcia talks about her family, there's nothing but warmth in her voice. "They're wonderful," she says. "They love people, they treat people right. They're just wonderful people. And that's how I am. And that's pretty much how I ran this place."

Chapter Eleven

THE BACK DOOR

CONSENT IS FUCKING MANDATORY!

BLOOMINGTON, IN

The Back Door is hard to find. The bar is quite literally accessed through the building's back door, not visible from the street. A dark alleyway leads us around the building to a brightly lit patio, where murals of the Golden Girls and an astronaut riding a unicorn indicate we have successfully located the only queer space within a fifty-mile radius of Bloomington, Indiana.

Smoove Gardner, cofounder and owner of the Back Door, greets us upon arrival. She's clad in a bright blue Adidas tracksuit and a pair of purple and green Adidas sneakers. "I'm a dyke that wears a uniform. Two outfits: shorts and a T-shirt or tracksuit, that's it," Smoove tells us. She has fifteen tracksuits: "all different colors. I tend to go for the slightly faggier ones," she adds. Perhaps the most distinct feature of Smoove's outfit is the T-shirt she sports underneath her unzipped sweatshirt. It features an artistic rendering of a naked woman in the sky; she's beaming up a figure from the earth into the opening of her spaceship-body—her vagina.

Smoove also rocks a handsome horseshoe mustache. "The mustache is because I got tired of dealing with it," she explains. "Menopause is also not hurting the cause." Smoove loves the look, although she does add: "people always think I'm trans." There's nothing wrong with this, of course, but she clarifies, "I'm a lady with a mustache."

Smoove's aesthetic matches the Back Door's interior. The bar used to be a VFW bingo hall, although it bears no resemblance to the original space.

The walls are painted with zebra stripes, the floor with a black-and-white star pattern, and the back wall of the stage features a unicorn silhouetted inside a white heart, framed by a lush, velour curtain. A disco ball hangs from the ceiling, and throughout, rain curtains and tinsel shimmer. The vibe is very much Lisa-Frank-walks-into-a-dive-bar.

If you spend enough time looking around, you also get a strong sense of the bar's values. Just inside the front door is an ATM that spits out exclusively one-dollar bills, so patrons can easily tip the nightly performers. A poster near the entryway reads THERE ARE TRANS PEOPLE HERE. The bathroom walls are covered with radical murals and collages, including a life-size photo of Angela Davis with a speech bubble saying, "radical simply means grasping things at the root," a poster of Zoe Leanord's poem "I Want A Dyke for President," and the words NO MERCY FOR THE PATRIARCHY in blocky pink-and-white letters.

The idea to open a queer bar in Bloomington first arose at the memorial of Smoove's friend Christian in July of 2012. It was there that Smoove met her soon-to-be business partner, Nicci B. "We were drunk at a wake. It was all of us in the garage at Christian's memorial, after his funeral," Nicci remembers. "He was a fabulous gay man and had lots of fabulous gay friends. And so, we're all mourning over a lot of vodka and a keg of beer and came up with the idea to start a queer bar."

In the early 2000s, there were a handful of traditional gay bars in Bloomington, but no inclusive queer spaces, and certainly no lesbian bars. At the memorial, Christian's friends swapped stories about being made to feel unwelcome in the town's many college bars. Wouldn't it be nice, the group thought, if there were a place for queer people to dance in downtown Bloomington? At first, the idea was nothing more than a pipe dream. After the memorial, Nicci returned home to Atlanta, and Smoove went back to her job as a statistician at Indiana University. But a few weeks later, Nicci got a phone call from Smoove and another friend of Christian's:

"Hey, we're actually doing this. Do you want to move to Bloomington?"

So Nicci packed up their life, relocated to Indiana, and opened the Back Door with Smoove in 2013. After about a year, Smoove and Nicci bought out their third partner. "He was a cis white gay man, and kind of had his own idea and agenda about things that Smoove and I didn't always agree with," Nicci explains. After his departure, the place "got a lot more feminist and a lot more queer in general."

One of the biggest challenges in the early years of the bar was contending with Bloomington's dangerous rape culture. Indiana University is known as a party school, and that atmosphere pervades the town of Bloomington. "There's this really, really dark and scary and sad culture of drinking [. . .] that allow[s] for a lot of abuse to happen," Nicci explains. "Apparently, roofies are very easy to come by in this town and that's something that happens to people fairly regularly. [. . .] Nightly, I would hear stories about this happening to people here." Rape and sexual assault were horrifyingly normalized. "That's what girls get if they go out to a frat party," Nicci would hear people say around town.

Nicci and Smoove never expected this culture to seep into their own space. "We knew that there was a problem in Bloomington in a larger capacity. But I know that I greatly underestimated what was happening within our own walls," Nicci says. In April of 2014, Nicci got a phone call from the local women's shelter.

"We've had four instances of sexual assault in the last month that people say originated from your bar," the woman on the phone told Nicci.

"That made me want to throw up and cry at the same time," Nicci recalls. Nicci and Smoove sprang into action. With the support of the women's shelter, the entire staff went through a bystander intervention training program. They also started a call-and-response chant that the host would shout at the end of every show.

"Consent is what?" the host would yell.

"Fucking mandatory!" the crowd would respond.

The most drastic action that Nicci and Smoove took was instituting what they called a wall of shame. "If you were violent in this space, if you violated people's boundaries, if you were known as a sexual offender [. . .] then you got your picture [and name] printed out, and you got put on the wall of shame," Nicci explains. Only the most serious offenses would land someone on the wall. This wasn't a means of publicly humiliating belligerent drunks or poor tippers. This was a way of letting "the public know who to look out for and also, who is definitely not allowed in."

The wall also signaled to certain community members that the Back Door would be a safer option compared to other bars in Bloomington. "There were plenty of people in town at the time that felt nervous just to go out," Nicci remarks. But, at the Back Door, patrons could identify their abusers on the wall of shame, which offered a sense of protection.

It was an effective strategy. "Public shaming, it can be very helpful, if you're using it in the correct way," Smoove notes. Of course, those being publicly shamed were less than thrilled. "People would get shitty and threaten us with lawyers," says Smoove.

Nicci recalls some frightening backlash: "There was about a year and a half that was a serious battle, where people were angry and coming for Smoove and I personally. A few people got pretty stalkery. A restraining order or two was filed."

The wall of shame had the ultimate intended effect: it changed the culture itself. "Shady people knew to just stay the fuck away from the Back Door because there would be consequences. At the very least, [there would be] public recognition that you're a violent predator," Nicci declares. Eventually, the wall itself was no longer needed. "Once we established the culture that things absolutely were not going to be tolerated, we took [the wall] down and moved on from that."

Yet, ensuring that the bar feels equitable to all is an ongoing, ever-evolving process. In 2018, several drag kings and nonbinary drag performers noticed a discrepancy in the way they were treated as compared to the way the traditional drag queens were treated. Drag king and burlesque performer Verna Vendetta discovered at one performance that the drag queens never paid for drinks.

"I haven't paid to get into this bar or for any drinks since I showed up the first night here in heels," one queen told Verna.

Meanwhile, the drag kings had been paying for their own drinks, in addition to paying the bar's entry fee, even on nights they performed. "[Free drinks] is a small thing," comments another drag king, Corvin. "However, it was a very concrete thing that we could point to [. . .] like, look, this is how you are reinforcing misogyny," Corvin posits.

Verna, Corvin, and four other drag kings set up a meeting with Nicci to address their concerns, which also included inequitable bookings; it seemed more drag queens were being booked to perform than kings. According to Nicci, none of this discrimination was intentional. No one had directed security staff or bartenders to treat the queens and kings differently, and Nicci was booking the folks who were demanding gigs.

"I think a part of that was just the traditional drag queens came in and kind of took whatever they wanted, and I think some of the AFAB [assigned female at birth] performers were a lot more timid and didn't know to do that," Nicci reasons. Some of this, Nicci acknowledges, can be attributed to being socialized as women. "Whether or not that was their gender identity at the time, it's the way that we're raised. And I include myself in that; I'm also an AFAB person who is nonbinary. [We're raised to be] more demure and rule following, and I think sometimes that makes us feel taken advantage of."

In this radical, feminist, queer space, many felt it was management's job to combat this kind of inequity. But following the meeting with Nicci, Verna says nothing really changed. If anything, the dynamics between the kings and queens at the Back Door got worse. Rumors began to swirl.

"[The kings] don't work as hard to get into drag as we do," Verna heard from some of the queens, "and now we're all in trouble, the drag queens, because we don't get free drinks anymore."

Verna recalls this being at the heart of the queens' problem with the kings: "We had ruined the free drinking for them."

These issues are not unique to the Back Door. Misogyny often pervades drag culture and drag bars. "Drag culture is toxic," Nicci remarks. "It just is. I hope that we're changing that. And by we, I mean the collective we. But historically [. . . drag culture] has been dominated by cis gay men [. . .] and it's often misogynistic and transphobic and often racist."

Smoove goes so far as to argue that this isn't just true of drag culture—it's true of queer culture in general. "Everything about queer history, I mean, it's dominated by men," she says. "They had the money, they had the power, that is still a thing. Unless you're a man, you know, an AMAB [assigned male at birth] person doing drag, [your artistry is] not valid. [When] even RuPaul is saying this [message], it permeates everything."

This is not to say that drag doesn't have immense value to our community. As Nicci highlights, "it's also been a big fuck you to patriarchy. There has been space within drag life for queer joy and for radical things to happen. But it's not an uncomplicated art form by any means."

Performers like Verna and Corvin expected the Back Door to be a haven for a more radical approach to drag. "The Back Door was where I first felt consistently comfortable to be a queer person," Corvin says, "but over time, it just started to—like so many of our structures—replicate the same misogynistic, heteronormative bullshit, capitalist bullshit that our communities are trying to escape. And after a while, I felt less and less comfortable being a brown lesbian there."

While a more equitable drag culture is of course worth fighting for, Nicci had no easy solution. Soon after all of this, Nicci stepped down from their role as artistic director and made the move to California with their partner. The decision to go wasn't directly because of the drag debacle, but it contributed. "I burned all the way out," Nicci confesses, explaining how their mental health plummeted during their last year or so at the bar. "Dealing with a lot of different people and different needs all the time, you end up sacrificing your own because you're the person in charge, and the authority, and [you're] supposed to know what to do, and do the right thing, and then pour a shit ton of booze on top of it," Nicci explains.

In the years since, the programming and the culture at the Back Door have shifted immensely. When we asked Smoove about the drag conflict, she couldn't even really remember the details. "You're talking about drama in the drag world, that's like every day," she jokes. But in all seriousness, part of why it may seem fuzzy is that it's simply less of an issue now.

Overall, there are far less traditional drag shows at the Back Door these days. On Friday nights there are free dance parties. On Tuesdays there's queer line dancing. They've started a lesbian tea dance. "We've definitely leaned into the lesbian bar thing more," Smoove says of these shifts in their programming. "I think [we're] making a conscious effort to put more marginalized folks in our community in the spotlight." While it feels the rest of the country is doing the opposite, at the Back Door, they're "leaning even more into DEI," Smoove declares, laughing.

As for the drag shows that do still happen at the Back Door, it seems there's more of a balanced range of gender identities among performers. There's a recurring show called Beyond the Binary that's specifically for trans and nonbinary performers and is run by drag king and trans man Oliver Closeoff. Another show, Kinker, which Smoove describes as "scary circus clowns," is also drag king led. "[We're] just branching out more," Smoove says, "in terms of the kinds of queer joy we can offer to people."

Today, Smoove says she is semiretired. When asked what this means, she explains, "My first impulse was to say, like, absentee father, but it's not like that because I love them. I love the bar." Although she's less involved, she spends enough time there to know the changes have been appreciated. "I met a couple of dykes last month who had driven down like three hours to come to the bar," she says, "and they were just in love. They were like, 'This place is awesome.' So, I guess we're doing something right."

Chapter Twelve

WALKER'S PINT

BE NICE OR LEAVE

MILWAUKEE, WI

One of the first things I notice upon walking into Walker's Pint is a hand-painted sign above the bar. It reads BE NiCE OR LEAVE! in bright green-and-yellow block letters, and sits in a wooden frame adorned with an assortment of beer bottle caps. It's a sentiment I hear echoed at just about every lesbian bar we visit.

Here, on the wall of Walker's Pint, it's articulated with total clarity and simplicity, posted for all to see. This is intentional. Though the space is proudly a lesbian bar, owner and founder Bet-z has always wanted to welcome everyone. "Be nice or leave" is now the bar's official motto—a shift from its original motto "Lock up your daughters."

Cultivating an inclusive environment is second nature to Bet-z, who is a lifelong Wisconsinite with a warm, soft-butch vibe. Her liberal values paired with her old-school Wisconsin energy allow her to get along with everyone who walks into her bar.

Bet-z had her own first lesbian bar experience in Milwaukee, just six blocks from where Walker's Pint now sits, at a bar called Fannies. And yes, that's Fannies, as in the plural of fanny, not a bar belonging to a woman named Fanny. It was a night Bet-z will never forget.

It was 1993, and Bet-z went out with her then-girlfriend. "I walked in, and it was just all these women that were kind of like me," she notes referring to her own lesbian identity. "You had your girly girls, you had your butchy lesbians, [and you had your] older ladies that had their own little group of friends already. And there was dancing there." Her girlfriend, who had been to Fannies before, began showing her around. "She introduced me to this one woman who is still a great friend to this day. And she was a little tipsy," recounts Bet-z.

"Wow, you have a great smile," the woman said. "Smile for me."

So, Bet-z smiled. "And then she licked my teeth," Bet-z declares. She wasn't particularly bothered by it—she's not the type to be scared off by odd behavior. "I guess this is where I hang out now. I was welcomed immediately by these people with some weird ritual," Bet-z remembers thinking at the time.

That was the first of many nights Bet-z would spend at Fannies. In the 1990s, it was the place to be for lesbians in the Milwaukee area. It was more traditional and rigid than the inclusive lesbian bars we know and love today. Most gay spaces in the Midwest back then were segregated by binary gender. "There wasn't a lot of blending," Bet-z explains. At Fannies, "if you were a boy and you wanted to come in, you'd probably want to go in with a woman. That's just how it was back then."

Like most queer spaces of the time, Fannies was discreet. Unlike Walker's Pint, which is on a main street, Fannies was tucked away in a more industrial part of the neighborhood, "by the recycling center and where the semis park," Bet-z describes. "It [had] no windows and [was] in this more dark, hidden place."

In 1997, Fannies was severely damaged in a fire.[1] The bar reopened the following year with flyers that read: "Fannies has always been open to the entire community," a departure from its previous identity as a women's bar. Fannies survived for another few years but never returned to the popularity of its lesbian glory days.

In October of 1997—the same month of the infamous Fannies fire—another lesbian bar opened in town. It was called Dish and was advertised as "a new night spot & party house for women."[2] Bet-z got a job bartending there, despite having no previous experience. "It was: get thrown to the wolves and you either sink or swim," she recalls. A mixed metaphor, but Bet-z swam.

A year after she was hired, Dish rebranded as a "basic club," as Bet-z calls it. She continued bartending there for a few more years but desperately yearned for the type of lesbian space that no longer existed in Milwaukee. She didn't always feel safe in straight spaces. "I'm six feet [tall], I have short hair, I have a deep voice. I don't really blend very well. [I would] get picked on [. . .]

when I [went to] straight bars," Bet-z explains. "I just learned to deal with it over the years, no big deal, whatev. But we felt better going to lesbian bars."

In 2000, Bet-z started searching for a space to open a bar of her own. "I wanted to have a place that, if and when I did have a girlfriend, I could feel comfortable going there," she says.

Combing through real estate listings in the local paper, she discovered a downtown bar with a patio for rent. She toured it on her thirtieth birthday and "fell in love with it immediately," Bet-z recalls. It was in Walker's Point, Milwaukee's unofficial gayborhood, surrounded by other LGBTQ+ bars and businesses. "Across the street is Fluid, which is a boys' bar. Diagonal across the street is LaCage, which is a mixed dance club. [. . .] There was a bunch of boys' bars all around," Bet-z says. "I knew if I opened it up here, my people would feel more comfortable coming."

The building had another feature that was a priority for Bet-z: windows. "All the other gay bars that I had ever been in were always in dark caverns. [. . .] For this bar, I wanted windows," Bet-z states. Blacked-out windows, or spaces that lacked windows altogether, were common in queer spaces of the twentieth century, when anonymity was often a matter of safety for patrons. But this was a new millennium. "I didn't care who looked in," Bet-z says. "I wanted us to be able to see what was going on [outside] and just feel like normal people because we're just normal people. [. . .] Nowadays, you want to look in and see me kissing my wife and you have a problem with it? That's on you. You looked in my window."

On Friday, July 13, 2001, Walker's Pint officially opened. For the first decade or so of the bar's existence, Bet-z herself was there every day, often behind the bar. She has since retired from bartending, but she still spends a fair amount of time at the Pint, as it's come to be called by the community. "I'm old," Bet-z remarks. "Being out until two in the morning isn't my jam anymore. I'm more of a daytime party person."

Bet-z's daytime parties often double as fundraisers, supporting an array of causes and groups, from the local domestic violence shelter to the Special Olympics to kids in foster care to animal welfare organizations and more. She's been doing this for decades, and in 2021, she formalized her philanthropy with the creation of her nonprofit, the Forward Please Project.

In 2004, Bet-z organized one of the bar's early fundraisers to support breast cancer research at the Susan G. Komen foundation, in honor of regular customer, Annie, who was fighting breast cancer herself. Becky, Annie's partner, describes the scene: "There were probably eighty people in the room [. . .] and Bet-z just could get on the stage and put the microphone in her hand, and she's got people reaching in their pockets."

When Annie started to lose her hair, she turned to her community at the Pint once more. "One day it just was falling out on my shoulders," Annie describes. Loose strands kept finding their way into her mouth while she was trying to eat, and she knew it was time. Becky made a phone call. That night, about a dozen friends showed up to Walker's Pint and shaved their heads with Annie out on the patio. "It was very helpful for me. Because it's a scary time. And to have so much support was very important."

Today, Annie has been cancer-free for twenty-plus years. She and Becky still visit the Pint on occasion, making the drive from their home in Fontana. "I like to drive," Becky tells us, "and [Annie] doesn't mind sitting in the passenger seat and taking a nap."

They've built up a bit of a reputation at the bar. "It's nice, even today when we walk in, people who we kind of know will recognize us and know who we are just by the fact that we've been coming in for so long," says Becky.

"We, being a little older than the rest of the crowd, I think have actually helped some of the younger ones," Annie details. This is part of why Annie and Becky are so well known around the bar; they take the time to get to know the Pint's patrons, often lending a much needed, parent-like ear to young folks whose own parents fail to do the same.

Bet-z's parents used to get to know young people in the same way. "They'd sit down and talk with customers, and people would call them Mom and Dad," Bet-z says.

Bet-z's parents have given the Milwaukee queer community more than just emotional support. They actually bought the building in which Walker's Pint resides. "That's how Walker's Pint is still there," states Bet-z.

Once a fairly desolate industrial area, Walker's Point is now considered one of Milwaukee's hottest neighborhoods.[3] Still, Walker's Pint endures. When the former building owner asked Bet-z if she wanted to buy the building, she turned to her parents, knowing this was the only way to secure the bar's future amid a rapidly changing neighborhood. It was an easy decision for them. "They knew how important that space was," Bet-z says, "and they didn't want that to go away."

Chapter Thirteen

BLUSH & BLU

THE MYTH OF THE LAST LESBIAN BAR

DENVER, CO

When we visit Blush & Blu, also known as Blush in 2021, it feels like another typical lesbian bar on our road trip. We spend an evening there playing pool, eating donuts from the Voodoo Doughnut shop next door, catching up with some Denver-area friends, and chatting with regulars.

While we were there, Sarah connected with a cute bartender named Beccah. Beccah had recently come out of the closet, and not only was Blush & Blu her first bartending job but that night was her first night working. She was a flight attendant and, in pursuit of queer community, had taken a one-night-a-week gig at Blush.

"I was really loving [the] social engagement and meeting new people. It was just such a great place to build community," Beccah recalls in a more recent conversation. She loved it so much that she ended up leaving her flight attendant job to work at the bar full time. Yet, two years after our visit on Beccah's first day, she quit, publishing a post on Instagram that would spark a community boycott of Blush & Blu.

We connected with Blush & Blu's owner, Jody Bouffard, ahead of our 2021 visit, and it's easy to see how one could be charmed by her. Her long, dark hair flows past her shoulders, and she rocks an effortlessly laid-back, ChapStick-lesbian style: button-downs, blazers, and lots of tattoos. She's aloof in the way that makes you lean in, wanting her to reveal her secrets, and she paints a picture of her bar as an inclusive place. "My staff is very diverse," she tells us. "Half of them are lesbian, half of them are nonbinary, and some of them are trans."

Jody's story of rising through the ranks of Denver's LGBTQ+ nightlife feels inspiring too. In 1996, at nineteen years old, she got a job at a local nightclub as a go-go dancer. Soon she became a barback, then a bartender, and by 2000, at just twenty-three, she was managing another LGBTQ+ nightclub in town.

She talks about finding community in the bars: "Everybody there was in kind of the same boat as I was in the '90s, as far as family rejecting us." Jody had come out a few years prior, at sixteen. "My mom completely rejected me and my lifestyle," she says.

In some ways, Jody says her childhood prepared her for a life in the bar industry. "The truth of the matter is that both of my parents were severe alcoholics. So, from a young age, I was making drinks. [. . .] I could never control my parents' alcoholism, so being a bar owner, I try to control everybody else's around me," she confesses.

At the time of our visit, Blush & Blu, which Jody founded in 2012, was the only lesbian bar in Denver. We walked away feeling like it was a good one. However, just two months later, in November of 2021, news broke about a lawsuit against Jody and the bar. Three former LGBTQ+ employees were suing for mistreatment and underpayment. The lawsuit argued that Jody "willfully weaponized the so-called 'safe space' and the 'family' at Blush & Blu to create a culture of obligation where workers were required to accept mistreatment and brazen underpayment as a 'service' to the bar and broader queer community." The suit also alleged racial discrimination.[1]

What had we—as cis white queer people, only in town for a few nights—missed at Blush & Blu? What had really been happening there, both behind closed doors and out in the open? Jordan Feltner, one of the three plaintiffs in the lawsuit, helped us fill in some of the gaps.

New to Denver and its queer scene, Jordan began frequenting Blush & Blu, where his then-partner worked as a bartender. Jordan's own employment at the bar began in 2012, in a very informal, amorphous way. Jody would buy him a shot in exchange for taking out the trash. Next, he found himself filling in for the door person. This gradually grew into regular work, sometimes as security, sometimes as a barback, sometimes as a bartender, but always under-the-table.

The bar's strong sense of community pulled him in, despite the payment structure raising red flags from the beginning. "You kind of take what you can get because you become friends with everybody who works there, and [you] become friends with all the regulars, then you care about the bar and you want to support the bar," he explains. At first, it was easy to excuse making only five to seven dollars an hour in cash because "if it helps out the bar, it helps out the community."

And the community was extremely important to Jordan, who came out as trans during his time working at Blush & Blu. While staff members and regular customers provided a much-needed support system, Jody "was not very good at gendering me correctly when I came out," Jordan says. "She didn't respect it." Although the exterior of the bar was painted in the vibrant pink, white, and blue of the trans flag, Jordan would later discover that, behind closed doors, Jody had been blatantly intolerant of his identity.

"Jordan's not trans, she's just a confused lesbian," Jody had said to another bartender, who eventually recounted the interaction to Jordan.

Over the years, the "culture of obligation" and the lack of adequate compensation became more and more untenable for Jordan and his coworkers. "If you went in there on your day off and something needed to be done at the bar, you were expected to do it and not be on the clock or get paid for it," Jordan details. This sometimes even extended to jumping behind the bar to fill in. "Whether or not I had been drinking," Jordan adds. "It was kind of like a running joke until it wasn't funny anymore, that when you're there, you're working."

Jody often justified this extra, unpaid labor as being in service of the community. Jordan describes a sentiment of "this is our home, treat it like your home," that was cultivated within the space. "If you're at home, and you see some trash on the ground, wouldn't you pick it up?" was the logic behind helping out when off the clock.

If employees were making a living wage when they were on the clock, perhaps pitching in off-the-clock would have been acceptable. But according to the lawsuit filing, employees often weren't even making minimum wage.[2] "If you're making a tipped wage, but you don't make enough tips to compensate between the tipped wage and the actual minimum wage, the employer is supposed to make up that difference. And that never happened," Jordan explains. "So, there were shifts where you work eight hours and you walk out with forty bucks."

What's more, the lawsuit alleges misuse and theft of employee tips. The complaint states that Jody participated in the tip pool and regularly took cash out of the tip jar for Blush or personal use, despite it being against the Fair Labor Standards Act for managers and supervisors to do so.[3]

When employees asked questions about their compensation, according to the lawsuit, "Bouffard would tell them that paying higher wages and other costs and fees would threaten Blush's ability to stay open, insinuating that if workers complained, workers would lose their jobs, and the queer community would lose Blush as a gathering space."[4]

The lack of standard wages and recordkeeping at Blush & Blu spelled even more trouble for employees when the bar was forced to close at the onset of the COVID-19 pandemic. "Since she didn't have any employees on the books, no one got unemployment," Jordan says.

When state restrictions were lifted at the start of the summer of 2020, Blush employees, desperate for income, were eager to get back to paid work. Soon after the bar reopened, though, Jody announced she alone would be bartending Fridays, the busiest nights. This was the last straw for one of Jordan's coworkers, Ashley, who promptly quit.

Others followed suit, including Jordan and Hannah, the third plaintiff in the lawsuit. Ashley's decision to leave Blush was not just about losing the busiest shift of the week. As a Black woman, Ashley had been contending with another set of issues at the bar, and with Jody herself.

The lawsuit states that Ashley faced discrimination "based on race and color," including "severe and pervasive derogatory, racialized comments" from Jody. The most notable example of such remarks is that Jody would often say she had "jungle fever," a derogatory way of expressing a sexual or romantic preference for Black partners.[5]

When called out on this type of behavior, Jordan says that Jody "would downplay it and say it's not that big of a deal, or since she didn't say the N-word, that it wasn't racist, and that she loves Black people."

Apparently though, even the N-word wasn't off limits for Jody. As the lawsuit details, "on one particularly memorable occasion, [Ashley] received a video of Bouffard using the N-word when yelling at a Black man on the street outside of Blush."[6]

Having finally quit their positions at Blush, Jordan, Hannah, and Ashley took to Facebook to share their experiences. They wanted to expose what was happening behind the scenes at Blush, explain why the community would no longer find them working there, and encourage people to stop supporting the bar.

Seemingly, though, Jordan, Hannah, and Ashley faced more backlash than the bar itself. "DMs just started going crazy," says Jordan, as Jody's friends and acquaintances jumped to her defense. These weren't random trolls on the internet, these were community members. "We cut ties with a lot of people that we thought were friends."

After leaving Blush, Ashley had difficulty finding work at Denver's other gay bars. According to Jordan, Jody had been telling other bar owners "that [Ashley] was a thief and that she was stealing and that's why she didn't work for Blush anymore." Most believed her. "I mean, Jody dubs herself as the gay mayor of Denver," Jordan adds, highlighting her influence in the community. Ashley did eventually secure work at another queer bar, but only after sitting down with management and explaining the situation.

Even with the filing of the lawsuit—and the press coverage that came with it—not much changed at Blush & Blu. Jody gradually brought on new staff members to replace the group that quit. Beccah was among them. She recalls not knowing much about the lawsuit initially. "I didn't really have friends out here yet," Beccah explains. "I was really out of touch with all that. It wasn't until I had been there for like a year that I started connecting more with people and getting the lowdown."

The more time Beccah spent at the bar, the more she also started to see for herself that something wasn't right. "If you're a white lesbian, you don't see the problem. You simply don't. You know, I can even say maybe I picked up on things too late," says Beccah, who herself is Latina, though self-admittedly benefits from the privilege of being femme and white passing.

"I hosted a Latin night on Wednesdays," Beccah shares, "and so I would have a lot of my friends come—Puerto Rican friends, Colombian friends. And one of my friends who's Puerto Rican, she came up to the bar and she was crying because Jody's wife had made her feel like she was profiled." Clocking Beccah's friend's braids, Jody's wife had followed her around the bar, keeping an obviously distrustful eye on her.

"That was when it really hit me," says Beccah. She immediately confronted Jody's wife about the incident, explaining why the behavior was hurtful and inappropriate. "She laughed it off," Beccah recalls.

Beccah considered quitting on multiple occasions, but like Jordan, the sense of community kept her coming back. "A lot of what kept me there was just the people. My regulars. I had such great people that would come in," Beccah says. "The community that I had built there was so strong, and I didn't want to leave."

But on November 3, 2023, Beccah hit her breaking point. "I had experienced all of that: abuse of power and the unprofessionalism, the racial profiling of my friends. And then the political climate, it just blew me over the edge," she describes.

Another interaction with Jody's wife prompted Beccah's moment of reckoning. The topic of Palestine had come up in conversation, and Beccah recalls Jody's wife saying: "Oh, fuck those people. Fuck Muslims. They ruined my country."

In shock, Beccah immediately went to find Jody downstairs. According to Beccah, Jody was cold and unsympathetic. Rather than addressing her wife's behavior, she accused Beccah of unprofessionalism for telling her coworkers about the incident.

"I can't work for you. You guys are bigots," Beccah told Jody.

Like Jordan, Ashley, and Hannah had, Beccah took to social media to share her experience. "I just kind of wanted to be, like, peace out guys. This is why I'm not going to be there anymore. Because I'd been there for two years and people were used to seeing my face," says Beccah. "And then it kind of blew up."

Her Instagram post quickly circulated through the Denver queer community, and the comments came flooding in, most in solidarity with Beccah. Someone, in the comments, mentioned boycotting the bar. "And then that turned into an actual boycott," Beccah recalls. "[It] turned into something bigger than I had anticipated. I guess my story was the catalyst for that, but it wasn't actually my decision to boycott Blush."

In the aftermath of her post, Beccah began connecting with former staff members like Jordan, Ashley, and Hannah, who had recently settled their lawsuit out of court. Beccah says that talking about their experiences together has only made her feel more strongly about speaking up.

Beccah also took legal action of her own. Rather than suing, she opened a complaint with Colorado's Department of Labor. In May of 2024, the Denver Auditor's Office determined that Blush & Blu had been underpaying its employees and ordered them to pay restitution and penalties. In October, Jody settled with the city, agreeing to repay a total of nearly

$60,000 to a set of thirty-three employees, and to begin complying with applicable Colorado labor laws.[7] That same month, Blush & Blu closed its doors for good.

Among the thirty-three employees involved in this later settlement were some individuals who initially participated in the backlash against Jordan, Ashley, and Hannah. "I got messages from them afterwards, apologizing," Jordan says. Paraphrasing, he says the messages read: "I didn't believe you at the time or I didn't want to believe you, but now this is happening to me."

The difference in impact between Jordan's and Beccah's posts comes down, in part, to timing. When Beccah quit in 2023, much of the community was already galvanized by activist movements such as Free Palestine, and more conversations were happening about racial equity and what we should expect from our queer spaces. "It doesn't matter if you are in a marginalized group. There's still power dynamics within those groups. [Those] who [have] resources to create those spaces have a higher responsibility to manage them and run them better," asserts Beccah.

Whereas back in 2020 and 2021, "it was at the time where people were trying to rally around supporting businesses in the community that had suffered through the pandemic," Jordan reflects. What's more, when Jordan, Ashley, and Hannah first spoke out, there was a nationwide interest in the scarcity of lesbian bars. Throughout 2021, Blush received press with headlines that read "Inside Colorado's Last Lesbian Bar: What it takes to keep Blush & Blu afloat"[8] and "Denver is home to one of just 21 lesbian bars in the U.S.; here's why it matters."[9]

But as Jordan points out, "Just because you're the last lesbian bar in Denver doesn't give you license to treat your own community poorly. We cannot expect the cis, heteronormative world to treat us the way that we want to be treated when we can't even expect that from our own community." When we get so wrapped up in the fear that our gathering places are disappearing, we sometimes forget to question whether those spaces are serving us in the first place.

The idea that Blush & Blu deserved unconditional support, regardless of how it treated employees and patrons, just because it was the last lesbian bar in Denver, was a dangerous one. It also wasn't true. Denver was already home to an array of other sapphic-centric spaces, like the queer- and women-owned Lady Justice Brewery and the queer and feminist independent bookstore Petals and Pages. And just months after Blush & Blu closed its doors, Denver welcomed both a queer-women-owned women's sports bar, the 99ers, and a new lesbian bar, The Pearl (originally called Pearl Divers). These two bars are living proof that new spaces can emerge when old ones fail us, if only we are brave enough to speak up when something doesn't serve us and bold enough to dream up something better in its place.

Part Three

THE GREAT QUEER PILGRIMAGE WEST

Chapter Fourteen

MONA'S

WHERE GIRLS WILL BE BOYS

SAN FRANCISCO, CA

San Francisco has long been considered a gay mecca. Over the years, we've heard countless tales from queer people who fled small towns and rural areas to head west, in search of safety, freedom, and community. Many landed in San Francisco, which today ranks among the most LGBTQ+-friendly cities in the world. So how did the West Coast, San Francisco at its heart, become such a haven for the queer community? For queer women, it all began with one individual: Mona—a woman with much to teach about surviving, thriving, and making space for lesbians in a world that would have much preferred we didn't exist at all.

Mona never intended to open a lesbian bar. She wasn't a lesbian herself, although over the years, many asked if she was. "You're what you are. I can't be gay, because I'm not," Mona says in an oral history recorded by author and historian Nan Alamilla Boyd in 1992 while conducting research for her book *Wide Open Town*. "But what's that got to do with friendship and all that?" Mona continues, a hint of a transatlantic accent in her voice.[1]

A self-identified bohemian, Mona was an ally to the queer community. The slogan for bohemians, she says, was: "We are not offended at how the other half lives."[2] Over the course of Mona's life, she would have four husbands and five bars. Along the way, however unintentional it may have been, she laid the groundwork for generations of lesbian spaces in San Francisco to come.

At age seventeen, in the late 1920s, Mona made her own pilgrimage to San Francisco from Santa Rosa. In her younger years, Mona wore her hair in a stylish, short, curly bob with bangs, and could be spotted in either eclectic ensembles of skirts, bralettes, flowers, bangles, and beads, or long fur coats and gloves.[3] She rented a studio in what was called the "Monkey Block," a residential haven for bohemians of all sorts. Short for Montgomery Block, the building occupied an entire block of Montgomery Street in San Francisco's Financial District. Originally built in 1853 as an office building, it drew in folks with its cheap rent and basic accommodations: "housekeeping rooms," as Mona calls them, which lacked their own kitchens and bathrooms.[4] Mona's room had a hot plate for cooking meals and some simple furnishings.

Mona describes the residents of the Monkey Block as "all kinds of kids and artists and writers, mostly that were struggling," though some were already beginning to make names for themselves.[5] Mark Twain, Robert Louis Stevenson, and Emma Goldman were among the Monkey Block's more prominent occupants.[6]

The Monkey Block was where Mona first felt a strong sense of community. For birthdays and special occasions, they would throw building-wide parties. "We locked the front door," Mona recounts. Musicians would bring out their instruments and play. "[We] moved the piano out and danced up and around the hall and people would hear the noise and come up," Mona describes, laughing.[7]

During these early years in San Francisco, Mona undertook a number of odd jobs and money-making schemes to cover her meager monthly expenses.

One of her more lucrative scams was posing as a sex worker outside a fancy hotel with her friend Helene.

"There's always men looking for girls," Mona remarks, slyly.

The operation involved getting men to fork over cash for a room up front, pretending to book it with the receptionist, and then sending the men up by themselves so as not to be seen entering together. But instead of following the men up as they promised . . . "We had the money in our hand. We'd run like hell!" Mona exclaims with a laugh.

In her early twenties, after a few years of scraping by in this manner, Mona met Jim Sargent at a party in Fresno. "I wasn't interested at all. He followed me 'til he got me," Mona recalls, and she doesn't mean just following her around the party. Jim actually trailed her all the way back to San Francisco. He was a football player in the process of divorcing his first wife. Mona had been married before too, though she says her first marriage doesn't count because she was very young and it only lasted about three weeks. Eventually, in what was a second marriage for them both, Mona and Jim wed.

In 1933, with Prohibition on the cusp of being repealed, a friend of Jim and Mona's approached the duo about opening their first bar.

"Mona knows everybody, and you've played football," Mona remembers their friend cajoling as he pitched the bar business to Jim.

"We'll call it Jim Sargent's," Jim said.

"No, you go play football. We're calling it Mona's," the friend replied.

Mona and Jim did not have the money to open a bar on their own, but their friend offered to fund the entire endeavor. So, with that, the first iteration of Mona's many bars and nightclubs was born.

In December of 1933, Mona's opened at 451 Union Street, on the southwestern slope of Telegraph Hill. It featured simple wooden booths and wooden picnic tables. Large murals of naked women spanned the upper halves of the walls—at this point more suggestive of a free-love, bohemian crowd than of lesbian patronage. Prohibition had just been repealed, and people had been waiting nearly fifteen years to be able to buy and sell alcohol legally again in the US. From the very beginning, the bar "was always packed because it was new—things were just legal that year," Mona says.

Technically, the weekend Mona's first opened, they were still breaking the law. "[Selling alcohol] wasn't really legal until a Monday or something, and we opened on a Saturday," Mona recalls. She had sent off her application for a liquor license but hadn't bothered to wait for it to arrive. The day they opened, a police officer came by and asked to see the license.

"I thought it would be here, and I had plans, [so] we're open," Mona stated matter-of-factly.

Mona suspects that the officer let the early opening slide because he knew her. The Monkey Block was not far from Telegraph Hill. "I said hello to everybody. I still do," Mona reflects. As Mona's friend who bankrolled the bar had suspected, Mona's connections in town were key to the bar's success. Not only could she get away with what others couldn't; she also knew exactly how to throw a party and how to draw in a crowd.

"I had free food from 5:30 to 7 [p.m.]," she recalls. "We'd have a big bowl of soup, French bread, and butter. That was it. That was for all my artist friends." Much like today, the promise of free food was enough to get Mona's broke artist friends—of whom she had many—to come out to the bar.

Word traveled fast, and after about two years of business on Union Street, Mona had outgrown her existing space. "So, I moved to Columbus Avenue," Mona recounts. This second location had sat empty for a number of years before Mona took it over in 1935. "It had a nice long bar and a few booths," Mona describes. "We put in barrels and sawdust." Presumably, the barrels served as makeshift high-top tables, while the sawdust was used to coat the floor—a common practice in bars back then because it absorbed odors and could easily be swept up at the end of each night. The bar became known as Mona's Barrelhouse.

"We were crowded every night," Mona says, although she's adamant about the fact that it wasn't a nightclub. It was "just a hangout for artists and writers," she explains. "I never wanted a nightclub with dancing and so forth. I hated nightclubs."

It was Mona's Barrelhouse that first began attracting a lesbian clientele, although Mona insists that it was entirely by accident. "I didn't know about lesbians," Mona reflects. "I had heard they were called lady lovers. I had heard and I paid no attention."

Mona speculates that gay women started frequenting the bar because the rest of the crowd was tolerant of queer culture. "With the bohemians," Mona figures, "[lesbians] found people that understood them."

At first, Mona did nothing to intentionally cultivate this accepting environment. It was simply the bohemian way. "The girls came in and they were nice, and then I was nice to them," Mona says. Then, one day one of her lesbian customers approached Mona in tears. "She told me about herself and said her folks shut the door in her face."

Instinctively, Mona offered the woman a job.

Now, with a lesbian waitress on staff, more and more gay women began frequenting Mona's Barrelhouse. Mona didn't mind in the slightest. "I thought, what the hell's with people calling them fruit or queer or something? And I couldn't understand because I knew them as person[s]," Mona reflects.

Other gay women joined the waitstaff, and soon Mona had a surprising revelation about them, though it had nothing to do with their sexuality. "We had a piano player that always played for some entertainment," Mona recounts, "and so [. . .] we discovered [the waitresses] could sing."

Some of the singing waitresses began to don full suits and sport butch haircuts. In today's language, we would call them drag kings, but at the time, they were referred to as "male impersonators." Before long, gay and straight folks alike began flocking to the bar to witness these performances.

Mona says the demographics on an average night were about "one third gay, one third our regular crowd, and one third tourists." The "regular crowd" she speaks of were the bohemians, and by "tourists," Mona doesn't mean out-of-towners. She's referring to straight San Francisco locals who were excited by the idea of a night out with the "little tomboy girls" and the "nutty bohemians," as Mona endearingly refers to them.

Around 1938, after two years at the Barrelhouse, Mona contracted tuberculosis. After spending eleven months on bed rest in Santa Rosa, she finally returned home to San Francisco. "[I] came back to find the A.H. [asshole] I was married to had not paid bills and my furs were missing," Mona remembers.

Not only had Jim bankrupted the Barrelhouse; he was also cheating on her and had been physically abusive throughout their marriage. "I was a battered wife, but you didn't tell in those days," Mona says. "I had scars all around. [. . .] I was in the hospital once for three days," she confesses in a shockingly casual tone. So, Mona divorced him.

A few months later, she received a proposition from a man named Charlie Murray, who owned a club at 440 Broadway and wanted to partner with Mona to tap into her existing clientele. Mona agreed, and they rebranded as Mona's 440 Club. Of all Mona's bars, this one was her most famous. Yet, it's the one with which she had the least involvement. She leased her name to Charlie but rarely spent time at the bar herself. "I was too sick anyway. I was still not supposed to be doing a lot of things," Mona recalls.

Still, the lesbians—both staff and patrons—followed Mona to her new spot. "By that time, I had more waitresses, most of who[m] had cried on my shoulder because their folks had shut the door on their face, called them queers and so forth," Mona remarks. At Mona's 440 Club, much of the waitstaff were masc-presenting gay women. The bar's tagline, printed on matchbooks and cocktail napkins, became "where girls will be boys."

Throughout the 1940s, an array of male impersonators and big-name lesbian performers took to the stage at Mona's 440. Nightclub singer Beverly Shaw, wearing her signature tuxedo jacket, bowtie, skirt, and high heels a la Marlene Dietrich, would croon jazz numbers.[8] Gladys Bentley, who got her start in Harlem in the 1920s, would play the piano and sing the blues in her signature white tuxedo.[9]

Of course, straight tourism only grew at Mona's 440. In fact, a company called Gray Line Bus Tours offered formal tours for straight folks looking to experience San Francisco's exotic gay nightlife scene. The tours made stops at places like Mona's and Finocchio's, another popular gay club known for its female impersonators, or drag queens as we would call them today.[10]

While this kind of tourism was good for business, it wasn't always appreciated by the gay and lesbian community. Historian Lillian Faderman tells us that "for the straight community, it was fun, it was exotic." But she says, "I think most of us would find [it] very troubling today, and maybe lesbians found [it] troubling in those days too. It was straight people looking at the queers." She is sure to clarify that "*queers* in those days was not a term that the community chose for itself. It was a hostile and exoticized kind of term."

In the mid-1940s, Mona left the 440 Club and bought into another bar and restaurant which catered to LGBTQ+ folks. It was back on Union Street, near her first location, and called the Paper Doll. She stayed there for about a year, and around this time, she met husband number three: Whitey Burke.

Mona describes Whitey as "a merchant, seaman, and fun artist." It was perhaps her most meaningful relationship thus far. "It was a real love affair," she reflects.[11]

However, before going back to sea, Whitey told Mona, "I don't want you back in clubs again."[12]

But Mona was never one to allow a man to dictate her decisions. So, when she got a call that a bar was for sale right across from where Mona's 440 used to be, she made an offer. By the time Whitey returned, Mona had opened her fifth and final bar: Mona's Candle Light, the first business that was solely hers. By this point, simply having the name Mona on the bar was enough to create a buzz. One article from around the time of the bar's opening reads:

"The mysterious woman named Mona has added excitement to San Francisco's nights for many years. [. . .] You can meet her any night at her new Candle Light Cafe. The Cafe is, Mona says, 'A place where people from all walks of life can meet their old friends.'"[13]

When Whitey returned home, Mona made him a bartender. "That was my mistake," she admits.[14] See, Whitey had a drinking problem, and by his side, Mona's own drinking quickly spun out of control. To make matters worse, Whitey was a violent drunk.

A headline in the *San Francisco Examiner* on June 6, 1949 reads, "'Mona' Beaten by Mate." The article continues: "Mrs. Ramona Burke, 37, the 'Mona' of Mona's Candle Light at 473 Broadway, was hospitalized last night after she was beaten by her husband, Frances 'Whitey' Burke, 38. She required eight stitches about the face at Central Emergency Hospital. The altercation took place at the nightclub, where Burke tends bar, in view of about thirty patrons."[15]

What is particularly shocking about this incident is that it was Mona herself who was arrested, on charges of intoxication, rather than Whitey for his blatant abuse.[16] It was around this time that Mona began questioning both her relationship with alcohol and with Whitey. One morning, after she awoke with a particularly nasty hangover, she picked up the newspaper and noticed a listing for Alcoholics Anonymous.[17]

"When I sobered up, I did it for me," Mona declares, "and you can only do it for yourself."[18] Mona divorced Whitey and sold the Candle Light around the same time, both decisions related to her newfound sobriety. Mona and Whitey remained friends until Whitey lost his battle with pancreatic cancer in 1991, but the sale of the Candle Light Café marked the end of Mona's career in nightlife.

At the time of Mona's interview in 1992, she was married to her fourth husband: John Hood. "This husband is so good, but he's no laughs," she remarks, and underneath the joke, it seems she loves him. They remained together until Mona passed in 2001,[19] and with John, who had three children from a previous marriage, Mona became a family woman.

Before she and John had even married, Mona fought for custody of John's youngest daughter, Barbara. John was living in an unsafe neighborhood at the time, and Barbara's mother was, in Mona's words, "a religious nut." In a custody hearing, Mona was questioned by John's soon-to-be-ex-wife's attorney. "They made it look like I was some kind of a lesbian 'cause I had the club," Mona recalls.[20] The attorney grilled Mona about where Barbara would sleep in her home. Mona played dumb, pretending not to understand the insinuation in his question.

I imagine at this point in Mona's life, she was used to answering questions about her sexual orientation. Despite her many marriages to men, she fielded such questions often. She maintained, always, that she was straight.

But was this out of truth or necessity? Certainly, she could not have gained custody of Barbara had she admitted she was anything but heterosexual. And it's exceedingly unlikely her bars could have thrived with an out gay woman at the helm, given the fact that liquor licenses could be revoked just for serving gay patrons during the early twentieth century.

Mona's great-niece, Beth Lemke, tells us that within the family, Mona's sexuality was never discussed. In fact, it wasn't until after Mona's passing that Beth learned her great-aunt's bars and clubs had all catered to the lesbian community. On her own quest to investigate Mona's legacy, Beth came across one woman who believes Mona may have been queerer than she let on. Her name is Rhoda Pack Curtis.

Rhoda and Mona were friends, and according to a conversation between Beth and Rhoda, there was at least one instance of flirting happening on Mona's end. "In Rhoda's mind, Mona definitely liked women and Mona had girlfriends," Beth tells us.

There is no other evidence to support Rhoda's claims, no accounts from other patrons or rumors printed in the local papers. Only the memory of a ninety-something-year-old woman. But it *is* true that a woman in Mona's era would have needed to make a choice between being out and creating space for out folks. You couldn't have done both.

Chapter Fifteen

MAUD'S

THE BEST OF TIMES, THE WORST OF TIMES

SAN FRANCISCO, CA

Unlike in Mona's time, the subsequent generation of lesbian bars in San Francisco were owned and run by out queer women themselves. One of the most famous lesbian bars to follow Mona's was Maud's, owned and run by Rikki Streicher from 1966 until 1989. Maud's was known throughout the country, and when it closed, it was purported to be the longest-running lesbian bar in existence. Though Rikki declared the lesbian bar era over with the closure of Maud's, her influence continues to shape queer and sapphic spaces today. The bar's final days were chronicled by filmmakers Paris Poirier and Karen Kiss in the documentary *Last Call at Maud's*, which served as my own introduction to the Maud's legacy, and this generation of the lesbian bar.

"I've always felt that bars were the most honest, open, free place that women could go," Rikki states in the film. "This bar [. . .] it's probably a composite of all of the bars that I've gone to and all of the good things that I found in each one."[1]

Mona's spaces in particular had been central to Rikki's early lesbian bar experiences. Mona had taught Rikki much of what she knew about the business, and the two had become friends. In fact, Rikki was there in the room with Mona during her 1992 interview, along with another friend, Reba Hudson. At one point the interviewer, Nan Alamilla Boyd, reads from a newspaper clipping about Mona's Candle Light: "The little girl waitresses look like boys. And the little girls who sing sweet songs look like boys. And many of the little girl customers look like boys." Then, Nan looks up and gestures to Rikki and Reba. "That was you two!" she exclaims, and the group devolves into laughter.[2]

Rikki and Reba were indeed among the "little girl customers" who looked like boys. The two met at an all-night party in Malibu, Los Angeles, in 1945, and that very weekend, Reba would be the one to get Rikki to San Francisco.[3] Rikki, as so many women did, had recently made the journey from the Midwest to California. By the time she was nineteen years old, her parents had both passed away. So, instead of going back to college in Denison, Ohio, following Easter break, Rikki boarded a Greyhound bus for California.[4]

Something had drawn her out West, although she wasn't yet sure what it was; she had never even heard of homosexuality. "I was not a lesbian when I got here," Rikki recounts in her own 1992 interview with Nan Alamilla Boyd, "although I always dressed in a tailored way, and wore pants whenever I could. Riding britches for days, right?"[5]

In Los Angeles, Rikki got a job in a darkroom, developing photos. There, she quickly befriended a photographer named Maria. "She kept talking about her husband, Tommy, the drummer," Rikki recounts, "and she never invited me to her home, which was a contradiction of the person that she was."[6] Rikki was puzzled by this, until one day, Maria gave Rikki some film to develop. "I put the negatives in the enlarger, and there was something unusual."[7] The image was of a person wearing swimming trunks and no top.

Upon closer examination, Rikki thought to herself, "This is not a man. This is just not a man. But it's got to be a man. It's Maria's husband, right?"

Eventually, Rikki came to the only logical conclusion: "This Tommy the drummer, her husband, was not a man."[8] Nonetheless, Rikki developed the photos.

When she returned them to Maria, she asked, "This is your husband?"

"Yes," Maria said casually.

"Tommy?" Rikki asked.

"Yes," Maria replied.

"Tommy's a woman?" Rikki asked.

"Yes," answered Maria.[9]

Rikki recalls the end of their conversation with a laugh: "And then I went off to think about *that* for a while."[10] The next day, Maria invited Rikki to dinner, and Rikki said yes. Maria and Tommy soon introduced Rikki to the world of gay and lesbian nightlife. Immediately upon walking into her first lesbian bar, Rikki knew she had found her community.[11]

It was in the Los Angeles nightlife scene that Rikki first met Reba. "Meeting Reba was certainly an adventure for me," Rikki reflects.[12] Somewhere in the middle of the weekend-long bender that kicked off their friendship, Reba found out Rikki had never been to San Francisco, and insisted they go immediately.

Without so much as changing their clothes, she and Rikki boarded a train that very weekend. Eighteen hours later, they arrived in San Francisco. "And [I] never left," Rikki says. "I had found out I wasn't straight by then."[13] As is a rite of passage for many lesbians, Rikki did one thing when she got to San Francisco: "I said 'Aha,' and cut off my hair and became a dyke."[14]

Rikki spent the next twenty years immersing herself in San Francisco's vibrant lesbian scene. She spent time at Mona's 440, "the rock of the women's bars," as Rikki calls it, as well as Mona's other bars.[15] She also frequented the Chi Chi, which she says "was owned by two Catholic football players from St. Mary's, but was a total lesbian bar."[16] Another go-to spot of hers was Tommy's 299, a few blocks away, and owned by Tommy Vasu, who was "a dyke, no question," Rikki says.[17]

In 1965, a friend told Rikki about a bar called the Study that was for sale in San Francisco's Cole Valley neighborhood. Rikki decided to buy it, and in April of 1966, she opened Maud's, a name inspired by the work of artist Noel Coward. The community often referred to it as Maud's Study, owing to the bar's previous name and the large sign on the building's exterior reading "The Study" that Rikki left up for a number of years. "The Study" soon evolved into the coded phrase "the library," which closeted women would sometimes use when talking about the bar in public. To an outsider, there was nothing gay about asking your friend to go to the library with you!

Maud's was a near-instant success. "It was a little neighborhood bar that was international," Rikki says. Lesbian communities all around the world knew of Maud's.

A key part of this success was how Rikki celebrated and took care of her patrons. She maintained an interest in photography and lined the walls of the bar with photos of the community. Her own transformation—from femme to butch—was memorialized in side-by-side portraits: one in which she has long, curly hair, and the other, taken a year later, with her short, boyish crop. There were images of patrons at softball games and collages of shots from various events and parties. This was long before queer people were represented in mainstream media, so it was rare for lesbian life to be captured in photos. To be able to walk into Maud's and see yourself and your community represented on the walls was meaningful.

For so many people, Maud's was home. "Maud's was a place where people *lived.* I stayed open 365 days a year," Rikki explains.[18] At Maud's, she began a tradition that is carried on by many queer bars today: keeping the doors open even on Thanksgiving and Christmas.

"[If] you have no place to go for Thanksgiving or Christmas because you don't have any family or you're not welcome there, Rikki Streicher would have a meal at that bar," shares Mandy Carter, a former Maud's regular and bartender. Mandy was precisely the type of person Rikki was trying to accommodate.

Mandy was born in New York in November of 1948, the youngest of three children. "After I was born, our mother left and never came back," Mandy tells us. She and her two siblings, Ronnie and Delores, landed at the Albany Children's Home.

When Mandy was eight, the home shut down. "Because we were Black, they placed me, my brother, and Delores into a Black foster home down in Chatham Center, New York," Mandy recounts. This particular foster home only took in boys, but with so few Black foster families in the system, and in the interest of keeping the three siblings together, they made an exception.

However, when Mandy hit puberty, she was sent away to the Schenectady Children's Home, her foster mother citing concerns that Mandy would get pregnant on her watch. The same had happened to her sister, Delores, the previous year. While Ronnie and Mandy would finally reunite fifty years later, as of 2025, they're still searching for Delores.

After graduating high school and aging out of the system at eighteen, "the home said, 'well good luck, you're on your own,'" Mandy recalls bluntly. With eighty dollars in her pocket, she boarded a bus to New York City. "I knew no one, got into the Y, walked the streets of New York City, slept in Central Park, but this is '67. It wasn't just me. That was the Summer of Love in New York City."

The Summer of Love was a counterculture hippie movement that celebrated peace, love, and freedom of expression. Think music from the likes of Jimi Hendrix, the Bee Gees, Pink Floyd, and the Beatles, or psychedelic drugs, bell bottoms, and tie-dye.

Mandy has fond memories of her time in New York City, but as summer came to a close, she was ready to move on. "Everyone was going to San Francisco," she says, a twinkle in her eye. It's true that San Francisco was really at the heart of the Summer of Love. During the summer of '67, hundreds of thousands of young people flocked to the West Coast. Mandy and her friends were among them. "We put our thumbs out and hitchhiked out to San Francisco."

Even before Mandy began her journey west, she had heard of Maud's. But when she arrived in the city, she was only nineteen: two years shy of being allowed inside. Counting down the days until she turned twenty-one, Mandy would sit across the street, gazing longingly at the women entering and exiting Maud's.

"On my twenty-first birthday, November 2nd, I went into Maud's for the first time in my life," she exclaims, "and it was extraordinary." Mandy approached the bar and struck up a conversation with the bartender, who bought her a birthday drink, and with that, Mandy knew she was home.

That same year, 1969, another young woman set foot in Maud's for the first time: Jeanne Clark. Like Mandy, she had ventured across the country with a small group of friends. We meet Jeanne in her San Francisco apartment, which looks more like an art gallery; her original paintings and drawings cover the walls. She tells us that she knew she was gay from the age of eleven, but as a schoolteacher in Florida in the 1960s, she couldn't be out publicly.

"It was a scary thing to commit to being a homosexual. I was suicidal when I was twenty-one," Jeanne confesses. But by 1969, she was ready to embrace her sexuality. "You're twenty-six years old. You want to get a little love by then. You've been waiting since you were eleven years old, that's a long time to wait," she declares with a small chuckle. "So, [my friends and I] headed west in my little Rambler."

"There's a really great bar. It's Maud's, and there're really beautiful women there, and you should go," a friend told Jeanne when they stopped in Chicago.

That's all she needed to hear. "I went every night for a year because I didn't know what else to do as a young lesbian trying to figure out the world," she admits.

For the first few years of Mandy's and Jeanne's patronage of Maud's, all the bartenders who worked there were gay men. "Women could not be bartenders. That was the ABC [Alcoholic Beverage Control] law," Mandy explains.

While, as at Mona's, women could waitress, they wouldn't earn the right to bartend in the state of California until the 1971 landmark case *Sail'er Inn Inc v. Kirby*. Sail'er Inn Inc. owned a topless bar and restaurant in Los Angeles called the Classic Cat, and they wanted to be able to hire topless female bartenders. They won their case, but not before California's ABC Board added a new rule: bartenders had to be fully clothed.[19] There would be no topless bartenders at the Classic Cat, but thanks to them, bars like Maud's could finally hire women. So long as they kept their shirts on.

Of course, Rikki jumped at the opportunity to hire her customers, offering to train anyone who was interested, including Mandy. According to Rikki, she was one of the only bar owners in the community to hire women of color in the 1970s. "It happens to be the individual that matters, and how they come wrapped is neither here nor there," Rikki says. "You could be a Black asshole or a white asshole; it makes no difference."[20]

Maud's was an invaluable community space for women like Mandy and Jeanne and countless others, yet there was also a troubling undercurrent to the lesbian bar scene of this era. "The whole gay community was into drugs in a big way. Women were into coke. Men were into speed. If you can generalize in such an awful way, that's the way I would generalize," Rikki recalls.[21]

Alcoholism and addiction were huge unspoken issues in the community. "Bars were what I knew to do," Jeanne says, describing the culture. "We weren't worried about getting drunk. We weren't worried about any of that. We were all doing it together. People were drinking. Nobody's worried about alcoholism."

A decade after Jeanne arrived in San Francisco, that changed. "When I was thirty-six, a lot of women kind of disappeared," she recounts. As it turned out, they had all gone to Alcoholics Anonymous (AA). Unofficial gay AA groups began popping up in San Francisco at the end of the 1960s, and by 1974 gay groups were officially listed as such in the AA directory.[22] When Jeanne decided to get sober in 1979, gay and lesbian AA groups had spread to cities across the country, presenting an option for queer community outside of the bars. One evening at Maud's, Jeanne and her friend Iris decided to go to a meeting together.

Iris got sober immediately. It took Jeanne another five months to fully commit, but she kept going to meetings. At first, to attend more than one queer meeting in a week, Jeanne would have to travel: one night in the Castro, one night in Berkeley, one night up in Mill Valley. Then in the 1980s, sobriety in the LGBTQ+ community took off, with no shortage of local gay AA meetings. "I remember Rikki saying to me that all of her customers were marching down the street behind the Living Sober banner," Jeanne remarks of the '80s.

In 1989, Rikki announced that Maud's was closing. It wasn't just because much of her customer base had gotten sober, although that certainly played a part. Rikki thought the era of the lesbian bar in general was coming to a bittersweet end. Plus, she didn't own the building and rent on the space had skyrocketed. When asked on the 1992 interview tape why she closed when she did, Rikki simply replies: "Because times had changed. [. . .] Sometimes it's time to go. And that was the case over at Maud's. I almost let it go too long, but I stopped just in time."[23]

Rikki didn't want the space to remain a lesbian bar under different ownership, but she did want to ensure it stayed community-centric. She sold it to a straight man from the neighborhood named Tom Frenkel. Tom opened Finnegan's Wake, assuring Rikki that everybody would be welcome there, including any Maud's regulars that remained. "Because I'm not a person who wants anybody to be kept out of my places, except for assholes and jerks, okay?" Tom tells us when we visit Finnegan's Wake in 2022, echoing the ethos of the contemporary lesbian bar.

The year after she sold Maud's, Rikki was diagnosed with cancer. Perhaps on some level, she already knew she was sick, contributing to her almost spiritual sense that the time to close Maud's had come. Rikki passed away on August 21, 1994, at the age of sixty-eight.[24]

Before she passed and after Maud's shut its doors for good, Rikki chopped up the original bar into small pieces of wood and made plaques. She gave the plaques to patrons and bartenders like Mandy, to commemorate their space. To this day, one hangs on the wall of Finnegan's Wake. It reads: "R.I.P. MAUD'S 1966–1989. It Was the Best of Times—It Was the Worst of Times. It Was Our Time."

But of course, Rikki's legacy, and that of Maud's, lives on. She may have felt that the era of the lesbian bar was over in 1989, but more than three decades later, it seems clear that what had ended was only a specific version of it: alcohol fueled and secretive. Countless queer and sapphic spaces have opened in the years since Maud's closed, expanding our very definition of the lesbian bar. In 2025, a bar called Rikki's opened in San Francisco. It's a queer-owned women's sports bar—something I doubt Rikki herself could have ever imagined existing. The name is a tribute to Rikki Streicher and the way she championed queer women and women's sports. In photos on the bar's website, Rikki grins alongside the Maud's softball team and clutches a video camera on the softball field—making space for queer women's joy and capturing it too.

Chapter Sixteen

WILD SIDE WEST

WHEN LIFE GIVES YOU GARBAGE, PLANT A GARDEN

SAN FRANCISCO, CA

The longest continuously operating and still-open lesbian bar on our list stands proud atop a hill in Bernal Heights, San Francisco. Hanging from a metal bracket that juts out from the building is a wooden sign with the phrase "Wild Side West, since '62" printed in a western-style font. Pat Ramseyer first opened the bar in Oakland, California, in 1962 with her then-partner Nancy White, naming it Wild Side, after the sapphically charged film *Walk on the Wild Side*. In 1964, the pair moved the bar west across the bay to North Beach in San Francisco proper, tacking "West" onto the end of the name, and in 1976, they relocated to their permanent home in Bernal Heights.

As the story goes, Pat and Nancy brought the original physical bar down from the North Beach location, loading it onto two trucks and precariously transporting it over the many hills on the way to Bernal Heights. "Janis Joplin, Bob Dylan all used to hang on that bar to drink, so that came with it, you know? Their spirits are there," Billie, the current owner of Wild Side West, shares with us.

The bar made it relatively unscathed, but the new neighborhood didn't respond too kindly to Wild Side West's arrival. "The very first day we were there, we got bricks thrown through the windows because we were gay. And we were women. And they did not want a lesbian bar to be there at all," remembers S.M., a regular customer who followed Pat, Nancy, and the bar from North Beach. We later learn that the neighbors got so extreme, they would dump all sorts of garbage on the sidewalk in front of the bar, including the occasional toilet.

Pat remained unbothered. She boarded up the windows, thanked her new neighbors for the planters, and decided to make a garden. She carted the junk out to the backyard, where everything became either a flowerpot, an art installation, or both.

Today, Wild Side West's backyard is its most magical feature. It's a level below the bar itself, and a wooden staircase leads you from the back door down into the garden. Trees, plants, and pieces of lattice divide the garden into smaller nooks, like restaurant booths. Plants grow out of ceramic urinals, toilet bowls, and old shoes. The headlights of a vintage car are mounted on the side of the stairs. Mannequin legs hang artfully from trees.

You can see Pat's decorative touch inside the bar too. The walls and ceiling, painted in a deep shade of red, feature an eclectic mix of art and antiques. In one corner, there's an upright piano on top of which sits the bottom half of a mannequin tiled in bottle caps. An art installation in the center of the room features an assortment of single shoes—all of which once belonged to Pat—mounted on the brick fireplace. Aesthetically, this bar is perhaps where the three of us feel most at home out of all the places we've visited. The pool table beckons welcomingly, the backyard feels intimate and wonderous, like a place I would have built fairy houses as a child, and the mix of theatrical masks, sports posters, and naked ladies on the walls cater to all our varied interests.

Pat was a collector of things. "She wanted whatever you were tossing out," says S.M. "She'd see a nail on the street, she had hundreds of thousands of dollars, but she would pick up the nail and put it in her pocket because she thought she might need it."

Beyond the indelible mark Pat left on Wild Side West, she remains somewhat of a mystery. She was an extremely private person. As S.M. notes, "She never exuberated happiness. She never exuberated sadness. She had everything inside of her." It's not that she was reserved. "She was always loving to smoke marijuana, and she was always laughing and honking and picking up instruments and wanting to play. [. . .] She was an entertainer," S.M. clarifies, but one who kept her inner life closely guarded. "Nobody knew how old she was. Nobody. She never talked about anything about herself whatsoever. Never." In 2010, when Pat passed away, her obituary revealed that she was seventy-five.

Aside from Nancy, who passed a year before Pat, Billie probably knew Pat better than anyone else. But when it came to her personal life, even Billie was kept at a distance. "She told me little bits and pieces," Billie says. "I didn't get that deep with her because that was her personal stuff. And I didn't want her to think I was trying to snoop."

Pat and Billie met in the late 1980s. The military had brought Billie to San Francisco; she was stationed at the Presidio, at a time when you could not be openly gay in the army, though she says she never had a problem. "All my time in the military, they thought I was gay, but they never would say anything to me," Billie remembers.

Being stationed in San Francisco, Billie eventually found herself at Wild Side West's Bernal Heights location, where she first met Pat, who was perched at the end of the bar, sipping a hot toddy. "She'd always look at me and just stare at me, and then I'd look at her, and then she'd turn away," Billie recalls.

Finally, Billie approached Pat. "Can I buy you a drink?" Billie asked.

"Oh, you're gonna buy *me* a drink? I'm the owner," Pat said.

"Yeah, where I'm from, I buy people drinks even if you're the owner," Billie replied.

Over their shared drinks, Pat revealed the reason she kept staring; she thought Billie—with her tough, military, butch style—was a police officer. Billie assured her she wasn't, and Pat relaxed. Over the years, the two developed a close friendship. "We had a really deep connection," Billie says. They were alike in many ways. Billie, too, values her privacy, and Billie and Pat's mutual respect for one another's boundaries is perhaps what made them so close.

"Pat really liked Billie, and I'm sure it was because Billie didn't share with Pat very much about herself," S.M. assesses. Unlike Pat, S.M. often needled Billie for details about her life.

"Hey, Billie, what do you do for a living?" S.M. would ask.

"If I tell you, I'd have to kill you," Billie would always reply, stone-faced.

"You felt like she really fucking meant it," S.M. says, laughing, "and I'm sure that Aunt Pat loved that line."

An open book, S.M. could not have been more different from Pat and Billie, but she too formed a close bond with both over the years. Pat herself was behind the bar during S.M.'s first visit in 1970, back at the North Beach location. "I was scared to death. My teeth were chattering. I was twenty years old but since I was six feet tall, I knew I could pass for twenty-one. So, I ordered a beer [. . .] and then I felt like I was at home for the rest of my life," says S.M. "The bar was our family," she notes of the North Beach queer community. "In the early '70s, that's how we met and that's where we socialized."

Like the bar itself, S.M. had also recently moved west, arriving in San Francisco that very year "in a car full of queens who ran like hell to get out of Texas," as S.M. puts it. She grew up in what she describes as a "little tiny town [where] they'd take you out and shoot you" if they knew you were gay. As a teen, she was far too scared to act on her proliferating queer desires, but she did begin to push the boundaries of traditional gender norms.

"I wanted blue jeans like my brother wore. So, I went to JC Penney's," S.M. recounts. But they wouldn't sell a teenage girl a pair of boy's blue jeans. "I made the salesclerk, this old frumpy lady, call my father, who was head of the phone company. And he had a lot of clout. And he told 'em to 'sell my daughter whatever she wants.'" Not because he was supportive of his daughter's right to self-expression; he just wanted her out of his hair. "And that's how I got my first pair of blue jeans. I needed my father's permission."

After graduating from high school, S.M. wore her blue jeans all the way to Dallas, where her mother had enrolled her in fashion merchandising college. There, she befriended her roommate Kathy, a heterosexual but liberal and accepting Californian, and Tommy and Greg, two gay coworkers at the clothing store where she worked. "These fantastic queens in the display department," as she refers to them.

Kathy had grown up in San Francisco, and in 1970, decided to move back. "Not without me!" exclaimed S.M. The two crammed into Kathy's tiny two-seater Corvette and caravanned out to California, with Tommy and Greg following close behind in their Chevy Nova station wagon. S.M. thought they would make quite the scene pulling up in San Francisco that June. "On the road I bought a purple fringe jacket in Wyoming [and] boots that came up to my knees from Taos, New Mexico. Tom and Greg had bought tons of jewelry. They had it around their necks—silver and turquoise," she describes.

But they weren't in Texas anymore. "Nobody even looked at me," S.M. recalls with awe, "and it just blew my mind. [. . .] Everybody else was wearing Led Zeppelin and eating acid in Golden Gate Park. [. . .] Finally

I could be who I wanted to be. And nobody was going to even look at me or judge me."

Still, S.M. couldn't immediately shake the prejudice, hatred, and fear she had left behind in Texas. During that first month, San Francisco held their first ever Gay Day Parade, a precursor to contemporary Pride. "All my gay guys got all dressed up with their feather boas and all this kind of stuff," S.M. details, but she warned them not to go. "They want all the gay people in one place and they're just gonna kill us," she feared.

Wild Side West was one of the few places she felt safe in the city. She found out about the bar through word of mouth. "I kept badgering all of my gay friends, all the queens I was hanging around with," S.M. remembers, asking, "Where do the women go?"

Finally, someone told her about Wild Side West. "Any lesbian bar you went to in the early goings, they never had their name on the outside. [. . .] You had to know what you were doing to get in," says S.M. North Beach was "a seedy part of town, where they had topless girls dancing and all that kind of stuff," she describes. Without an exact address, she wandered up Broadway until she came across a group of women gathered outside of a "girlie club," as S.M. calls it, slang for a strip club or brothel. S.M. asked for directions to Wild Side West, and the crowd pointed her one block over. They likely were familiar with the bar not just because it was in the neighborhood, but because they patronized it themselves. This iteration of Wild Side West was a refuge for the many women who worked in the area as strippers—gay and straight alike—to come in for a drink where they wouldn't be bothered by men.

Finally, S.M. found the bar: "There was this heavy leather curtain. It took all my strength to push it to the side. [. . .] It was almost like breaking in, and I think [Pat] did that purposely. She didn't want people falling into her bar thinking they could come and have a drink there. It was a special place for girls to go." And so began S.M.'s forty-plus year friendship with Pat.

In the final years of Pat's life, both S.M. and Billie were among the few people she allowed into her inner circle. "Pat had actually battled cancer twice. She never let anybody know. She just did it on her own," says S.M., who only found out when Pat asked her for a ride to chemo.

Toward the end of her life, Pat rarely left her apartment above the bar. "She'd come down when nobody was here," says Billie. "She didn't want anybody to see her with the oxygen tank on." She had emphysema, and in the last year or so, she could barely get out of bed. The people closest to her, Billie and S.M. included, would go up to her apartment to visit.

"She always still had a twinkle in her eye," says S.M. "Maybe she'd have half a beer, and she'd always want to smoke."

Pat never lost her sharp wit or her sense of humor. "We'd have to call the ambulance every week or two to get her to the hospital," says Billie. Whenever an ambulance was passing through the neighborhood for other purposes, Pat would joke, "My taxi went by!"

Billie was Pat's primary caregiver, moving in with her for the last six months of her life. Billie also stepped in to help manage the bar, as it was Pat's main source of income. The two never talked about Billie taking over the bar in any official capacity. In fact, they never discussed the fate of the bar at all, except for one conversation, years earlier.

Speaking hypothetically, Pat asked Billie who she would give the bar to if it was hers. "You give it to somebody you think would take care of it. Whoever wanted to cherish it," Billie answered.

"Would you change anything?" Pat asked.

"No, why would you change it? Why would you fix something that's not broke?" Billie answered.

One day, shortly before Pat passed, an estate executor came by to speak with Billie. Downstairs in Wild Side West, perched on bar stools at the bar that had travelled down from North Beach decades earlier, they discussed Pat's affairs.

"You know, she's going to leave [the bar] to you," the executor told a shocked Billie.

Billie was humbled, honored, and overwhelmed. "I never wanted to be a bartender. I never wanted a bar," Billie reflects. "I had enough bar back in the '80s and '90s. I had my full of it."

When Pat passed away in 2010, the bar was officially Billie's. Of course, they planned a huge memorial at Wild Side West. "We had about three hundred people come. We had to open the side doors, and the garden was packed. You could hardly walk around," Billie recalls. "She was like our mother, our aunt, our mentor, our daddy, whatever. She was there for us," Billie says of what Pat meant to the community. At the memorial, she noticed a group of older women seated in a corner. They didn't quite fit in with the rest of the crowd, and nobody seemed to know who they were. Finally,

Billie asked them about their connection to Pat. As it turned out, they were the strippers from North Beach who used to frequent the old Wild Side West. Pat had protected them, and they had come to pay their respects.

In the years since Pat's passing, Billie has kept her word, not changing much about the bar. She cleaned and repainted, ridding the space of thirty years of cigarette smoke. "The best part is, when you put your elbow down on the bar it didn't stick anymore," says S.M., laughing. Otherwise, the bar looks just as Pat left it.

At first, Billie wasn't certain about the bar's future. "Let me run it for a couple years. See what happens," she remembers thinking. But the community wasn't going to let Billie off the hook that easily. Gay and straight people alike came to her in droves, begging her to keep the bar open. So, she decided to keep at it for a few more years, waiting to see if maybe the bar would start making some money.

More than a decade and a half later, the bar hasn't started turning a profit. But something else has shifted for Billie. "I started liking it," she says. "This is not so bad after all. [. . .] It's kinda like family. [. . .] It's a haven, it's a refuge. [. . . We] do the same thing Pat and them did, as long as you behave and [aren't] an asshole, then you're good to be in here," she adds, voicing a familiar sentiment.

"That's what Pat wanted. She wanted that bar around so she could haunt it," S.M. says. "She's still there listening. I know it. [. . .] And *Billie* says it. And if Billie says it, then you know the freaky incident happened. Because Billie's got her feet on the ground, [she's a] no bullshit kind of woman."

"I was sitting here talking to one of the bartenders," Billie describes, "and me and him were standing there and all of a sudden a glass came flying at him." There's a shadow Billie's staff often report seeing in the basement, too. "Well, that's just Pat and them checking on you, 'cause when y'all do me wrong, she's watching ya," Billie says with a laugh.

Chapter Seventeen

GOSSIP GRILL

WELCOME HOME

SAN DIEGO, CA

Moe Girton, owner of Gossip Grill, never intended to open San Diego's only lesbian bar. "I actually turned Betty's into a women's bar by accident," she tells us, referring to Baja Betty's—a bar which primarily catered to gay men—where Moe had been hired to bartend in 2004.

Moe had been working in LGBTQ+ nightlife in San Diego since 2000, when she got a job doing coat check and security at The Flame, an iconic lesbian nightclub. Bored by this role, she worked her way up to a bartender position and immediately fell in love with bartending. Charismatic and outgoing, Moe has a soft butch vibe and a crisp, classy style. "I was always a big social butterfly, going to the bars and meeting up with people and having drinks. And [bartending] was a great way for me to make money but also be in the environment," she explains.

She was good at it, too. "I started doing a lot of flair work back then," Moe says. "Flipping bottles, juggling, blowing fire, [. . .] fun little tricks." Soon, she was the star bartender at The Flame, with her own dedicated clientele. But when the nightclub sold to a developer and closed its doors in 2004, Moe applied for a position on the opening team of Baja Betty's in Hillcrest, San Diego's gayborhood.

With the closure of The Flame, and soon thereafter the closure of San Diego's only other lesbian bar—6 Degrees—the queer women of the city had nowhere to go. "Oh my God, I'm gonna date myself," Moe exclaims before detailing how she'd post on MySpace to let her community know when she'd be bartending. "Little by little, all the women started coming in to see me," she adds.

The gay men of Hillcrest were not altogether pleased. "[The women were] kind of scaring off some of the boys in the neighborhood," Moe says. "Back then, [bars were] still kind of segregated. You know, the women stayed with the women, the men stayed with the men."

"I had to get rid of her at Baja Betty['s], she turned it into a lesbian bar! They all came to see her," jokes Stefan Chilcote, then the manager, now Moe's business partner. "So that's when we were like, okay, let's open a new place for Moe," Stefan adds.

After Stefan pitched the idea to Chris Shaw—one of Baja Betty's owners—they made Moe an offer: they would open a lesbian bar for her to run. "I quickly turned them down three times," Moe says. She wanted partial ownership, and she wanted to call it a women's bar, not a lesbian bar. "Lesbian really is too small of a box to be successful and survive long term. So being a women's bar is the giant umbrella and underneath 'women's bar' is lesbian, gay, straight, bi, trans, pan, asexual. Anybody that identifies with the woman in them just a little bit, this bar is for you," Moe explains. In 2009, once Chris and Stefan agreed to her terms and gave her full creative control, they opened Gossip Grill, or simply Gossip as it's often called.

More than a decade later, Moe still maintains Gossip's identity as a women's bar, but of course, she welcomes everyone. "We have a sign on the door that says we don't care if you have a dick, just don't be a dick," Moe says. The space itself has a welcoming spirit. "It really kind of sucks you in. It's like a vortex. It's very common that people are with us for four or five hours. [. . .] We're not just a bar. We are, number one, a community center. [. . .] You know, we have the big neon sign that says, 'Welcome Home, Beautiful.' That's us. We're home. It gets me all teary-eyed."

When we visit Gossip Grill in 2021, we find Rudy and Lisa Ramrod, two longtime regulars, beneath the "Welcome Home, Beautiful" sign in the open-air half of the bar. Rudy is clad in a flame-patterned, Hawaiian-style shirt. Lisa is in all-black with red cat-eye glasses. She has short purple hair and dark purple lipstick. For the couple, Gossip is home in many ways. "We personally are here *a lot*," Rudy says.

Rudy and Lisa run the San Diego Kings Club, a group of drag artists that perform monthly at Gossip. Rudy is an original member of the group, which began in 2000 at the Flame. In 2017, the Kings Club made Gossip their home after Moe agreed to host their show.

For Lisa, Gossip is also somewhat of a spiritual home. "We consider [it] one of our sanctuaries," she says. By 'we,' she's referring not to her and Rudy—nor to the San Diego Kings Club—but to the Sisters of Perpetual Indulgence. The Sisters of Perpetual Indulgence are an activist and charity group, and an international order of queer and trans nuns that can be traced to a 1976 drag troupe in Iowa called the Sugar Plum Fairies. After the drag troupe borrowed some retired nun habits from a local convent for a drag version of *The Sound of Music*, troupe member Ken Brunch headed west, moving to the Castro in San Francisco, which by then boasted a thriving gay community. The nun habits went with him. On Easter Sunday of 1979, Ken and two of his friends decided to dress up in the nun habits and parade around the neighborhood. That day, the Sisters of Perpetual Indulgence were born.[1] The trio quickly realized that their nun getups garnered them something powerful: attention. And they decided to channel that attention into mission-driven work.

"We are considered nuns to the LGBTQ+ community," Lisa explains. "We take vows, we promise to take care of everyone around us." Their mission has remained the same since the 1980s: "to Promulgate Universal Joy, Expiate Stigmatic Guilt, and expose the forces of bigotry, complacency, and guilt that chain the human spirit."[2] As Lisa puts it, their purpose is "basically to get rid of guilt and spread love."

In their early years, the Sisters of Perpetual Indulgence created street theater performances in support of social change. They participated in a 1980 Three Mile Island march in San Francisco, protesting nuclear power in the wake of the Three Mile Island plant accident. They hosted a bingo night benefit for gay, Cuban refugees.[3] They performed at parades and art festivals.

"And then [the] 1980s hit," says Lisa. One of the four main founders was the first of the group to start showing signs of illness. At the time, this mystery sickness was being referred to as a gay cancer. Today, we know it as AIDS. "People were not visiting family members in the hospital. Nobody would go and sit. Nobody was claiming the bodies. Nobody was doing anything for anybody at the time," Lisa details. The Sisters knew they had to do something to help their community. "So, they would start sitting with people in the hospitals," says Lisa. "They would go in and they would deliver, you know, almost a last rites, a blessing, and sit with them. Because nobody else would."

As soon as more information about HIV/AIDS became available, the Sisters made it their mission to educate people. On June 18, 1982, a report out of the Los Angeles area suggested that the disease was being sexually transmitted.[4] Just nine days later, the Sisters published the first ever pamphlet on safer sex for gay men. It was titled "Play Fair!" and featured a variety of cartoon bearded and mustached nuns educating about safer sex and STDs.[5] "Play Fair!" was groundbreaking in many ways. It was written by and for the gay community, and it used humor and sex-positive language rather than shame. In fact, the last STD listed in the guide is guilt itself. "This STD is subject to home remedies," the pamphlet reads. "Sister Roz Erection recommends putting your guilt in a blender set at 'annihilate' for about five minutes, then flushing whatever's left down the toilet."[6]

Over the years, the Sisters' looks evolved from simple nun habits to more elaborate drag ensembles. Today, their signature garb includes long headpieces and white face paint. The headpieces vary from house to house. Each chapter of Sisters across the country—and around the world—has a specific shape to their headpieces.

"We kind of look like really fancy clowns," says Lisa. "Imagine a drag queen but in white face with lashes and jewels and gems." Some wear traditional black-and-white Catholic nun habits, some wear rainbow habits, and most embellish their looks with their own flair: glitter, colored eyeliner, chunky jewelry, feather boas, corsets, and so on.

While at first, the Sisters were all gay men, they eventually began accepting women as well. "Yes, they let girls in," Lisa affirms. "They let everybody in. All colors, shapes, sizes, identity." Lisa herself joined in 2013. She was in the hospital when she first discovered the Sisters. Lisa lives with Crohn's disease, fibromyalgia, and a rare genetic bone disease called osteogenesis imperfecta. On February 3, 2013, she went into the hospital with an abscess in her colon.

Six weeks later, she woke up from surgery with an ostomy bag and a significant period of recovery and life adjustments ahead of her. Lisa remembers thinking, "Okay, we have a bag. Let's go. Let's rock and roll. [. . .] How do we do this? How do we make this work?"

During her stay at the hospital, Lisa stumbled upon the Sisters via a friend's Facebook page. "This was a near death experience. I was given a second chance. This is a time you can really do some good. So, I told my friend, 'I want to join the Sisters.'"

Lisa's friend walked her through the four stages to becoming a fully professed Sister. "We very much go on trend with the Catholic nun matriculation as you become a nun, so it's Aspirant, Postulate, Novice, Fully Professed," says Lisa. The process starts with attending a meeting and declaring your interest in joining, which is exactly what Lisa did.

On November 26, 2014, Lisa became a Fully Professed Sister of Perpetual Indulgence. "I got down on my knees. I looked in the mirror. And I promised to take care of my Sisters and my community and myself even when it wasn't easy," Lisa recounts. In turn, the Sisters took care of her. "I needed the Sisters more than they needed me," Lisa confesses, recounting the first time she ever let anyone see her ostomy bag. She was at a pool party with some of the Sisters, and a friend encouraged her to get in the water, reassuring her that no one cared about her bag.

Today, Lisa's very comfortable with her bag. "Most people have a butt hole. Mine just happens to be on the front," she states matter-of-factly. As a Sister, her ministry—her personal mission—is helping others with invisible illnesses. Over the years, she's met and supported many people with ostomy bags. "I will talk about shit with anybody. I don't care where it comes from, we'll just talk about it," Lisa declares.

As for the Sisters of Perpetual Indulgence as a whole, they currently have over eighty houses worldwide.[7] They continue to fundraise and hold events for all kinds of causes, but primarily, their job is to just show up, listen, and be unapologetically themselves. "Some houses, like ours, we call it a manifestation of presence," says Lisa. "We are manifesting our joy, and we are just here."

Gossip Grill, at its core, aligns with the Sisters' mission wholeheartedly; it's a place where people can simply *be.* That's why the Sisters consider it a sanctuary space. "When we sanctify a place, it means it is welcoming to everybody. This is where you can walk in and you are going to feel safe," Lisa explains.

Like any holy place—churches, temples, mosques—Gossip Grill is where the community turns for comfort in times of need. The bar houses a disco ball shrine for people who have passed, and whenever someone loses a loved one or a community member passes away, their picture gets placed inside the ball. "So, they're always dancing, they're always a part of our lives," Moe reflects.

And just like Cubbyhole and so many other lesbian bars we've seen, Gossip makes sure it is available in times of overt crises. "It doesn't matter what is going on. We will stay open," Moe proclaims. After the 2016 mass shooting which killed forty-nine individuals at Pulse, an LGBTQ+ nightclub in Orlando, patrons came out to Gossip in droves. In September of 2011, a mass power outage wiped out electricity for up to six million people in Southern California, Arizona, and Mexico.[8] "Nobody knew what to do," Moe says, "so everyone just started showing up to Gossip."

Soon, Moe's business partner, Chris Shaw, arrived with a borrowed generator. "We plugged in the lights; we plugged in a DJ booth. [. . .] It was magical," Moe recalls. As the night went on, Gossip got busier and busier. "Next thing you know, we have a line down the street," Moe says. "We were at full capacity. [. . .] And everyone just kept saying, 'I didn't know where to go. I didn't know what was going on. So, I just came home.'"

Chapter Eighteen

REDZ

SHIT COME, SHIT GO, I'M GONNA BE MYSELF

LOS ANGELES, CA

Redz, or Redz Angelz as it's known today, sits on a quiet street in East LA. As the name would suggest, the exterior is painted bright red. A Mexican flag hangs in the window, and when Sarah, Jen, and I step inside, we are the only people speaking English. The many rainbow flags which line the walls indicate it's a queer bar, though it's also a neighborhood spot where all sorts of folks mingle, gay and straight alike. We are here because of the bar's history: soon after opening its doors in the 1950s, Redz became a lesbian bar that catered primarily to the area's Chicana community.

If you walked in on a Friday night in the late 1950s, you might find regular customer Nancy Valverde perched on a leather bar stool, dressed in a pair of pants and a button-down shirt. What sounds like an ordinary scene was actually a stubborn act of resistance. As a young adult, Nancy was constantly harassed and arrested by the LAPD for violating masquerading laws. Masquerading laws were originally introduced to prevent people from disguising themselves for the purposes of committing a crime, but by the mid-twentieth century, they were used to police gender presentation.

Throughout the 1950s, Nancy spent dozens of nights in jail over her refusal to wear what was traditionally deemed "women's" clothing. Nancy was more comfortable in a pair of pants and a collared shirt.

"I want to see you in a dress," LAPD officers would tell her over and over again.

"Sit down and wait, because you're going to get tired," Nancy would reply.[1]

While the 1960s would see the first waves of LGBTQ+ people flocking to the West Coast as a safe haven, Nancy was already there in the decades prior, quietly but willfully protesting for the right to live authentically. Today, she's often referred to as a "pioneer"—a fitting term for the woman who paved the way for liberated gender expression for generations of queer folks to come.

Leading up to our trip in the fall of 2023, we began trying to reach Nancy, who was ninety-one at the time and living in an affordable LGBTQ+ senior housing complex called Triangle Square Apartments. A friend of hers told us that Nancy would be open to an interview and provided us with detailed instructions to reach her over the phone. We had to call, wait for the answering machine, introduce ourselves, and then stay on the line until Nancy picked up. Moving across the room took Nancy a lot of time and effort, and this process meant she wouldn't have to rush to the phone. It also meant she could screen her calls; if she wasn't interested in talking, she didn't have to bother getting up.

Sarah called numerous times, leaving long and awkward messages: "Hi Nancy, it's Sarah Gabrielli from *Cruising* podcast. . . . Um, I guess I'm just going to wait and hopefully we can talk. . . ." Long awkward silence. "Um . . . okay, if you get this message, feel free to call me back. Or I'll try you again later. Thanks!" Apparently, we were being screened.

On our last day in LA, we decided to swing by Nancy's building to drop off a card and flowers: an apology for the long messages on her machine and a final invitation to connect for a phone interview whenever she was feeling up for it. The security person in the lobby buzzed us up to make the drop ourselves.

That's how we met Nancy Valverde. She recognized us immediately as the girls who had been calling her. We insisted we were just there to drop off flowers and apologize for clogging up her voicemail, but she ushered us in to do an interview right then and there. An especially generous offer, seeing as she'd been having a bad day.

"What a bitch. It's been a bitchy day, huh?" she declares as we walk in the door, her voice dry and warm, threaded with an unmistakable East LA Chicana cadence. Nancy settles in her recliner, next to the oxygen tank that she relies on to breathe, and we sit opposite her. She's been battling cancer for some time, but she's still very much the fiery woman who once flouted heteronormative standards, whether she was picking up women at Redz or standing up to LAPD harassment.

Part of why Nancy let us in that afternoon, despite the "bitchy day" she'd been having, was her deep commitment to the LGBTQ+ community. She explained to us that when the community had requests of her, she always wanted to oblige, because she didn't have any queer elders to guide her when she was young. But I'll always wonder if there was another reason Nancy let us in that day: if she also knew it might be the last time she told her story. Just six months later, on March 25, 2024, Nancy passed away in her home at age ninety-two.

Nancy was born in 1932 and spent the early years of her life in Deming, New Mexico. "It's a one-horse town, and the horse is dead," she deadpans. Already, she was wearing pants. "The winters were very harsh," she describes. "They put [most little girls] in stockings way up to here and then pants because it was so cold [. . .] and so I was used to that kind of attire."

At nine years old, her family moved to Los Angeles, where her father was drafted into a defense job during World War II. They settled on Clover Street, just a few miles north of Redz, in the Mexican American neighborhood of Lincoln Heights.

"In those days, they call[ed] them barrios. It's Mexican ghettos," Nancy comments. "Very united," she adds, referring to the close-knit nature of the community. When she first arrived, she had to earn the respect of the rest of the neighborhood youth, who picked on her as the new kid on the block. Already, Nancy was not the type to go down without a fight. "I hit back," she says, a glint of mischief in her eyes.

It didn't take long for the neighborhood kids to accept Nancy into the fold, but she still felt different. "I found myself a very strange kid," Nancy reflects, "because little girls would look at little boys and [. . .] I would admire little girls."

It was here in East LA, in the early 1940s, that Nancy first ran into trouble for the way she dressed. "I went to school one day with pants on and they sent me home," she recounts. In sixth grade, at eleven years old, Nancy dropped out. Not only because she hated wearing skirts and dresses, but also, as one of five kids in a family with very little means, she needed to work. "I didn't get enough to eat at home, and so I had to go and scrounge around," Nancy remembers. "I was always looking for a job."

Her first job was working for a Mexican bakery, helping in the kitchen and making bread deliveries throughout the surrounding Mexican American neighborhoods. "You know where the Chavez Ravine is?" Nancy asks, referring to the land on which Dodger Stadium now sits. "That used to be three neighborhoods up there, Chicano neighborhoods too. Palo Verde, Bishop, and La Loma. And they forced them out to build that, would you believe? I don't put one foot in that stadium," Nancy spits.

Nancy only ever saw ten dollars a week for her work; the rest of her earnings went straight to her mother. In the afternoons, after she finished her daily deliveries, Nancy sought out supplemental income in other ways.

As a teenager, she would drive neighborhood sex workers to their tricks and back.[2] It was a good gig; Nancy would make a few bucks, get her gas tank filled, *and* get to hang out with some beautiful older women. This was how she met her first lesbian. One day, a woman asked Nancy to take her to pick up her girl. Nancy assumed she meant her daughter, but when they arrived, she discovered it was actually the woman's girlfriend. With relief, Nancy realized she wasn't alone in her own growing feelings of attraction toward women.

At fifteen, Nancy met her first girlfriend: another teenager who already had experience with other women. This relationship empowered Nancy to stop caring entirely about what other people thought of her. She began more intentionally exploring her style, using her extra earnings to buy tailored men's clothing. "I dressed to please myself," she states simply.

It was around this time in Nancy's life that people around her realized she was gay. "I never came out to no one. They just knew. My mother knew," Nancy explains. "She found out that I was gay when I wouldn't take off the men's attire."

"Why don't you get a gun and shoot yourself?" her mother told her.

So, Nancy sought acceptance elsewhere. The Chicana lesbian community was "very hidden," as Nancy describes it, but it existed, mainly in the bar scene. "We went to the bars to socialize because there was no other way," says Nancy. For her, and many of her friends, going to the bars was never about drinking. In fact, that's why Nancy liked Redz so much: "You could buy a beer and just have it there all night and you could talk and socialize and everything. They didn't push the drinks on you."

Nancy was in her early twenties when she first discovered Redz, or Redheads, as it was called back then. The bar has cycled through a number of names over the years, from Redheads, to Reds, to Redz, and as it stands today, Redz Angelz.

"We never expected it to be a historical place," Nancy says, "but it lasted for a long time. All the other bars closed. Redz was still there." When Redz first opened, it was not a lesbian bar at all. "It was a neighborhood bar. And a little old man owned it, Charlie," describes Nancy. Charlie was always kind and welcoming, and so "more and more lesbians started going there."

For a while, it was a mixed crowd, but then Charlie "made the mistake of hiring a lesbian," says Nancy, "and we just took over." When straight men arrived at the door, Nancy and her friends would turn them away. "No, it's a girls' thing now," they would say. Charlie never seemed to mind this shift in the bar's clientele. "He was the best, one of the best men that I've met," Nancy proclaims.

Nancy always felt safe in Redz. Despite the prevalence of police raids back in the 1950s, she was never arrested in the gay and lesbian bars. Outside the bars was another story. Nancy was seventeen when she was arrested for the first time. She was standing on the sidewalk in Maravilla, an East LA neighborhood, in front of a brickyard. She'd come to meet a friend, but the brickyard was closed for the day, and the gate was locked. "I was yelling from the sidewalk to my friend [. . .] when the police came. And right away they turned me around and put [me in] cuffs," Nancy recounts.

They took Nancy to an East LA substation and locked her in a cell. "The cop came up to the bars and he tried to reach for my parts, you know, and I jumped back," she recalls. It was then that she noticed the cell had drapes, and that she couldn't be seen by anyone outside. "Shit, they can do anything they want to me here," she remembers thinking. "So, I sat on the wooden bench, and I started hitting it, making a bunch of noise."

What she didn't realize was that on the other side of her cell wall, there was another cell full of men. Soon, the men began yelling at her: "Shut up! Knock it off."

"This is Nancy from Eastside Clover," she shouted back. At seventeen, Nancy was well known within her community. "I'm very loyal to my friends," she explains. "I became famous because [I was] just a shut-your-mouth kid." In other words, she wasn't a snitch. "Never knew nothing, never saw anything. Better that way."

When the men heard her calling for help from her cell, they recognized her as a friend to be protected.

"Hey, Nancy! What's the matter, Nancy?" they called back.

"This fuckin' cop here, he tried to touch me," she yelled.

At this, all the men erupted into a cacophony of their own. "I want a female officer," Nancy repeated over and over again, until finally, one was sent over to her cell. She informed Nancy that she was being sent to the jail downtown for masquerading.

"What the hell is masquerading?" Nancy thought. She would soon learn that it simply meant she was wearing clothes designated for the opposite gender.

This incident was the first of many masquerading arrests for Nancy: "When I was going to barber school, they would arrest me almost every Friday." This was the worst day to be arrested, as it meant spending the weekend in jail, a fact the local officers were no doubt well aware of. These arrests also meant she would be absent from barber school on Mondays.

After many weeks of this cycle, Mrs. Lewis, the owner of the barber school, called Nancy into her office. "Well, there goes my schooling," Nancy thought to herself, "because I had lied on the application that I had never been to jail." But she explained herself, and Mrs. Lewis sent her back to class. A few days later, Mrs. Lewis called Nancy back into her office.

"Nancy, I spoke to every officer within a three-mile radius. And I told them, you don't bother my students going or coming to school," Mrs. Lewis told her.

Mrs. Lewis had convinced the LAPD to stop arresting Nancy, but it was only temporary. After finishing barber school, the arrests began again.

Through all this harassment, Nancy never once considered changing the way she dressed. "I was determined to be myself, regardless," she asserts. "Shit come, shit go. I'm gonna be myself. I don't care what anybody says. I support myself. Nobody supports me. I buy these clothes. And why would anybody come and tell somebody else how to dress?"

In 1959, Nancy was arrested for the last time. She was in an empty bar, quietly playing pool. "The cops walked in. They pulled me out and they handcuffed me," she remembers.

"What the hell's wrong?" she asked.

"Masquerading," they replied.

This was the last straw for Nancy. She wanted to fight these arrests in court, so she went down to the local law library to research masquerading laws. There, Nancy discovered a case from 1950. "This woman had already taken [masquerading laws] to the state Supreme Court, and it had been thrown out. [. . .] She had already fought it," Nancy informs us.

Specifically, the court had ruled that masquerading laws could only be enforced if the perpetrator was disguising themself for the purposes of committing another crime. Feeling vindicated, Nancy sought out legal representation to fight her most recent charge. The lawyer who stepped up to take her case was a young Black man named Arthur Black. "[Black people] were fighting for their rights. [The police] were arresting them left and right, in Alabama and all over. And now, he's gonna defend a Chicana lesbian?" reflects Nancy, describing the troubling racial politics at the time.

By the end of the afternoon, the case was dismissed. "That was the last time I was arrested," Nancy remembers.

More than a decade after that final arrest, Nancy opened a barbershop of her own. There, she made it her mission to provide a safe haven for the queer kids in the neighborhood. "The kids would come to my shop and tell me they were gay. They wanted to tell their mother[s]," Nancy recounts. Based on her own experiences, Nancy had a cynical, but perhaps practical, response: "Your mother already knows. She's in denial. [. . .] Just keep quiet. Go to school. Learn [. . .] and then just live your life."

While she would never spend another night in jail, Nancy would spend the rest of her life recovering from the trauma she had endured at the hands of the LAPD. A cop had kicked her in the back during one of their routine arrests, resulting in chronic pain. After nine years of running her barbershop, her doctor told her she needed to retire.

The psychological effects of police harassment lingered with her, too. At ninety-one years old, she was still wary of the cops. She detailed a minor traffic stop a few years prior, before she got sick. This small encounter upset her. "I try to take precautions around them," she told us, "I know how abusive they can be."

In June of 2023, the City of Los Angeles tried to make things right with Nancy. The city council voted to rename a square downtown after her, in honor of her advocacy for the LGBTQ+ community. At the unveiling, Commander Ruby Flores apologized on behalf of the LAPD: "Sadly, rather than working to protect this community, the LAPD of that time was not always kind to our gay, lesbian, transgender, our nonconforming Angelenos. This mistreatment of our citizens was wrong and should never have happened."[3]

Nancy wasn't well enough to attend the ceremony; her sister Lupe went in her place. The *Los Angeles Daily News* quoted an alleged statement from Nancy, in response to the unveiling: "I'm very humbled. I didn't know I was making history."[4]

But that's not what Nancy told us. "I'm shocked," she exclaims, when we ask her about the square, and her voice is laced with incredulity. "I want some money for it. I don't want an apology." Just six months before her passing, Nancy is undeniably sharp. She knows what she's endured, and she knows what justice should look like.

"I lost jobs because of [the LAPD]," she states.

"Have you ever said anything like that?" Sarah asks her.

"No, I haven't told them anything ever. I'm very disgusted with them. I think it's a lot of bullshit myself. Make themselves feel good. I'm not impressed at all."

Nancy's legacy—of her lifelong fight to live and dress authentically in the face of police harassment—is better honored within the walls of Redz Angelz than with a city plaque and a lukewarm apology. Today, nearly seventy-five years after Nancy first set foot in Redheads, many in the LA Latinx drag community spend weekends at Redz Angelz. Queens and kings alike take to the stage, unapologetically themselves, wearing whatever makes them feel powerful. And thanks to Nancy, they do it freely and without fear.

Chapter Nineteen

THE WILDROSE

THE HEART OF THE HILL

SEATTLE, WA

When Bryher Herak, cofounder of Seattle's sole lesbian bar, The Wildrose, first arrived in the city in 1973, the experience of going to the local LGBTQ+ bars wasn't all that different from the experiences Nancy had in LA a few decades prior. "You would get busted walking over to the bar. You would get jaywalking tickets," she explains. "Then you'd go inside, and the cops would come in, and they'd line you up, and they'd check IDs, and it was kind of a nasty scene." Nonetheless, Bryher was immediately hooked on Seattle. "[I] absolutely fell in love with that town at that time," Bryher reflects, and she wasn't the only one.

Like San Francisco, Seattle saw an influx of queer folks during the 1970s. "It was part of a general migration that was happening," Ruth Pettis, local Seattle historian, explains. Not just LGBTQ+ people, but progressive thinkers of all genders and sexualities flocked to the Pacific Northwest. "There were radical groups that had put out the word that Seattle was going to be the site where the revolution breaks out. [. . .] If you were in certain circles, you would hear this buzz going on. But it wasn't necessarily something that was being proclaimed in newspaper headlines," Ruth details.

Ruth herself came to Seattle from Boston in 1977. "What was different about Seattle, and maybe for the West Coast in general," she begins, "was that the bars—the gay bars—were owned by gay people." Today, this is nothing out of the ordinary, but back then it was unusual in other parts of the country. "In places like New York and Boston, you'd have to go to someplace where it was always rumored that it was Mafia run. [. . .] Our public spaces [were] at the behest of some other group of people who ran [them] for profit," Ruth details.

For Bryher, the plethora of lesbian-owned-and-run establishments popping up all throughout the city was certainly part of the appeal of Seattle. "There was the Lesbian Resource Center. [. . .] There was It's About Time bookstore, there was Red and Black bookstore, there was the Coffee Coven," she rattles off.

Bryher grew up in rural Montana in the '50s and '60s, where despite the lack of lesbian community, she was already defying gender norms as a child. Raised on a farm with eight siblings, Bryher couldn't stand the housework that was expected of her. "I wanted to always be out in the field with my brothers," she remembers, "and so I convinced them that I should get to do that."

As a preteen, Bryher recalls driving the tractor through the fields and thinking to herself, "Oh, I'm bisexual." She was an avid reader and had recently come across the word in a book, misinterpreting it to mean "half man, half woman." The descriptor fit, she felt. "I do all the work outside that the men do, and I do all the work inside that the women do," little Bryher reasoned. Though she'd gotten the word's definition wrong, this was the first time she'd ever considered her own gender or sexuality.

Bryher didn't fully grasp her sexual orientation until around 1969 in her twenties, when she started law school in Washington, DC. There, she became involved in legal and political activism, crossing paths with the likes of Bella Abzug, who in 1970 ran for a House seat with the campaign slogan "This woman's place is in the House . . . the House of Representatives!"[1] Bryher also met Gloria Steinem, already famous for her feminist writings. "I was working with the National Women's Political Caucus. [. . .] The gay movement was just starting. Women were just coming out. I mean, not that we haven't always been around," Bryher muses. For the first time, she saw gay women existing in community rather than on the fringes of society; she saw queerness tied to political identity, not just listed in the dictionary as some form of sexual deviance or mental illness.

If in DC Bryher's gay identity and her political efforts began to overlap, in Seattle they became inextricably linked. Discussing her work with the ACLU and the Lawyer's Guild, Bryher says, "They asked me to work with them on the first lesbian mothers' case." The case centered around two women, Madeleine Isaacson and Sandy Schuster, and their custody battles with their ex-husbands.

Madeleine, mother of two, and Sandy, mother of four, met in 1970 at a Pentecostal church in Seattle. The pair fell in love, leaving their husbands and taking their children with them. In a highly publicized case, the husbands sued for custody. "The men, of course, just immediately made it an issue of 'lesbians are unfit parents,'" Bryher recounts. "The wonderful thing is, these were not unfit women, parents. They were fabulous. They were good parents, and we were able to prove that at trial."

Initially, the mothers were granted custody of their respective children but were ordered to live separately. In a clever loophole to an unjust ruling, they secured apartments across the hall from one another, technically meeting the court's order. In an appeal that would eventually go to the Supreme Court of Washington in 1978, the husbands protested, claiming that while the women maintained separate apartments, they were in fact living together.

That year, Bryher was a part of Madeleine and Sandy's legal defense. "We brought in experts from all over the country, and it was probably a three-week trial," she details. "The attorney from the other side was a man named Clay Nixon. He always wore white. Everything white. A three-piece suit, white hat with a pink carnation, and always had a Bible." Bryher remembers him in such vivid detail, perhaps because he came up to her personally on the first day of the trial.

"I understand you're the lesbian on the legal team," he said to her. "Well, I'm gonna get you."

"He never got me," Bryher laughs. "It was just an intimidation tactic, and it didn't work." Sandy and Madeleine won their case, retaining custody of their children.[2] It was the first custody ruling in favor of a lesbian couple in the country.

"It changed everything," Bryher declares. "It's still a case that's quoted. It's still probably the most important lesbian mother case ever. The Supreme Court of Washington supported the view that [. . .] you had to look at what was actually in the best interest of the child and not use sexuality as the basis for best interest."

Four years later, having established a successful law career in Seattle, Bryher decided she wanted to open a bar. Despite all the groundbreaking work that was happening for queer folks in the city, and the multitude of gay-male-centric bars and clubs, Seattle lacked a lesbian bar. "It's really important that there be a lot of social places for lesbians to meet and hang out together. And you could certainly do that through working with the Lesbian Resource Center, or Take Back the Night, or all of these different political or social organizations," Bryher explains, "but a bar is where people are a little bit looser. They're cruising. It's a place to be comfortable in another kind of way."

Bryher teamed up with four other women who shared her vision. She describes how the five founders were acquainted: "We were all in one group or another or all sleeping with each other's partners or whatever else we were doing."

Their bar would be different from the other LGBTQ+ spots in the city. The women wanted a place where they could feel proud to bring their parents and families. "If they could deal with us, we would create a space that we thought they might like as well," Bryher notes. They aimed to be "a little bit more inclusive, to not be in a dark alley, and to serve food and be open to the public." None of this would dilute the bar's identity, though. "It was a women's bar; it was a lesbian bar. If you were okay with that, you were welcome," Bryher says, echoing the sentiments of many lesbian bar owners before her, and many lesbian bar owners to come.

After nearly two years of searching, they found the perfect space: the ground floor of a three-story building on the corner of East Pike Street and Eleventh Avenue, with big windows and plenty of natural light. It was also close to the gay men's bars they knew in the neighborhood, Capitol Hill.

Today, Capitol Hill is considered one of the trendiest neighborhoods on the West Coast.[3] It's also Seattle's gayborhood. Back in the 1980s, though, it was fairly desolate. When Bryher and her cofounders signed the lease for The Wildrose, one of the only other businesses on the block was a tattoo shop, owned by Lamar Van Dyke, who happened to be their friend.

Seattle had captured Lamar's heart too, after having spent much of the 1970s traveling North America by van with a group of lesbians. The group called themselves the Van Dykes, a last name that Lamar eventually legally adopted.

Whenever they could, the group would stay on what was known as "women's land." "There were these encampments all around the country," Lamar explains. "Women were doing this everywhere. They were going out into rural areas and setting up spaces where they welcomed traveling women, but it was women-only land."

"There was this publication called *Lesbian Connection*," begins Lamar. "*Lesbian Connection* had a list of contact dykes in various cities in America." In any given city, Lamar and her friends could call up the local contact dykes and ask where they could park their vans and stay. Often, they were sent to the nearest women's land.

"There was this whole underground kind of world that you could move around in very easily, and lots of women were moving around in that world," Lamar reflects. "We lived on water and air, and we shaved our heads," she recalls wistfully. "We were just saying 'Fuck you' to everything we had ever been taught."

In 1980, Lamar landed in Seattle. "My van broke down," she says, "and it would not be fixed. Every dyke mechanic in town worked on it. I took it to the dealership. It was supposedly fixed twenty times and every time I would get in it, [. . .] it would just stop." Lamar's van, it seemed, wanted her to stay. "I was just passing through," she thought at the time. "I am still here," she adds with amusement. "It was the best place ever for me to be. It all worked out."

By 1984, Lamar had her own tattoo shop on East Pike Street. She recalls a friend walking in one day that year and asking, "What would you think if we bought the bar next door?"

"I would think I had died and gone to heaven!" Lamar answered.

Of course, that bar was The Wildrose. Bryher and her cofounders essentially ran a GoFundMe through word of mouth to get it up and running. "We each had to find like $10,000," Bryher explains, "and so most everybody went to friends and borrowed $1,000 here, $1,000 there, until they had their $10,000 together."

Their cobbled-together crowdfunding campaign conveniently doubled as a publicity campaign. "Right there you've got thirty women we probably owed a thousand bucks or two thousand bucks to. So, they all knew about it. They invited their friends, and the word just spread," says Bryher.

The bar opened with a New Year's Eve party ringing in 1985. Lamar remembers popping over from her shop next door to find the women getting ready. "They were polishing the bar," she says. "All of them had on black pants and white shirts and black vests and pink bow ties. [. . .] Oh and they had cummerbunds too, they had pink cummerbunds," Lamar describes vividly. "They had painted the underneath of the bar pink. And they had tablecloths on the tables and little candles. [. . .] They transformed it." Despite all their preparations, the women didn't feel ready. "They were a *wreck*," Lamar emphasizes.

"Do you think anybody's going to come?" Lamar remembers them asking.

"I just laughed and said 'Uh huh. Yeah. I think so,'" Lamar recalls. "I came back like an hour and a half later. And their bow ties were sideways; their cummerbunds were twisted. They were going a hundred miles an hour. The place was packed."

None of the women had any experience running a bar. "We didn't even know how to change a keg, let alone get the cash register to work," Bryher admits, "but we had a line around the block. We had probably three hundred people there, and it was a blast."

The bar faced its fair share of trials and tribulations in its first decade of life, but Bryher was determined to keep it afloat. She bought out her partners after the first year and a half, and by the mid-1990s business was stable. In 1995, Bryher was able to purchase the building that now houses The Wildrose.

She sold it five years later, in 2000, before moving back to Montana to be closer to her disabled twin brother, but not without taking steps to secure the future of The Wildrose amid a rapidly changing neighborhood. "Believe it or not, this lesbian bar helped gentrify the neighborhood, for better or for worse. I mean, if you call a lot of gay businesses gentrification, but of course I do," Bryher declares.

Next door, Lamar's tattoo shop was one business to eventually fall victim to the neighborhood's swift development. "Someone new bought the building," Lamar says, "and she decided to double my rent, which sort of pissed me off." So, Lamar sold her shop. Bryher wanted to avoid this fate for her bar, so when she sold her building, she made sure The Wildrose and the building's other businesses had good, long leases with fair terms, so they could stay for as long as they wanted. "Some of them are still there and some aren't, but that was really important to me, because we were community, we were family," Bryher remarks.

We visit The Wildrose in fall of 2021, stepping in past a sandwich board that reads "36 years of beers and queers." It's just after opening and late afternoon sunlight filters in through the bar's large windows as we sit down with owners, Shelley Brothers, who later passed away in February of 2025, and Martha Manning. The pair tell us they are certain Bryher's choices back in 2000 are the reason the bar has been able to survive. When Bryher owned the building, "she kept the rent down so that all the poor queers could have a cool place to live," says Shelley. "[Bryher] didn't just run out and sell it to a developer who at that point could have knocked it down, probably with not a lot of opposition to 'em," Shelley adds, her voice deep and gravelly yet also soft.

Although the building has changed hands again since the 2000 sale, Shelley wasn't worried about The Wildrose's future. If anyone tried to tear down The Wildrose today, Shelley insists "people would probably go crazy because this block is one of the [only] original blocks basically up here on the hill. I know I'd be out there chained to the trees saying, 'You're not gonna take this building down!'"

Chapter Twenty

THE SPORTS BRA

EVERYONE WATCHES WOMEN'S SPORTS

PORTLAND, OR

The idea to open the world's first women's sports bar began as a joke for Jenny Nguyen, the boldly influential, lesbian owner of the Sports Bra. "We would want to go out and watch women's sports games," Jenny says of her and her friends, "and it was constantly a battle. Every time we went to a sports bar, the game we wanted to watch was never on." Sometimes, if they requested it, bar staff would put their game on, but not always. "I feel like my experience with that is very universal for [any] women's sports fan trying to watch sports out in public," Jenny affirms.

As a lifelong basketball fan and former player herself, Jenny's event of the year is the NCAA Women's Basketball Championship. Back in 2018, Jenny remembers trying to watch the championship game with her friends at a local sports bar in Portland. "We get in there [. . .] and this place had probably thirty TVs. None of them had the game on. And it was kind of empty in there."

So, as they always did, they asked the bar staff to put the game on. The staff obliged, but they put the championship game on one of the smaller TVs in the back corner of the space. "The game ended up being this ridiculously awesome comeback from behind," Jenny exclaims. Right before the final buzzer, her team scored the winning basket. "Our entire table goes nuts," she describes. "We jump up and down, we're screaming. And I remember taking off my hat and throwing it across the bar in excitement. And I looked out across the bar and no one else was celebrating with us. They were looking at us like we're nuts."

Still high on Notre Dame's epic win, the friend group made their way out to the parking lot. "Oh my God, that game was incredible," Jenny commented.

"Yeah, it would've been better if the sound were on," her friend replied.

Jenny stood there in shock. "I had gotten so used to watching women's sports in a way that was completely compromised, that something as big as not having sound on, I didn't notice it," she reflects.

"The only way we're ever gonna have the opportunity to watch women's sports in its full glory is if we have our own place," Jenny said to her friends in frustration. It wasn't a serious proposition; the group laughed, and on the ride home, Jenny and her then-girlfriend continued to jokingly fantasize about a women's sports bar.

"What would I call it?" Jenny wondered aloud. "The very first thing that came to mind was 'the Sports Bra,'" she says. "All we were doing is taking a traditional sports bar and changing the channel. So, all I'm doing is taking the word sports bar and changing two letters," Jenny points out.

For years, the Sports Bra remained an inside joke among Jenny and her friends, not realizing the phenomenon it would later become. At the time, the bar usually came up in moments of exasperation. "Oh, at the Sports Bra this game would be on," they would fantasize. "Oh, at the Sports Bra the women's bathroom would be clean. At the Sports Bra they'd have gluten-free buns."

Despite her lifelong love of women's sports and her wealth of experience in the bar and restaurant industry, Jenny never wanted to open her own place. "Hell no. Never,'" she stresses. As anyone who has ever worked in the industry knows, and as we've previously witnessed at countless other lesbian bars, opening a restaurant is a massive undertaking. "I don't love anything that much to work that hard," Jenny always thought.

Then, in 2020, "the rug kind of got pulled out from under everybody," Jenny recalls. "It forced me, and I feel like it forced a lot of people, like millions and millions of people, to reevaluate their priorities, [. . .] their role in the world."

It wasn't just the COVID-19 pandemic. The rise of activism and social movements like Black Lives Matter and Me Too had Jenny questioning her own values and responsibilities. "I started to get really frustrated with how I wasn't contributing anything positive. So, I started cooking in the kitchens downtown for homeless youth. [. . . I] volunteered a bunch [. . .] but it didn't feel like enough," she notes thoughtfully.

Jenny's then-girlfriend was the one to suggest she channel her energy into the Sports Bra. "I literally laughed in her face," Jenny remembers. "I was like, I don't understand how something like that could make any kind of a difference, because in my mind, it had only been a joke. A place for my friends and I to hang out and watch games. That was it."

But the idea stuck in Jenny's mind. "Within months, I was completely obsessed with at least the possibility of doing it," Jenny says. So, she began researching, curious to see what had been successful for other women's sports bars. Yet, after scouring the internet, she couldn't find a single one.

In July of 2021, she met up with a mentor of hers, who was involved in running more than a dozen restaurants in the Portland area, some of them traditional sports bars.

"I'm thinking about opening a women's sports bar, a bar that only plays women's sports," Jenny told him.

"What's your timeline?" he asked.

"A year and a half, two years," Jenny answered.

"No, you need to do it right now," he told her.

On the front lines of the restaurant industry, he saw how women's sports viewership was exploding, and he understood that Jenny's vision would satisfy an unmet need in the Portland community. One of his sports bars showed National Women's Soccer League games whenever the Portland Thorns played. On those particular nights, they would have to turn people away at the door.

While he had full confidence that the Sports Bra would succeed, the investment world felt differently. "I got denied by every traditional lender," Jenny says, "three big banks and two SBA loans." They all cited the same three reasons for their denial. One, the pandemic was still wreaking havoc. Two, bars and restaurants were closing left and right, and most loans were going toward keeping existing establishments alive, not opening new ones. And three, Jenny had never done anything like this before. No one had. "We love it, but literally, you can't get us to write a check for it," Jenny heard over and over again.

Jenny didn't have support from her parents, either. "They did not want this to happen. And it was a hundred percent fear based," Jenny explains.

"I'm the only child of Vietnamese immigrants, and so it wasn't that they thought it was a bad idea. They just thought it was so risky, and they didn't want me to put everything into it and lose it all."

Jenny's parents, Thu and Tuong, both immigrated from Vietnam to Minnesota as teenagers in 1975, where they met and soon married. Before Jenny was born, they headed west to Oregon, settling in Portland for—believe it or not—the warmer weather. There, Thu and Tuong each worked multiple jobs to give Jenny the best possible opportunities, enrolling her in private school and sending her to college. "They wanted me to be a doctor or an engineer or a dentist," Jenny says.

When Jenny told them about the Sports Bra, it was far from the first time she had defied their expectations. "I'm forty-two years old, and I've had a lot of moments in my life where I came to my parents with something big and they absolutely hated it," she shares.

At seventeen, Jenny came out to them as gay. "I remember going to bed one night and being like, 'I'm gonna tell my parents tonight,'" Jenny recounts, "and I basically picked a time [. . .] 11:20 at night. And I had like this little Sony radio clock next to my bed, with the digital numbers and the blinking colon." The clock read 11:15 p.m., and Jenny told herself that when it hit 11:20, she would get out of bed, walk upstairs, and tell her parents. "I spent the next five minutes just staring at that blinking colon and getting sweaty."

At 11:20 p.m., Jenny summoned her courage, headed upstairs, and—sobbing—told her parents she was gay. "We'll love you no matter what. We just want you to be happy and we want you to be safe," Jenny's dad told her. Jenny's mom was less supportive, asking if Jenny was sure or if this was just a phase.

It would take Jenny's mom nearly a decade to fully accept her daughter's identity, during which Jenny came to her parents with another piece of big, frightening news. She wanted to be a chef. She called her parents from college to tell them. "They hate[d] everything about it," Jenny recalls. "They basically were like, 'We didn't flee a war-torn country on a boat and almost die for you to be a servant to somebody,' 'cause to them, a chef was the help."

Their disapproval—of her sexuality, of her career as a chef, of the Sports Bra—always boiled down to fear. "Very scary," Jenny's mom Thu tells us, describing her feelings of doubt when Jenny first broke the news about the

Sports Bra. "Because nobody['s] ever done that before. And also, she's a woman, she's [an] Asian minority, and she's gay."

"That was hard for me, to not have my parents be behind it," Jenny confesses, "and every day they were trying to talk me out of it." Still, without the emotional support of her parents or the financial support of a big bank or loan, Jenny persisted. She emptied her savings account, started asking friends and family for donations, and began looking for a venue.

Jenny fell in love with the fourth place she saw. "As soon as I walked through the doors, I could see where everything was gonna be. And that feeling of just knowing, I was like, I'm gonna sign the lease," Jenny asserts. "I had enough money to last for maybe two months." Not nearly enough of a cushion to get a bar and restaurant up and running, but she took a leap of faith and signed the lease anyway.

Then, she launched a Kickstarter. "I knew I needed $48,000 to make it to five months, and that was me being really frugal," Jenny remembers. But Kickstarter is an all-or-nothing crowdfunding platform; if you don't meet your goal, you don't get any of the money. So, Jenny thought asking for the entire $48,000 was a recipe for failure.

"I'm gonna ask for 30[K], 30[K] sounds like an okay number to ask strangers for," Jenny told her girlfriend at the time. But then how would she come up with the remaining $18,000? her girlfriend asked. "I'll figure it out, I can beg somebody else," Jenny insisted.

"And then, she gave me a piece of advice that I will hold onto forever," Jenny adds, "which is, 'You should ask for what you need.'" So, Jenny did. Slowly, donations started rolling in, mostly from friends and acquaintances.

On the third day of the Kickstarter, Jenny got a phone call from Brooke, the editor of the online food magazine *Eater PDX*. Brooke had gotten an alert that a new bar and restaurant on Broadway called the Sports Bra had applied for their liquor license, and thinking there must have been some sort of typo, she wanted to know more. "Is it supposed to be the Sports *Bar*?" she questioned. Jenny explained her concept for a women's sports bar, and Brooke was hooked. "We're going to write this story today," she told Jenny.

Two hours later, Jenny got a text from her mom: "Have you looked at the Kickstarter?" Examining the donation graph, she noticed small increases for days one and two and then, on day three, a huge spike. "It was like a straight up-and-down line," Jenny tells us. As Jenny stared at the screen, flabbergasted, her phone buzzed with another text. It was Brooke, telling her they'd published the *Eater* article. "Immediately, my phone starts going off and it's like *KGW* and *The Oregonian*," Jenny remembers.

News about the Sports Bra, and their fundraiser, spread like wildfire. By day nine, Jenny had hit her $48,000 goal. By the end of the month, she had more than double what she needed.

Beyond earning more than the resources she needed to open, she also gained her parents' support. "After the Kickstarter skyrocketing, they completely one-eighty-ed. Because their fear was becoming alleviated by all the positive reinforcement we were getting," Jenny says.

In awe of the outpouring of media coverage and encouragement Jenny was getting from all over the world, Thu and Tuong started to get involved. "I didn't realize she has any support, besides us. But it turned out that it's very overwhelming, which I'm so thankful for," Thu reflects tenderly.

"I was getting comments and letters and emails from all over the country. There were people who wanted to donate money from like Belgium and Australia and couldn't because of whatever Kickstarter rules are," Jenny explains. There were messages from parents of daughters who play sports, thanking Jenny for creating this space. Messages from older women who played sports before Title IX, who never in their lifetime thought they would see a women's sports bar. Messages from men who had never realized this type of bar was missing.

On April 1, 2022, the bar officially opened to the public. "The first month or so we were open, we were so busy. Like chaos. It was slam packed," Jenny describes. "We'd open to a line, and we would shut the door on a line. The wait was like two hours, constantly. It was nuts."

Once inside the Sports Bra, you're thrust into the world of women's sports. The bar's many TVs, which *only* show women's sports, have games playing whenever possible. In fact, during our visit, we see a group of people looking to watch the men's soccer World Cup get turned away. Women's sports memorabilia cover nearly every inch of the bar. There are jerseys, flags and scarves, signed soccer balls, baseballs, and footballs. Shelves of trophies and medals. A pair of boxing gloves, a snowboard, figure skates. "Ninety percent of it is donated," Jenny tells us. "Half of it, at least, [has] a story that is extremely powerful."

In the years following the Sports Bra's opening, dozens of other women's sports bars began popping up throughout the country.[1] There is Rough and

Tumble in Seattle, Whiskey Girl Tavern in Chicago, Watch Me! in Long Beach, and A Bar of Their Own in Minneapolis, to name only a few.

The enthusiasm for the Sports Bra itself has not waned, either. The bar is franchising across the nation, beginning with locations in Boston, Las Vegas, St. Louis, and Indianapolis. "To this day, I still get people wanting to donate money to me and I'm like, oh no, we're not taking donations," Jenny says. "What's wild is that I thought that I was filling a small niche, a wedge of women's sports fans. And it turns out, a space like this is actually very intersectional in who it's impacting and who it resonates with for all different reasons."

The Sports Bra is big within the queer and lesbian community, regardless of their interest in sports. Sadee, who's working behind the bar the day we visit, tells us she's not much of a sports fan herself. She's here for the queer community. Still, she gets a kick out of telling folks that they don't show men's sports. "A lot of times people will call and be like, 'Do you play the Oregon State game?' I'm like, 'Only if it's women's!'" she exclaims gleefully.

While the Sports Bra is an undeniably queer haven and is strict about only showing women's sports on the TVs, everyone is welcome, regardless of gender or sexuality. "We have people with families and their husbands coming in, and everybody's watching," Jenny says.

Minors are allowed in the bar until 10 p.m. because Jenny recognizes how much a community like this would have meant to her as a kid. Witnessing the impact the Sports Bra has on young people is a highlight of Jenny's days. "So many young girls drop out of sports thinking that there's no future for them in it," Jenny asserts. "One time there was a dad in here with two daughters, and we had gymnastics on, [. . .] and I remember these two girls, they didn't blink. They were just staring at the TV. And I walked by, and the dad taps me on the arm. And with tears in his eyes, he just thanked me for creating a space where his daughters can see their future on TV."

The Sports Bra has become a family affair for Jenny, Thu, and Tuong as well. Her dad began helping with small repairs, and her mom "weaseled her way in" too, as Jenny puts it.

"I try to come in every day," Thu tells us. She used to be a bank teller, so she handles tasks like counting out the register, changing money at the bank, and tipping out the staff each day.

"We spend two, three hours here every day together, which is more than we've ever spent," Jenny says, "and sometimes it's really hard, 'cause she's a mom still." Meaning, often Thu has ideas that Jenny doesn't want to hear. "Because the ideas are totally ridiculous!" Jenny exclaims. Jenny goes on, telling us that Thu has tried to introduce some labor-intensive Vietnamese recipes to the menu, and even directed Jenny to purchase a rice cooker. Instead, the Sports Bra pays homage to their Vietnamese heritage in simpler ways, with menu items such as "Aunt Tina's Vietna-wings: over a cabbage slaw" and "Mom's Baby Back Ribs: Vietnamese-style, clay pot pork ribs."

At the end of the day, Jenny appreciates her mom's involvement. As do the rest of the staff, to whom Thu has become "the restaurant mom," Jenny says. "She went from having one child to twenty children. [. . .] Everybody here calls her Mom. Everybody calls my dad Dad."

"I don't know where that come from," Thu says, commenting on the parental honorifics she and her husband get around the bar, "but we get used to it and yeah, we love it."

"I have never seen my mom happier," Jenny tells us. "Never in my entire life.

"I am just overwhelmed with emotion, and I don't speak English very well, so I keep it to myself. [Jenny has] so much courage. I don't know where she got that from. [. . .] She doesn't get that from me or her dad. [. . .] It's all her [. . .] I'm very lucky to have a daughter like her," Thu says softly. "Proud is an understatement."

Chapter Twenty-One

DOC MARIE'S

WE FIGHT BECAUSE WE CARE

PORTLAND, OR

If there's one thing queer people are good at, it's arguing with each other. Since the very beginnings of the LGBTQ+ community, there have been disagreements about who should and should not be included within it, what rights we should be fighting for, and how we should go about that fight. Take the dykes that protested Cubbyhole's early inclusivity or the more recent online outrage about Henrietta Hudson's new slogan. Or you might consider the tensions that arise every year in June surrounding whether or not Pride should be a corporate-backed celebratory parade or a radical protest march. Every year, around the same time, there are also arguments about what sparked Pride in the first place; online discourse about who threw the first brick at Stonewall has become so prevalent, it's now a meme.[1]

There's always been a push and pull between respectability politics and radicalism too. While the homophile movement of the 1950s and 1960s employed an assimilation strategy to earn rights for the LGBTQ+ community, the Gay Liberation Front of the 1970s turned to direct action protests. In the early 2000s, some fought for marriage equality while others argued that we shouldn't conform to such a heteronormative, patriarchal institution.

The story of Doc Marie's—the Portland lesbian bar that fractured from within just one day after opening—isn't an anomaly, or simply a product of our current internet-era and politically correct culture. It's part of a long-standing legacy of LGBTQ+ infighting, which ultimately stems from our deep investment in our community.

In December of 2022, we received a slew of angry messages and comments online simply because we went to Doc Marie's. We explained that the goal of our visit was to uncover what really happened and provide listeners with an unbiased account. But the haters didn't seem to care. "Oh word, y'all already knew and you went there anyways. Never mind. LMAO," one individual replied before blocking us. It seemed that to some, setting foot in Doc Marie's was a crime, and we had committed it. Still, we remained invested in hearing all sides of the Doc Marie's story.

In some ways, perhaps explicitly branding a bar in Portland as lesbian was doomed from the start. A 2016 *Willamette Week* article pointed out that it meant "stepping into a minefield of identity politics."[2] As a liberal hotspot with a substantial queer population, many in Portland feel the label *lesbian* to be rooted in the gender binary, potentially excluding gender-nonconforming people and trans people. The article went on to highlight various lesbian nights at local bars that changed their names to be more inclusive, as well as the local, lesbian-owned bar Escape which has avoided the label "lesbian bar" despite its large clientele of queer women.

It seemed, however, that Doc Marie's was going to be different. From the start, it was branded as "a lesbian bar for everyone," and in general, the community was thrilled about this new venue. "Everybody was talking about it. Everybody was like, 'Oh my God, we're getting a lesbian bar in Portland!'" says one local community member Robin, who was there on opening night.

We connected with Brandy, a long time Portlander who was hired as bar manager at Doc Marie's in May of 2022. She had been working in the food service industry in Portland for fourteen years. "I knew what it was going to take [to open]. It's a lot of work," Brandy tells us. Despite having told herself in the past that she never wanted to be on a bar or restaurant opening team again, Brandy was enthused about the prospect of working at Doc Marie's. "This was way different, it was a lesbian bar," she exclaims.

Doc Marie's, named after Portlander Dr. Marie Equi—the radical out lesbian, abortion provider, and labor reformer of the late nineteenth and early twentieth century—was the brainchild of Olga Bichko. Olga spent her young adulthood in New York City, and its lesbian bars, before heading west for a slower pace. Her style and energy project a mixture of polished city sleekness and Pacific Northwest ease. Olga was born in Latvia—then part of the Soviet Union. Her family immigrated to the US when Olga was seven and her brother, Dmitri, was twelve. Though a five-year age gap may seem small, it has made a world of difference in how they have each experienced life in the US; while Dmitri speaks with an Eastern European accent, Olga does not. Despite any differences between them, Dmitri has always been one of Olga's biggest supporters.

Laughing, Olga tells us how Dmitri was the first person she ever came out to: "Before I even fully wrapped my head around it, I just called my brother [. . .], and I was kind of freaking out a little bit."

"I have news," she remembers saying to him.

"What is it?" he asked.

"It's about, like, dating," said Olga.

"Women?" he questioned.

"Yeah," Olga affirmed.

"Awesome! Yeah, fuck yeah!" was Dmitri's response.

"He really gave me the absolute best coming-out moment that I could possibly have, because it was not just accepting, but celebratory," reflects Olga.

Dmitri became Olga's business partner, as well as the bar's chief financial investor. He "had always wanted to do something that mattered, something that was consequential," Olga says. So, when she asked him if he wanted to open a lesbian bar with her, it was an easy yes.

Neither of them had any experience running a bar, but as we've seen time and time again, experience isn't necessarily required. "We were absolutely in the throes of a huge learning curve," Olga emphasizes. To compensate, they hired two salaried employees, intending to rely on their extensive industry experience: Brandy as bar manager, and a kitchen manager. "We were very open with that in our hiring," adds Olga.

At first, things went smoothly. Brandy appreciated Olga's transparency and her willingness to defer to their expertise. But tensions soon surfaced. The managers were taking on more and more responsibilities that they felt should fall to ownership. Meanwhile, Olga and Dmitri, who were still working their full-time jobs to fund the bar, had always intended to rely on these two salaried employees to handle the bulk of operations.

To their credit, Olga and Dmitri did respond promptly to some of the managers' early concerns. They cut ties with two problematic business partners, raised the kitchen manager's salary to match Brandy's, and even sent both managers $1,500 bonuses to compensate them for contributions that went beyond their job descriptions. Olga also agreed to handle some larger tasks, like resealing the upstairs floor after a leak.

Still, frustrations mounted. "With what we did, we should have had some level of ownership," Brandy asserts. When she voiced this concern to Olga and Dmitri, they were actually open to the idea, but Brandy had growing doubts. "I wanted to invest in ownership of a lesbian bar [. . .] but I didn't feel confident about being on an ownership team with Olga and Dmitri," she says, reflecting on what she felt was poor communication and leadership from them. But already in the final sprint to opening, Brandy temporarily put her concerns aside.

Opening night arrived sooner than the managers would have liked. The staff hadn't been sufficiently trained, plumbing issues persisted, and much to Brandy's dismay, Olga hadn't had the floors resealed. The managers didn't feel ready. Still, Brandy felt pressure to stick to their scheduled opening date—not from Olga and Dmitri, but so that tipped staff could start earning income.

So, on July 1, 2022, Doc Marie's opened to the public. We talked to several people who attended that night. Most described long lines and water leaking where it shouldn't have been, but overall, many attendees were willing to forgive the local lesbian bar's slightly rocky debut.

"I think the business was just unprepared for what they were going to get. [. . .] There was so many people," says Robin, who waited for an hour and a half to get in. "But it was fine," she assures us. "We're chatting with other people in line. [. . .] It was a fun atmosphere and everybody was excited. I mean, there were some people mildly annoyed."

From Olga's perspective, the opening was a success. "There were no huge disasters on opening night," she proclaims. "A huge number of people turned out. It was absolutely amazing. People that came had a great time. There were some flaws, [. . .] which I think is really to be expected with a brand-new bar and hundreds and hundreds of people in it."

Brandy felt differently. "[Opening night] was my breaking point," she admits. The following morning, she and the kitchen manager quit. In addition to the mishaps and under-preparation that much of the community noticed, Brandy also cites a physical fight between patrons during which staff members reported hearing the N-word used. The managers promptly met with Olga and Dmitri to air their grievances before meeting up with the rest of the staff in the afternoon to explain their resignation.

"We honestly were all really shocked," recalls a former staff member. "Opening night didn't go perfectly. There were a lot of funny mishaps, and also just straight-up really unsafe and wild things that happened. But we all felt like we were having a fun time." Still, the staff listened intently as the managers described their experiences. "If someone that you trust tells you that someone is dangerous and manipulative and doesn't care about the community, [. . .] then you need to take that seriously," the same former staff member elaborates.

The entire opening staff decided to quit as well, developing a set of demands to present to Olga and Dmitri as the Marie Equi Workers Collective—a group they previously formed as a bargaining unit. Brandy and the kitchen manager were not technically a part of the collective, as their salaried roles placed them in management. The group demanded that Olga be removed, that fifty-fifty ownership through sweat equity go to Brandy and the kitchen manager, and that Dmitri remain a silent investor until funds could be secured to purchase the business from him outright.[3]

That Sunday, July 3, the collective met with Olga and Dmitri in front of the bar to read these demands aloud. They then presented them in written form via email, requesting a response within twenty-four hours. "It was so, honestly, just crazy to us that we didn't feel like this was anything that we needed to interact with in any meaningful way," Olga remarks. "It's not staff asking for changes. It's them saying that we are so bad that we need to give over the bar to them."

When the twenty-four-hour deadline passed, the Marie Equi Workers Collective took to the internet, publishing the set of demands, along with a set of grievances, on Instagram. "The first time we saw anything about the grievances was online with everyone else," reveals Olga. Many of the grievances centered around Olga's character, accusing her of being an "unsafe person."[4]

The list included some objectively false or incomplete claims. One pointed to a pay discrepancy between the two managers which, as we know from Brandy, was resolved early in their employment. Another stated that Olga failed to provide adequate security on opening night. But Doc Marie's did have two individual security people present, and as Brandy herself explained to us, the only reason they didn't have an established security team was because ownership decided together, with the managers, to let go of the team Olga had originally contracted.

Perhaps the most troubling grievance on the list was the allegation that "the owner, while significantly intoxicated, enabled an openly racist aggressor." We know this stems from the fight between patrons on opening night, in which the aggressor was heard using the N-word to refer to a person of color. After this incident, Olga was seen talking to the aggressor. Olga, of course, says she was neither "significantly intoxicated" nor enabling anyone involved, and no other witnesses were able to tell us anything more about this interaction.

A few claims on the list point to valid concerns, such as clearly documented safety issues. "Electrical cords posing a tripping hazard, in an area with flooding" and "water leaking through subfloor onto the patrons in the basement," the list reads. An Occupational Safety and Health Administration (OSHA) complaint was filed regarding these issues. Yet, both were promptly addressed following the July 1 opening and fixed by the time the bar reopened to the public.[5]

Why, then, didn't Olga share proof that she was addressing all these alleged grievances? "You guys were the only ones that asked," she tells us, referring to our coverage of the story. "That's how I know that people are not searching for truth. People are not coming to have a conversation."

The internet didn't seem particularly interested in sorting fact from fiction. Soon after the Marie Equi Worker's Collective's initial posts went up on Instagram, other accusations began to circulate, including sweeping allegations of transphobia and racism. "I don't think the collective alleged that [Olga] was racist and transphobic," Brandy herself points out. Still, the backlash against Olga and Doc Marie's was swift and ruinous.

"It caught on, and it caught on immediately," says Olga. "I received so much deep, personal hate and malice. [. . .] I got death threats, and these were all things that came from within the community. [. . .] Once people get into that online mob mentality, that cancel-culture kind of thing, there might be an element of 'the ends justify the means,' so it's okay to be hateful, it's okay to be vile, it's okay to spread misinformation, because they deserve it. But we didn't. And nobody does. Cancelling is not a productive form of activism."

Soon, the Marie Equi Worker's Collective was facing their own set of online hate and backlash. Someone from within the group had betrayed them by leaking meeting notes to a podcast called *Blocked and Reported*, hosted by Katie Herzog and Jesse Singal.[6] Katie and Jesse are two cisgender journalists who are perhaps most known for their coverage of transgender issues, which many—myself included—condemn as blatantly transphobic. In a segment covering Doc Marie's, the two hosts spend about fifteen minutes reading aloud and criticizing the leaked notes, referencing members of the collective by name and publicly outing one individual as trans.[7]

On July 19, 2022, Libs of TikTok, an online platform being tracked by the Anti-Defamation League as one of the "biggest online amplifiers of anti-LGBTQ+ extremism,"[8] shared a post titled "Lesbian bar shuts down one week after opening because they weren't woke enough."[9]

"We were flooded with hate," one member of the collective tells us. It was particularly brutal for those named in the *Blocked and Reported* podcast. "They were receiving hate and death threats," the collective member says. "It's really, really heartbreaking because we did all this to protect one another, and to prevent transphobia from happening, and then someone from our own group did that and we really don't have any idea who it was."

While everything unfolded, the bar was shut down for six weeks. Olga, who had made the leap to quit her day job, tried her best to unplug from the internet and focus all her energy on addressing any legitimate issues while hiring a new staff.

Bartender Aundrenee, who we met on our December 2022 visit, was among this second round of hires. "I was very adamant about making sure that this was a safe space for me, especially as [. . .] a person of color," she tells us. She did her due diligence during the hiring process, asking Olga about everything she had heard and read about Doc Marie's online. "Olga was very informative, very honest, and just open about everything. And so, I built a lot of trust through that," Aundrenee remarks.

Aundrenee worked at Doc Marie's for about a year, before accepting a manager position at another bar in town, leaving on good terms. During that year, she observed many people walking into Doc Marie's skeptical and guarded, curious to see for themselves the site of such controversy. "But then I['d] see them next week, and I'm like, 'Oh, so you liked it here, that's awesome,'" she adds.

For Brandy, watching Doc Marie's from afar has been bittersweet. "I mean, it sucks. It's really irritating. Of course now you're gonna fix all the things that we wanted to fix," she says wryly. But even she didn't want to see the bar fail: "I hope that a lot of people found happiness in going there."

In October of 2025, Doc Marie's announced that Halloween would be their last night in business. They cited financial difficulties following a devastating year for small businesses and the queer community in general. But the Doc Marie's story cannot simply be boiled down to hyper-liberalism gone wrong, as *Blocked and Reported* or "Libs of TikTok" would have you believe. It's not a cautionary tale about how we will lose queer spaces if we hold them to too high a standard. Nor is it just a warning about the dangers of the internet for queer people, although I think all involved will think more carefully about how they engage online. Queer people have been arguing about our values since long before the internet even existed. It's a part of our identity.

"Part of the process of being LGBTQ is arguing with people that you love and care about and people that you are ultimately allied with," LGBTQ+ journalist Shane O'Neill tells us. In any identity-based group, there will always be disagreement about what the best path forward for the community is.

Shane has a theory on why we—as LGBTQ+ people in particular—seem to be so good at disagreeing: "We have better critical-thinking skills than other people. Otherwise, we wouldn't have even known we were queer," he reasons. "Being LGBTQ+ and realizing that you are means that you're inherently noticing something about yourself and noticing that it doesn't fit with a dominant society. And that primes you to question things more broadly in the rest of your life."

This especially applies to our queer spaces. "We as LGBTQ+ people care so much about our culture and care so much about our community and care so much about the venues that support and engender community that I think these things have greater significance than maybe straight people understand," Shane observes.

And this is a beautiful, albeit complex, thing: to care so deeply about one's community. But how do we hold our spaces to a high standard while also helping them to exist, survive, and thrive? How do we reconcile our desire for equitable, community-owned venues with the reality of the capitalist system under which we live? I certainly don't have an easy answer to these questions, but perhaps I can offer a place to start. We can begin by honoring and making room for our arguments, our desire for change, and our suspicions about the structures in which we exist. We must also ground ourselves in our idealism: our dreams of equity, justice, mutual care, and inclusivity. And we must be mindful of the tools we use to work toward those dreams, questioning tactics like public shaming and cancel culture but also respectability politics and assimilation. As Shane says, critical thinking is often central to queer identity. So, let's put our thoughts to good use.

Part Four

THE SOUTH

WE KEEP US SAFE

Chapter Twenty-Two

ALICE BRADY'S AND CHARLENE'S

LESBIAN BARS ARE POLITICAL

NEW ORLEANS, LA

You can't talk about lesbian nightlife in New Orleans without talking about Alice Brady—the first owner of a lesbian bar in the city—whose spaces in the '50s and '60s paved the way for generations of lesbian bars to come. However, despite her legacy, there's minimal information about her life on the internet. Fortunately, we've been able to piece together her story from conversations with her friends, family members, business partners, and lovers.

Despite the rich picture of Alice's life that emerged from our conversations, a Google search turns up only a single photo of her: the grainy snapshot published alongside her obituary.[1] In it, I'd estimate Alice to be in her fifties. She's not looking at the camera, and she appears to be laughing at something, or someone, out of frame. She has on a white collared shirt and thick, wire-framed glasses—the kind your grandfather might wear.

This collared shirt was on brand for Alice. "She always wore the same thing: loafers, a skirt, and usually a white short-sleeved shirt with a collar," describes Ellen Frayle, a local New Orleanian who became close with Alice in the 1960s. The pair dated for a handful of years and remained close friends until Alice's passing in 2012. There was one other distinctive feature of the Alice Brady uniform, Ellen tells us. The shirt always had a pocket. "Because in the pocket, she'd stick her cigarettes," Ellen reminisces with a small giggle.

Alice was born in 1927 in Birmingham, Alabama. She was named after her mother, Alice Pickels,[2] a schoolteacher who worked until she fell ill when Alice was a young teenager. Alice spent much of her early years moving from place to place, as her father, Wilson D. Brady, worked for the railroad. Eventually, he opened a boarding house and settled the family in Pineville, Louisiana, just outside of Alexandria.

As Alice's niece and nephew tell us, Alice was disenchanted with life at the boarding house. With her mother sick and forced to live with her father, a generally unkind man, she spent as little time at home as she could. Much to the dismay of her more straitlaced older sister Maude, Alice would stay out late each night, roller-skating under the streetlights. At age sixteen, she dropped out of high school. At age nineteen, she lost her mom to cancer. With nothing left to tie her to Pineville, she boarded a bus to New Orleans in 1946.

As the story goes, when Alice stepped off that bus with one suitcase and no money to her name, she was spotted by Dorothea "Torchy" Wilde.[3] Torchy took Alice under her wing and thus began a lifelong friendship. Torchy was just a few years' Alice's senior, but as a burlesque dancer, bartender, and singer, she was already deeply embedded in the French Quarter nightlife scene. She was thought to be in a relationship with the well-known burlesque dancer Stacy "Stormy" Lawrence, a rumor all but confirmed in death; the two are buried side by side with matching tombstones that read BELOVED.[4]

It was through Torchy that Alice got her first bartending job. She was a natural behind the bar. "People were drawn to her," Ellen says.

While there were no explicitly lesbian bars in New Orleans during Alice's early years in the city, there were numerous queer-friendly places, a few of which were run by gay women. The most notable was a jazz club called Dixie's Bar of Music, which Yvonne Fasnacht, widely known as "Miss Dixie," ran with her sister from 1939 until 1964.[5]

Miss Dixie didn't intend for her bar to be gay. Yet, as often happens when a queer person opens a space, the gays came anyway. According to a 2011 article reporting her passing in *The Advocate*, "Dixie's Bar of Music became a place where LGBT folks mingled comfortably with luminaries like Helen Hayes, Danny Kaye, Walter Cronkite, and more than one congressman."[6]

People flocked to Miss Dixie's for the music and mingling, not for any sort of backroom shenanigans, as she would allow nothing of the sort. Same-sex dancing was prohibited in bars across the country until well into the 1970s, including at Miss Dixie's. She also enforced a strict dress code: skirts for women and sports coats for men.

On the relatively rare occasion that the police raided Dixie's Bar of Music, it was widely known that Miss Dixie would post bail straight out of her cash register. "One time they raided her entire bar," says Diane Dimiceli, a New Orleanian who later owned her own lesbian bar. "They took over a hundred-and-something people to jail just because. I mean, [the police] always came up with some charge," Diane adds, referring to charges like disorderly conduct or lewd dancing, which were often used to criminalize gay people in public spaces. Miss Dixie "bailed every single one of those people out of jail. And brought them all back to her bar and bought them drinks."

Influenced by the likes of Miss Dixie, Alice opened a bar of her own in 1952: a little place on St. Louis Street called the Masquerade, which predominantly catered to gay women.[7] Like Miss Dixie, Alice enforced a strict set of rules in hopes of preventing police raids and arrests. At the Masquerade, women couldn't wear pants after 5 p.m. "The girls had to go home and change into a skirt or a dress," Ellen explains with incredulity. But she's not judging Alice for enforcing this rule. Alice was simply trying to protect her community at a time when women could be arrested for wearing men's clothing, and a pair of pants could spell danger.

At the Masquerade, many of Alice's customers were strippers she had met through Torchy on Bourbon Street. According to Ellen, the strippers adored Alice. "You'll find that a good portion of strippers are gay," Ellen declares, launching into one of her favorite Alice Brady stories. One year, knowing Alice couldn't afford to make the payment on her liquor license, one of the top strippers on Bourbon Street called Alice up and asked to borrow the bar for a night. Of course, Alice said yes.

The following morning, Alice found a cigar box sitting atop her desk. "When she opened it up, it was all this money. More than enough money to pay for her alcohol license," Ellen exclaims. The women had secretly invited all their clients and had thrown a fundraiser to keep Alice afloat. After about another year of business, the Masquerade did eventually close, but not before it made history as New Orleans' first known lesbian bar.

In 1957, following the bar's closure, Alice went to work for Mary Collins—an original owner of New Orleans' oldest gay bar, Café Lafitte—who had opened another gay men's bar called the Galley House.[8] Alice's official title was bartender, but as Ellen tells it, "Alice Brady was like Mary Collins' right-hand man. [. . .] She wasn't a financial partner, but you might as well say she was a partner."

From behind the bar, Alice, now in her late twenties, a stellar conversationalist brimming with confidence and charisma, became the main attraction at the Galley House, sometimes called "the Wrinkle Room" due to its customer base of older men. Although she worked there for less than a year, Alice built quite the rapport with these patrons, many of whom were wealthy, influential, and even famous.

The connections Alice made at the Galley House would be of the utmost importance when, later that year, she opened the bar for which she is most remembered: Alice Brady's. Its first location was in the French Quarter, across from the Old Ursuline Convent. It was small—downright cramped considering its popularity—but that didn't matter. Women felt safe there, safer than at the other queer bars in town, because Alice Brady was running the place and Alice Brady protected them.

This was no small feat. As postwar moral conservatism gripped the nation, the environment toward LGBTQ+ people in New Orleans in the late 1950s was incredibly hostile. Police raids of gay bars throughout the city had only grown more common throughout the decade. In 1958, New Orleans' Mayor Morrison created "the Committee on the Problem of Sex Deviates in New Orleans." The committee strategized to increase law enforcement and legal harassment of LGBTQ+ people in an effort to rid the city of homosexuals.[9]

Yet we're told that Alice's bars rarely, if ever, got raided. In part, this was certainly due to her numerous friends in high places. But also because she continued to enforce a dress code and other cautionary rules: no same-sex dancing or canoodling, and no drugs. So, even if the police did raid the bar, her rules limited their ability to arrest people. "She would rule over her bar with a baseball bat," local LGBTQ+ historian Frank Perez tells us. "If two women got a little too touchy-feely, [and if] she didn't know what their hands were doing below the bar, that bat would come down because [touching] was enough to get you not only arrested but shut down."

Her brusque, no-nonsense demeanor, and the protection it provided, is part of what people loved about Alice. However, anyone who was close to Alice was quick to tell us that she had a genuine soft side too. "All that gruffness, that was just a persona. That was the Alice Brady facade," Ellen reveals. Underneath was a person who put little value on material things. She was generous to a fault. Far more than money, Alice valued the people around her.

At the bar, she poured heavy drinks for cheap, covered cab fares for drunk customers, and on occasion, she even helped regular patrons make rent. "She probably would have ended up being very, very wealthy," Ellen proclaims. "She did not because she gave it all away."

In the late 1960s, Alice moved her bar business to a bigger space, located at 700 North Rampart Street, just three blocks from Bourbon Street. This was where Ellen and Alice got to know each other. "When she first opened [on Rampart Street], you still couldn't dance," Ellen remembers. However, as the years passed and other gay bars around town started to relax their rules around same-sex dancing, Alice's patrons took notice.

As Ellen recalls, "the girls" started pleading with Alice: "Come on, Brady, let us dance!" they begged. Eventually, Alice gave in. Ellen recalls being out one night when somebody stood up on the bar and said: "We have a major announcement: Alice Brady says you can dance!"

Slowly but surely, the New Orleans queer community was shifting. Still, Alice enforced a culture of caution at her bar. Despite—or perhaps because of—her many politician friends, she had a strict no-politicking-at-the-bar rule. You could dance but you couldn't organize.

But then, on the night of June 24, 1973, the New Orleans LGBTQ+ community was irrevocably changed. Something happened that would make the separation of nightlife and politics seemingly impossible, galvanizing an activist movement across the city. At the center of it all was a young woman named Charlene Schneider.

Charlene recounts that fateful night in a series of archival interviews filmed on a home video camera over the course of 1996 and 1997 by New Orleans LGBTQ+ activist Marilyn McConnell, which were later digitized and shared with us by the Newcomb Institute of Tulane University. Seated in a white, plastic lawn chair in her yard, smoking a cigarette, Charlene tells Marilyn about the evening of June 24, 1973, when she happened to be nursing a beer at none other than Alice Brady's.

It was an entirely unremarkable, sweltering summer evening, aside from the fact that Charlene's feet were killing her. That night she was wearing a pair of new white clogs as she and her friends walked to the Up Stairs Lounge, another New Orleans gay bar. "We went as far as the Galley House," Charlene recounts in her signature Southern twang. There, she decided her feet needed a break. She couldn't bring herself to ascend the steep staircase at the Up Stairs Lounge and stand around in the crowded bar. So, while her friends went ahead, Charlene stayed back to rest her feet at Alice Brady's.

A few hours later, she noticed a commotion on the street. Stepping outside of Alice Brady's, she learned that there was a fire at the Up Stairs Lounge. "We didn't think it would be a deadly fire," Charlene explains. "Certainly, a fire at the Up Stairs. Well, you don't think of anybody dying."

Another friend of Charlene's, "Joan that has the guard dog," as Charlene refers to her, volunteered to head over to the Up Stairs Lounge to check out the scene since she worked for the police department. "When that girl came back, she was as white as that table," Charlene declares somberly.

"Be glad you didn't go over there. I've been to a lot of scenes. I've never seen anything like this in my life," Joan told Charlene.

Thirty-two people died that night in the Up Stairs Lounge, making it the deadliest fire in New Orleans history. Seventeen of the victims were gay men, Charlene's seven friends among them. For forty years, this incident remained on record as the deadliest mass killing of homosexuals in US history, until 2016 when forty-nine people were shot and killed at the Pulse Nightclub in Orlando, Florida.

Yet—because so many of the victims were gay—the City of New Orleans didn't treat this tragedy with the weight it deserved. To this day, the New Orleans Police Department (NOPD) considers the fire to be an unsolved crime. But as we learn from journalist Robert W. Fieseler, the details of what happened that night have never been a mystery to the local queer community.

The investigation was mishandled from the moment it began. The chief suspect was Roger Dale Nunez, whom Robert describes as "this internally conflicted gay-for-pay sex worker." As Robert explains, despite the sweeping evidence—Nunez was at the Up Stairs Lounge that night, was kicked out of the bar shortly before the fire started, and was then spotted purchasing 7.5 ounces of Ronsonol lighter fluid, the very same substance that started the fire—Nunez was never charged. "[He] was never questioned by police, though he was caught and released by them in the most suspicious of circumstances," Robert evaluates. "This terrible tragedy was deemed this political inconvenience due to its queer overtones and [it was] permitted to become a historic mystery. They closed the case without even solving it."

The day after the fire, Charlene watched a police broadcast. She recalls listening to the chief of police say: "Well, you know how these people are. We don't know who they are. [. . .] They kind of move from place to place and they don't carry ID," as if to shrug off the whole thing.

"I'm thinking, 'Is this man nuts?' Professional people died in that fire," Charlene narrates, stressing each word with lingering disgust. She was devastated and outraged but not entirely surprised. The NOPD had a reputation for harassing the LGBTQ+ community, and Charlene had personally experienced their abuse.

Nearly a decade before the fire, in 1964, Charlene herself had been arrested in a bar raid. It was her younger sister Diane's eighteenth birthday, and they were celebrating at a gay bar in the French Quarter. The bliss of Diane's first gay bar experience was brought to an abrupt halt when police showed up for a routine raid. Initially, Charlene managed to get out of the bar untouched, until she realized Diane was still inside. So, she walked back in to be arrested with her sister. It was a noble act, but one that would cost Charlene her dignity and her job: a high-ranking position at the local NASA plant.

Knowing that her name would be published in the paper, and not wanting to be publicly outed, Charlene gave a fake name to the arresting officers: Charmania Cochrane. She stood to plead "not guilty" under this name, not realizing that the federal security officer from her job at NASA was at the hearing. She was rearrested on the spot for a felony charge of giving a false statement to police and subsequently terminated from her position.

Gay people, according to the common line of thinking at the time, were inherently more susceptible to blackmail because of their sexual identities. That's what Charlene's boss laid out for her on her last day of work at the plant. Even as a valued employee, her lesbianism made her an utterly unmanageable security threat to NASA.

This series of events was the beginning of a very dark time in Charlene's life. "She refused to leave the house," Robert details. "And even though the felony charge was eventually dropped against her, it didn't resurrect her previous employment, and she had this black mark on her resume." As Charlene was unwilling to explain her arrest and firing from NASA, most job opportunities remained out of reach. Desperate for work, she turned to the very thing that had gotten her in trouble in the first place: gay bars. As a bartender, she didn't have to explain her record and no longer had to worry about being outed and losing her job. Charlene's double life had become one. She spent both days and nights in the bar scene.

Charlene's experience was not a unique one in the LGBTQ+ community. At the time of the Up Stairs Lounge fire, being outed as gay was still ruining lives and careers. There were no laws in place to protect people from being fired for their sexual orientation. Yet, in the aftermath of the fire, much of the LGBTQ+ community felt it was important to hold a public memorial to honor their friends who had perished, despite the risk of being outed.

It proved challenging to find a church willing to accommodate them. But finally, a week after the fire, St Mark's United Methodist Church agreed to hold a service. Famous out gay pastor Troy Perry flew in from Los Angeles to host and assured the New Orleans community that there wouldn't be any news cameras; he would protect them. Charlene, along with nearly three hundred other people, showed up to the service. Charlene was still cautious about protecting her identity. "I wore a dress and a big orange hat. This big, so nobody could see my face," Charlene describes, holding her arms up on either side of her head.

Robert details the scene at the memorial: "Everyone is just swept up and feeling the energy and finally venting their grief in a public space with and amongst each other for their fellow queer brothers and sisters who died." Then, toward the end of the service, Troy Perry rushed back to the altar.

As Robert tells it, Perry announced to the crowd: "I know I promised you all would be safe. [But] they've set up television cameras out front and they're gonna photograph and video you all when you come out the front door." Perry went on to suggest that mourners sneak out the back door instead, but chaos broke out as the crowd began to debate their options.

Amid the uproar, a woman's voice cut through. According to Robert, the woman has never been identified and was only ever described as a "butch lesbian." She would forever change the course of gay rights in New Orleans with one declaration.

"I came in the front door, and I'm damn well going out that way," her voice echoed through the cathedral.

"Everyone hears her, and they cheer, and [. . .] they all walk out the front door of St. Mark's Church into the light of Rampart Street with Troy Perry, ready to face the news cameras and the world, and to out themselves collectively together," Robert recounts.

Charlene was among them. Something had shifted within her. "And that was the beginning. Right that very second," she reflects.

It was the beginning of her life as both an activist and a fearless, out lesbian. For the larger New Orleans gay community, it was also the beginning of a decades-long fight for equal rights, legal protections, and an end to police harassment. A decent portion of which unfolded within the walls of the bar Charlene would go on to open herself.

When Charlene first walked into the space that would become her bar in 1977, it felt like fate. The building had previously been occupied by Castillo Pharmacy, and their tiled letter Cs still lined the floors. Charlene called it an "omen." Like Alice Brady, Charlene made the decision to name the bar after herself. It was a way of very intentionally and publicly sticking her neck out for potential patrons, and a far cry from her choice to give a false name to the police all those years ago.

At the time of Charlene's opening, Alice was going on twenty years at the helm of her bar business. She was only fifty, but she'd been diagnosed with diabetes and was slowing down and thinking about retirement. "We talked about it so many times," says Ellen Frayle, who at this point was in a relationship with Alice.

Within the year, Alice decided to retire and sold the bar to Diane Dimiceli, another friend who'd been looking to get into the business. Under a new name, Diane's, she ran the bar for three and a half years until closing the doors for good in 1984.

Bored with retirement, Alice herself ended up bartending at Charlene's for a handful of years. Charlene must have deeply respected Alice and all she did to pave the way for lesbian bars in the city of New Orleans.

At their core, Charlene and Alice had the same mission: to create safe space for queer women. However, at Charlene's, politics weren't just allowed, they were encouraged. "She becomes this sort of street corner lecturer, and she would go out to the front, and whenever people stepped outside to have a smoke or whatever, she would educate lesbian youth about the Up Stairs Lounge tragedy," describes Robert. Charlene was passionate about the need for political activism within the queer community, so that the community would be able to protect itself when no one else would.

While Charlene was an unabashed advocate for the queer community, her tactics were often rooted in respectability politics, and in playing nice with politicians and police. "When I first opened the bar, I went to the police and I said, 'I'm opening up a gay bar. There'll be no fighting, no effing, no dope. If you have a problem, come to me,'" Charlene recounts.

It was because of Charlene's connections and her perceived respectability that she was tapped to run New Orleans' first annual Gay Fest—a political Pride celebration—alongside friends Mark Gonzales and Dick O'Connor. The more radical Pink Triangle Alliance had hosted the city's first ever gay Pride rally in 1978, but likely hoping the event could gain more mainstream traction, they handed it over to Charlene and her friends the following year.

While there are fair critiques of respectability politics, it's important to note that for Charlene, they really worked. Gay Fest grew each year, eventually morphing into Pridefest, today one of the largest Pride celebrations in the South. In the twenty-two years that Charlene's was open, there was only one documented incident of police harassment at the bar, and leveraging her political connections, Charlene was able to make the related charges disappear for her customers within twenty-four hours.

What's more, Charlene and her bar were deeply instrumental in securing the first legal protections in the Deep South prohibiting discrimination on the basis of sexual orientation in employment, housing, commercial spaces, and more. This was a fight that would take more than a decade to win. Gay and lesbian activists brought an antidiscrimination ordinance twice to the city council, in 1984 and in 1986, to no avail.

After the ordinance was shot down for the second time, Up Stairs Lounge survivor Stuart Butler and fellow activist Rich McGill returned to Charlene's bar for a drink. That night, Rich proposed that they put together a report proving that discrimination was happening and had been happening for a long time, refuting the doubts that some in the city council had voiced. The report is titled *Exposing Hatred*, and is dedicated to the Up Stairs Lounge victims and to Charlene.[10] In 1991, because of this report, the antidiscrimination ordinance finally passed. It's still in effect today, and in 1998 was expanded to cover gender identity in addition to sexual orientation.

Charlene sold her bar in 1999, but she and her life partner Linda Tucker took the party with them to Bay St. Louis, Mississippi. On the final day of our 2023 trip to New Orleans, Sarah and I drive out to Bay St. Louis to meet Linda in the house she once shared with Charlene. The two met in the summer of 1987 in Charlene's bar while Linda was visiting from Houston. They were immediately drawn to one another. After two years of a long-distance relationship, Linda left Texas and moved in with Charlene in Bay St. Louis, spending their weekends in the small apartment Charlene kept next to the bar.

When we arrive at the house, Linda shows us a small building by the pool. Inside, there's a little bar of its own. The ceiling is painted rainbow, and the walls are lined with framed photos and Charlene's memorabilia: the sign that used to hang above the bar, a framed poster of the bar's logo, and dozens and dozens of photos of Charlene, Linda, and all their friends. In the cement floor, they have even replicated one of the famous tiled Cs from Charlene's. Here, Charlene and Linda continued to play host to the New Orleans gay community after Charlene's closed, having been priced out of the building that housed it.

On February 20, 1999, people from all over the country flocked to Charlene's for one last night at their beloved bar. The place was packed with old friends, regulars, city and state officials that Charlene helped elect, and musicians who had played at the bar. One person was notably missing, though: Charlene herself.

"Charlene was really sick," Linda tells us. She hadn't been diagnosed with anything yet, but for months, she'd been growing increasingly tired and weak. She spent the majority of the evening resting in a friend's camper van parked just outside the bar, barely mustering the energy to come out and say hello. It was Linda who made last call, at around 2 a.m.: "I got up in the DJ booth, and I remember the words exactly. I said, 'I never dreamt that I would be the one who would be saying this, but last call at Charlene's.'"

It would take another five years for Charlene to get a diagnosis: myelodysplastic syndrome, which eventually progressed to leukemia. Charlene passed away on December 3, 2006, in the very room where Sarah and I sit with Linda.

On our way back to New Orleans, Sarah and I stop at Charlene's grave. Linda told us where to find it. A winding dirt road leads us to a chain-link fence and a sunlit clearing, surrounded by woods. There is no parking lot, no cemetery office, and not another soul in sight. A rusted sign over the unlocked gate reads "Bayou Caddy Cemetery" in gothic white lettering. With no map or plot number, just a description of Charlene's heart-shaped tombstone from Linda, we set out searching. It's quiet. The only sounds are the buzzing of cicadas, the chirping of birds, and the rustling of the leaves of the massive oak trees overhead. Finally, we spot her tombstone on the far side of the cemetery. "Charlene Ann Schneider, Aug 13, 1940–Dec 3, 2006," it reads. Then in capital letters across the bottom of the stone: "LET THE WORK I HAVE DONE SPEAK FOR ME."

Chapter Twenty-Three

LES PIERRES

THE HOME THEY BUILT

NEW ORLEANS, LA

Despite having a majority-Black population,[1] New Orleans lacked a Black-owned lesbian bar until Juanita Pierre and her partner, Leslie Martinez, opened Les Pierres on the corner of North Rampart and Pauger Streets in the '80s. "I decided we needed a place of our own," Juanita tells us. Although it's no longer around today, Les Pierres would go down in history as the first documented Black lesbian–owned bar in New Orleans—and quite possibly the entire South—offering a blueprint for centering Black queer women's lives in a world that otherwise marginalized them at every turn.

In the days leading up to our trip in 2023, we tried desperately to reach Juanita. After we finally get a hold of her on her landline, she invited Sarah and me over to her home in Uptown/Carrollton to talk. We had an address and a time: Sunday after church.

Juanita herself greets us at her front door, cigarette in hand, and welcomes us into her home in her distinct, raspy voice. "It looks a mess," she says, as we cross through the living room to the kitchen. "My housekeeper don't come on weekends."

Since her partner Leslie passed, Juanita insists that the place has not been up to her impeccable standards, though to us it looks perfectly neat and beautiful. "Leslie's been dead three years and three months. So, nothing's like it normally [would] be," Juanita tells us, adding, "'Cause I'm not a housewife."

Abruptly, Juanita then asks: "Y'all gay? Are you in the life?" and we assure her that yes, we both are.

Now that we have affirmed our queerness, Juanita reiterates: "I ain't never wanted to be a housewife." She says it with a smile and a twinkle in her eye; this is a detail she now trusts we understand. She's telling us something about her gender identity and her relationship with Leslie; Leslie kept the house, while Juanita assumed a more traditional masculine role in their relationship.

"I'm a typical boy-girl," Juanita elaborates. "Y'all got boy-girls in y'all lives. Y'all know how they are," she continues, and we nod in understanding, although most folks in our circles would opt for labels like *trans masc* or *nonbinary* or *butch*. "I'm no different from them. Just older and doing it at a slower pace now," Juanita muses.

Leslie was the opposite. "That lady was gorgeous. I have never seen in forty-five years her hair or her nails [undone], or no eyeliner [. . .] even when she was asleep," Juanita says. "I love ladies. I put up with women, but I love ladies. And there is a difference!"

We must look confused. "Y'all don't know the difference?" she asks us incredulously. "There's a big difference. Class and no class," Juanita distinguishes. "I taught my boys: you marry a lady. We taught our two girls: you marry a gentleman [. . .] and don't settle for anything less."

At this moment, Sarah and I are thinking about how distinctly unladylike we are, seated at Juanita's kitchen table with our unpainted nails, messy hair, and cutoff denim shorts. Neither one of us really fits into Juanita's binary sense of gender at all. But Juanita doesn't seem to mind, and neither do we. We're proud to be unladylike, comfortable in our own gender expressions.

We also recognize that Juanita's seemingly heteronormative framework for thinking about relationships and gender is a part of her own authentic identity. In her terms, if Leslie is the lady, then Juanita is the gentleman, a role she has embraced from a very young age. "Even when I played house, I was the daddy," Juanita confesses, reflecting on her youth. "[Once] my friend and I got naked, and I got a clothespin and stuck it between my legs, 'cause I was always *the man*."

Despite having this clear sense of her identity so early, Juanita married a man at nineteen, right out of high school. "I tried to do what was called 'the right thing' back then," she says. Juanita and her husband had three children together, though she never did let her marriage get in the way of her feelings for women. "I was married, but I didn't settle down. I tried. Just didn't work." For years, Juanita was dating other women while her husband thought she was working a night job. "I really thought it would have worked," she says, "but it didn't." Because Juanita met Leslie.

"I met Leslie at a men's gay bar. [. . .] I walked into this dark bar that night and I saw her on the dance floor," Juanita begins. She strolled right up to Leslie and said, "I'm gonna spend the rest of my life with you," then walked away. "I know y'all have heard [of] love at first sight. I knew that was my mate when I saw her. And that's what it was."

The next day, the two connected at a gathering at a mutual friend's house. Two days later, Leslie invited Juanita over for dinner. "The first meal she cooked for me was chicken cacciatore," Juanita recalls. "I'm *Black*, ya know? [. . .] I said, 'That's spaghetti and red gravy, why didn't you just call it that?' And we've been together ever since."

Juanita and Leslie dated for three or four years, during which Juanita's husband assumed they were just close friends. "You could tell your friend to give me some," he would often say to Leslie, referring to his lackluster sex life with Juanita.

"And me and Leslie would laugh about it because we knew it wasn't gonna happen," says Juanita.

Throughout those years, Leslie got to know Juanita's children. "The kids loved her," Juanita emphasizes. "I can't comb hair. So, every morning [Leslie] had to comb my daughter's hair to go to school. She brought 'em to school, she picked them up."

When the time came, Juanita included her children, then two, six, and nine, in the decision to leave their father and move in with Leslie. "'Cause if you're old enough to think, you're old enough to know the truth," Juanita reasons. "It's what I wanted to do, but it was their decision. I was not gonna thrust my children into something they didn't want. [. . .] I would've stayed there and just kept messing around. But they wanted to go stay with [Leslie]. They loved her." With her children's blessing, Juanita told her husband she was leaving him.

"I knew something was wrong with you," he responded.

"My children and I left with the clothes on our back [. . .] and we went home," Juanita recalls. To this day, Juanita is very close with all her kids: the three she birthed, plus her great-niece whom she and Leslie raised from infancy, and various other nieces and nephews whom they helped rear. Throughout our conversation, Juanita would pause to answer the landline whenever one of them phoned, inviting them over. Juanita's middle son, Michael, his wife, Kewanya, and Juanita's nephew, Anthony, all stopped by that afternoon.

Michael tells us more about the early days of Juanita and Leslie's relationship. He reminisces: "When [my mom] got with Leslie, even as kids, we understood it was a match. It was a yin and yang. They balanced each other."

Of course, not everyone embraced Leslie and Juanita's partnership as wholeheartedly as Michael and his siblings. "In the seventies and eighties, kids [were] very brutal [. . .] they were calling my mama some very rough words," Michael remembers. But he always stood up for her. "Inadvertently, I was fighting for gay rights before the gay movement," he says with a chuckle.

Michael knew his classmates' cruelty came from ignorance, and that he had something his peers were missing. "I'm surrounded by all this love that y'all not getting," he remembers thinking, "I got it on both ends now. I got two mothers I can go to whenever I'm ready."

Juanita is proud of the way she and Leslie modeled a healthy relationship for all the kids in their lives and is proud of the adults these children have all become. "[They] are products of gay environments [. . .] they were taught by two gay women how to live. How to live respectful, how to live successful," Juanita explains.

The pair also modeled entrepreneurial smarts. In a departure from their otherwise heteronormative gender roles, Leslie handled the family's finances, and she was good at it. It's because of Leslie's financial prowess that she and Juanita were able to open Les Pierres in the early 1980s.

As the two began making plans for Les Pierres, Juanita sought advice from a familiar friend of hers who had extensive experience in the business: Charlene Schneider. Juanita met Charlene in New Orleans' existing lesbian nightlife scene, frequenting the so-called white lesbian bars. "I would go to Dusty's, Charlene's, every damn female bar. [. . .] It was not *uncomfortable*," Juanita says, choosing the word carefully. But there is a difference between feeling uncomfortable and feeling at home, and Juanita wanted a bar for the Black lesbian community to call their own. Charlene thought this was a brilliant idea. "She was the one [who] mentored me on how to go about opening the bar," Juanita tells us.

In the newspaper, Juanita and Leslie found a spot where the rent was reasonable, a friend made them a sign, another built them a bar, and eventually Les Pierres was born. "The name originated from [Leslie's] first name, Les, and my last name, Pierre. So, it was Les Pierres," explains Juanita.

"I don't think we even had a grand opening. It was just word of mouth," says Juanita. "It was packed. [The bar] gave people of color somewhere to go, and then everybody else started coming. So, it was really mixed." There were some details of the bar that Juanita couldn't recall, so she invited over her friend Imelda to help fill in the gaps.

Imelda was a teenager when Les Pierres first opened. "I was too young to be in the clubs at the time. [. . .] I had to sneak past her," Imelda says, gesturing to Juanita.

Imelda has known Juanita for most of her life. "I've always been her little sister," she remarks. Growing up with Juanita and Leslie as role models was hugely important for Imelda. "Seeing how they were living, it gave me the ability to say, 'Yeah, I could live [like that],'" she explains. "To see them enjoy the gay life, and it was safe, [. . .] it made me feel welcome."

Surprisingly, this is not a point of pride for Juanita. "I felt bad about it," Juanita asserts. "I never want to be known for influencing someone to be gay. I really didn't."

But Imelda would have been gay with or without Juanita and Leslie. They just showed her it was possible to be happy and successful in addition to being gay. "I come from one of the worst projects in the world," says Imelda. "So, watching what they were doing, it enthused me."

During one college break, Imelda was finally old enough to get into the bar legally. "It was amazing," she recalls. "The first time I was able to go in and actually sit [. . .] and I [was] a good-looking stud at the time; I sat there and enjoyed the show."

Onstage at Les Pierres, you could find drag kings performing each week. "Oh, that's what y'all call it now?" Juanita remarks when we ask her about the drag king shows. "We called them male impersonators back then," she explains. Juanita ran the drag troupe, called La Femme. "You had to audition to get in La Femme. [. . .] We had rehearsals, and I mean hard rehearsals," she describes.

The weekly performances were elaborate. "La Femme had a choreographer. [. . .] We had a makeup artist, we had a spotlight guy." The performers usually dressed in full tuxedos. "I had a friend named Mr. Morgan [who] had a tuxedo rental place. So, he would let me bring the girls down there and pick out tuxedos," Juanita details. Each troupe member had a specific celebrity they impersonated. "I only did Luther Vandross," says Juanita. "We had one little girl [who] did Frank Sinatra. She was awesome."

For the final act of each show, La Femme always had "one of the boy-girls doing a female number," says Juanita. "We'd do Gladys Knight, we'd do Cherrelle, but one of us had to come out, as we said, in drag. 'Cause putting on a gown and a wig was drag for us."

When there wasn't a drag show happening at Les Pierres, the DJ was guaranteed to pack the dance floor. "They played whatever was happening at the time," says Juanita. "Being a Black bar, [they played] a lot of R&B. But they'd play anything you asked the DJ to play."

According to Imelda, the bar was known for having an older crowd. When she would tell her peers that she was hanging out at Les Pierres, they would make comments about it being an "old people" bar. "But what they didn't know is, we was having a ball," she adds.

One day each week attracted a much younger demographic. "Saturdays during daytime hours, that was my children's time," says Juanita.

"My mother would give us a chance to act like we were adults," Michael recalls fondly. "We got to sit at the bar drinking a root beer. We got to turn on the DJ equipment, the jukebox, we'd get to shoot pool."

"That was our bar, the family bar," Juanita declares.

When the bar closed at the end of the 1980s, Michael and his siblings felt the loss the hardest. "It took away our Saturday mornings," Michael notes sadly.

The bar's closing left a gaping hole in the community, too. "We still get people asking us to reopen," Juanita remarks.

Yet, Juanita never considered opening another bar. She seems to be the only one who doesn't express any grief over the closure of Les Pierres. "That's a closed chapter in my life," she says. "The building got sold, and I wasn't gonna pay the price they were asking. So, we shut it down." There was no last call, no big final event; Juanita isn't partial to that kind of sentimentality. "We just closed down one day [. . .] and we just kept moving," Juanita says matter-of-factly.

This type of pragmatic, no-nonsense resilience is typical of Juanita, and of many New Orleanians. "In New Orleans, what happened yesterday is yesterday. We not gonna worry about that. We just going [to] focus on the road up ahead," Michael says. This outlook has gotten the family through a loss far more astronomical than that of Les Pierres.

"Oh baby, you gonna love the finale," Juanita exclaims as we near the end of our afternoon together.

"I have a feeling I'm actually gonna *not* love the finale," Sarah says wryly.

"Yes you are. I loved it. It's a tearjerker," insists Juanita.

In 2005, Leslie slipped and fell on the two steps leading from the kitchen up to the bathroom. Juanita took her to the emergency room, and finding no broken bones, they sent her home. The following evening, Leslie went to work the night shift at a nursing home. Returning home, she nearly drove into the house. "Her legs were [. . .] blue," says Juanita, who rushed Leslie back to the hospital. There, doctors discovered that Leslie's body was full of blood clots, and she went straight into emergency surgery.

"Every Black, gay woman in the city of New Orleans was in that hospital that night. They were praying, they were singing, they were there," Juanita recalls. At one point, the hospital staff even came out and told Juanita some folks had to go—it was too crowded. Leslie made it through surgery, but she still had a long road to recovery ahead. They had amputated both of her legs, and she was on dialysis for her failing kidneys. "But she didn't give up and I didn't give up. I cannot tolerate giving up. You fight 'til you drop," says Juanita forcefully.

Juanita did not leave Leslie's side. "I lived in the hospital [for] three months with her," she recalls. "Family and the gay community, they were there twenty-four hours a day, seven days a week. [. . .] The gay community made sure I had breakfast, lunch, and dinner. Those that live close to the hospital [gave me] keys to their houses so I could go and shower."

For those three months, it seemed Leslie was teetering on the edge of life and death, until finally, Juanita was able to bring her home. Two days before Hurricane Katrina hit, Leslie was back in the hospital—not unusual in the months following her double amputation. Knowing they needed to evacuate, Michael and Juanita got her discharged and drove straight from the hospital to Pensacola, Florida. Less than forty-eight hours later, Hurricane Katrina made landfall in Louisiana as a Category 5 storm, killing more than one thousand New Orleanians, many of whom were trapped in hospitals without power.

A year later, Leslie and Juanita returned to their home in New Orleans. It had been gutted and rebuilt, not only because of damage from Katrina but also so that it could be made wheelchair accessible for Leslie. As the city continued to rebuild around her, something in Leslie shifted. "She just snapped back. She went from the weakest part of her life to what I call the strongest part of her life," Michael marvels.

Although she was in and out of the hospital, Leslie went on to live another fifteen years after her fall and double amputation. Through it all, she never stopped being "a lady," as Juanita would say. "Every single time she went to the hospital, somebody had to come and get her nail kit," remembers Michael's wife, Kewanya. "You cannot catch her with a chipped nail [. . .] at all times, up until the last day. Even when she was hurting, she still kept everything done."

Though she rarely complained, Leslie was certainly in a great deal of pain toward the end of her life. In January of 2020, Leslie went into the hospital for the last time. "She knew that her time had come," Juanita says. Everyone was there, gathered around her hospital bed to say goodbye.

"I love you," Juanita told her.

Leslie opened her eyes and said, "I love you too."

"Baby, if you're tired and you are ready to go, I'm gonna be all right. Go ahead," said Juanita.

"I knew it was time to let her go. She had suffered enough. She only stayed to make sure I was all right," recalls Juanita. "The minute I told her I'm gonna be all right, she took her last breath."

In classic Leslie fashion, she left detailed instructions for what she wanted when she was gone: her body donated to science and a budget-conscious funeral with a simple balloon release.

"I know she got her balloons," reflects Juanita tenderly. "Oh Lord, [there were] a lot of us and all of us had one balloon. And it was January, so you know the wind was blowing [. . .] but all those balloons from a circle of people gathered in one bunch. None of them separated. And they all went up to the point where we didn't see 'em no more. *Together.* And with the wind blowing. So, I know she got 'em."

Chapter Twenty-Four

BOYCOTT BAR

LESBIANS AGAINST DRUNK DRIVING

PHOENIX, AZ

Audrey Corley first met Melissa in 2004. The pair would soon find themselves in a fiery on-again-off-again relationship, but at the time Audrey was busy. She was just weeks away from launching Boycott, her new twice-monthly pop-up party for queer women. Back then, Audrey's mission was simple: get women together and give them a good time. But Melissa would change that. By the time Boycott opened its permanent location, Audrey had a new top priority: keeping people safe.

Audrey had been working in the Phoenix area nightlife scene since she got her first job bartending in college. By the early 2000s, she was working at the number-one women's bar in the city. After falling out with the owner, Audrey decided to branch out on her own, and eventually Boycott was born.

She spent months planning and promoting the first party. "I found a location in a restaurant that was kind of struggling," Audrey says. She pitched her event to the owner, guaranteeing that she could support the business by bringing in a packed house every other Saturday night. He agreed.

Now, Audrey had to deliver on the crowds she had promised. "I started out with these little business cards. That's how I promoted [Boycott]," she details. She spent about three months handing out cards to anyone and everyone she knew in the community, and given her previous years spent bartending, she had built up quite the network. The first party, on July 16, 2004, was a hit. "There was a demand for a more upscale event for women at the time," Audrey explains, and gregarious, funny, and tatted, Audrey knows how to throw a good party.

Eventually, Audrey moved Boycott to another bar called The Vibe, which was previously a predominantly lesbian bar called Ain't Nobody's Bizness. During the approximately three years that Boycott popped up at The Vibe, Audrey and Melissa finally got together. Audrey can't quite recall how it happened. "I just knew one day she wasn't there, and one day she was," Audrey states simply.

Melissa was twelve years younger than Audrey. "She was beautiful. She was African American and Latina," describes Audrey, who herself is Latina as well. "When she walked in the room, she owned it. She had that type of energy. Oh gosh, she was fun. [. . .] She could dance, she could speak Spanish, she was everything. She could cook. She just did it all. She was a good mom. Whenever you went somewhere, you couldn't miss that smile. You knew she was in the room."

While Audrey can't recount the first time she and Melissa got together, she vividly remembers meeting Melissa's son. One day, while she was setting up for one of Boycott's events at The Vibe, Melissa walked in and said, "I got something to show you." Audrey thought she was going to pull out a new pair of shoes, but instead, she held up a seven-month-old baby. "Here's my son," Melissa declared.

"I took him, and I walked around, introduced him to my staff at the time, and that was it. I was in love at first sight, you know?" Audrey recounts fondly.

Melissa's son became a huge part of Audrey's life. "He definitely was a game changer for me," Audrey explains. "My best friend always says, I was rolling around with bottles of liquor in my car and then—after I met him—it was car seats and baby bottles in my Tahoe."

Audrey's relationship with Melissa's son was more stable than her relationship with Melissa.

"[She] wasn't really a one-woman type of person at that time," Audrey asserts. "The only thing I can say that was always consistent with us was [her son], and the love I had for [him]. She knew that I was always going to take care of [him] and help out, and I adored him."

Once, while Melissa and Audrey were broken up and business for Boycott was especially slow, Audrey concocted a plan to drum up buzz for the party *and* get Melissa's attention. On a whim, she publicly announced that she was getting engaged and would be celebrating her engagement at that week's event. With the exception of one friend who was in on the joke, Audrey wouldn't tell a soul *who* she was engaged to. "We made a flyer [. . .] and it just blew up from there," recalls Audrey.

"I'm not really dishonest so it was kind of a hard joke to play at first. [. . .] For the two weeks leading up to it, [. . .] my staff just couldn't stop [asking questions]," says Audrey.

Nicole "Nic" Enniss, a longtime Boycott bartender and close friend of Audrey's, was among the inquisitive staff. "It's probably an internet bride," she remembers thinking at the time. Aside from this, Nic and her fellow bartenders had only one real guess as to who Audrey might be marrying: Melissa. But even Melissa swore she didn't know who Audrey was engaged to. "It was one of the best promotions in the world. It was genius. And Melissa showed up sure as shit," recalls Nic. Audrey's plan worked on all accounts.

"[Melissa] showed up pretty heated that night. [. . .] She was mad that I was marrying someone," Audrey remembers. "She was coming back to claim what she said was hers. Which was me."

At the end of the night, Audrey got up in front of everyone and announced: "I guess y'all want to see what I'm getting engaged to? I'm engaged to the bar!" Audrey and Melissa got back together that evening. "I think it was good for about a week, or two weeks, between us, and then it went up in flames," she says nonchalantly. Boycott, on the other hand, was a constant in Audrey's life. In a sense, the engagement was never a lie. "The woman I'm dating now calls [the bar] my wife. It's my true love," Audrey adds.

However, the year after the infamous engagement party, an accident prompted Audrey to temporarily walk away from hosting Boycott and from lesbian nightlife altogether. In 2010, Melissa was killed by a drunk driver.

"It was September 25th. [Melissa] and her new girlfriend were headed to work, and the drunk driver, [. . .] on the freeway, was going the wrong way and crashed into them. And they both died," recounts Audrey. One of the hardest parts about losing Melissa was that Audrey also lost Melissa's son. "Her ex-husband never let me be active in his life after that, so I never got to see him again," Audrey says.

Reeling from Melissa's death, Audrey knew she needed to hit pause on Boycott. "I was ready to stop and get out," she says. "I was pretty hurt. And

I just wanted to get away from it for a little while." She didn't leave the bar business altogether, but she wanted to take a break from the gay scene. So, she retreated to Glendale, where she opened a straight bar.

"[The straight bar] was in a real kind of rough neighborhood, and I was depressed, you know?" she explains. "For a gay woman, let's just say that it wasn't the area you really want to be in." But it was exactly where Audrey wanted to be at the time. In retrospect, she admits that her choices back then were, whether intentionally or subconsciously, self-destructive. "I was punishing myself for a little while," she says. "See, I thought they'd probably kill my gay ass over there. I was that depressed at the time," she exclaims with a wry laugh.

She wasn't wrong—Audrey did run the risk of harm in Glendale. "One time I had a guy, he kind of threatened my life. He was a gayphobe," she describes. He came by the bar multiple times and eventually pulled a gun on Audrey. Fortunately, her staff were there to protect her. They followed him home, intimidating him enough that he stopped coming to the bar.

In another incident, a man was shot directly outside the bar. Nic, who had followed Audrey to Glendale as a bartender, was there that night. A trained EMT, she rushed to start CPR; however, the cops on the scene stopped her, instructing her to wait for the ambulance to arrive. Nic suspects that they thought the incident was gang related. "The medics showed up, maybe minutes after that, and were mad that we weren't doing anything," Nic recalls. But it was too late. "The only thing positive that I can say is that at least that man didn't die alone. We were there. We were with him."

"We were out there for I don't know how many hours afterwards, just sitting there and thinking. It was [a] very traumatizing moment for all of us," Nic reflects. To this day, this experience informs the way the staff at Boycott interacts. "We watch each other's back, we take care of each other, we don't walk out without someone else walking us out. We're very cautious."

Audrey, too, credits her experiences in Glendale—the good and the bad—with preparing her to finally open Boycott as a permanent, brick-and-mortar bar. "What I thought was my curse turned out to be my blessing," Audrey often says. After seven years, she was finally ready to return to her roots in the lesbian community when she received an offer to buy a bar in Melrose. "Let's just go where your heart is," she told herself, "and it's always been in the [queer] community." So, she bought the bar.

In some ways, running Boycott is no different from running the straight bar in Glendale. "It's all people," Audrey proclaims. "Once you know how to deal with people, and you value people, you know how to treat people, that's really what it comes down to. [. . .] It's pretty much the same, except I have more women to pick out of now. I have a better dating pool," Audrey jokes.

Today, she estimates that Boycott's clientele is about 60 percent women. The other 40 percent is a mix of allies and queer folks of all genders. When we visit, Audrey and Nic are both behind the bar slinging drinks. They wear matching T-shirts that read "Boycott Bar" on the front and "Ass & Titties," Boycott's unofficial slogan, on the back. They also sport matching tattoos on their right forearms: a cocktail shaker, jigger, and martini glass connected by a heartbeat line, the kind you would see on an EKG machine. Audrey convinced Nic to get the tattoo. "You're not a real bartender 'til you get a tattoo," Audrey declares.

Audrey and Nic have something else in common: their shared mission to keep their community safe by preventing drunk driving. "What happened to Melissa changed my life a lot, but I also believe it saved a lot of lives," Audrey explains. "It has changed the way I run bars. [. . .] I take it real personal because I am directly impacted. You'll never forget that phone call that you lost someone you loved, you know? [. . .] Everyone thinks [. . .] it can't happen to me. But it really does happen to everybody. You go out there and you drink and drive, you put everybody in danger. [. . .] It's never worth it, but people still do it all the time."

At Boycott, Audrey, Nic, and the rest of their staff do everything in their power to stop people from driving home while intoxicated. "It is so hard being in this business, because that's what we do, we give you alcohol, and then at a certain point, you do have to go home. But I think because of that, we desperately try to make sure everyone is okay," Nic states.

"Our first policy is, we slow them down, cut them off," Audrey says, explaining what the team is trained to do if someone gets too intoxicated. From there, the staff decides how to get that person safely home. "We pay for [their] Lyft a lot of times [or] my staff will drive them home—all that's situational," describes Audrey.

They'll even take your car home too, so you have no excuse to try to drive. "One person will drive, another person will follow, and we'll make sure that you get home," Nic adds.

It's not always easy to stop a drunk person from getting behind the wheel. "There's no blanket way to handle it," explains Audrey. One moment, an intoxicated customer can be calm and collected; the next, they can be belligerent.

None of this deters Audrey and her team. As Nic explains, "If you come and you yell at me, I know you're intoxicated. You're gonna forget about it tomorrow, but I'm still gonna make sure that you're good now." If patrons don't accept a ride, the team has even been known to let the air out of people's tires. "We're not popping any tires, just letting the air out," Nic clarifies.

"I'm not able to protect everybody," Audrey admits, but she is confident that she's been able to protect some. "I guarantee you it has [saved lives] because people have come back and told me, and they've thanked me," says Audrey. "If we save one life in Melissa's honor, then we're doing what's right."

Chapter Twenty-Five

YBR PUB

FROM ALLY-RUN TO QUEER-RUN

TULSA, OK

At ten years old in Checotah, Oklahoma, Kevie Smith didn't know any gay people. In fact, she didn't even know gay people existed. "It was never talked about," she recalls of her small town in the 1970s.

While she didn't have a word for it yet, Kevie says she's always known she was gay. "I've been out since I was born," she declares. "Honestly, I thought something was wrong with me 'cause I'd never heard of gay people. I really thought maybe I was mentally ill."

It wasn't until Kevie moved to Tulsa at nineteen that she first laid eyes on another gay person. "That's when I finally heard someone say that I wasn't alone," she recounts. In Tulsa, she got a job working at a printing company where two other young women employees captured Kevie's attention. "They look[ed] like me, you know what I'm saying?" Kevie says, "and they kind of caught on that I was gay."

One afternoon in the lunchroom, they invited Kevie to go out with them after work. Not yet twenty-one, Kevie at first shied away from the idea, but her coworkers insisted. As Kevie climbed into the backseat of their car, one of her new friends declared: "We're going to the gay bar."

"What?" Kevie asked in shock.

"There's more of us out there than you know," she told Kevie.

Relief washed over Kevie. "I started crying. Because then I knew that I wasn't sick in the head, you know? There wasn't something wrong with me," she says.

"When I went to that first bar, I felt like I was home," she remembers fondly. The Tulsa gay bars wound their way through Kevie's young adulthood, and after two decades as a patron, she bought a bar of her own in January of 2000.

She agonized over what to name her new space. It had previously been a drag bar called Lola's and sat across the street from a long-standing head shop called Oz, established in 1969. *The Wizard of Oz* being Kevie's favorite movie, she knew she wanted a name that somehow fit the Oz theme. "It took us about three months to name it. Dorothy's, Tin Man, Munchkin Land," Kevie says, recalling the many names she cycled through before landing on Yellow Brick Road Pub, or YBR for short.

The name ended up coming from someone Kevie worked with at a local auto-parts shop, whom she describes as the most homophobic man she's ever met in her life. "[Every day] he would hear us talking about what to name [the bar]," Kevie recalls.

One afternoon, fed up with the never-ending discussion, he slapped his hand down on the table and exclaimed, "What the hell are they walking on through this whole movie?" The room fell silent.

"You know what? I think you just named the bar," Kevie replied.

A few months later, on April 1, 2000, Kevie opened YBR. "That place was packed out the very first night. It was pretty cool," Kevie remembers. From day one, she intended for the bar to be inclusive. "I opened it up to the public, for anyone. I felt like we were being too segregated in Tulsa. We needed to open it up to everybody. It did end up being about 80 percent lesbian, but we had straight people in there, we had all kinds of genders in there." Even Kevie's homophobic coworker stopped by to see what YBR was all about. "He was there on grand opening for one beer and left, so I think he felt a little pride in naming that bar," Kevie says with a smile.

Since that night, the bar has consistently remained a queer space, but its identity as a lesbian bar has ebbed and flowed. In large part, this is because ownership has changed over the years, since Kevie sold the bar six years after opening.

You can't miss YBR from the street; one whole side of the brick building is painted a bright yellow, and a large, yellow pylon sign reads "YBR Bar." When we visit in 2021, another yellow sign greets us inside. This one is smaller and handmade; the words "YBR: YEAH, YOU'RE IN A GAY BAR. ENJOY" are scrawled across in capital letters.

The space has a classic dive bar feel: deep red walls, an assortment of neon beer signs, two pool tables, and two dart machines. Both the bar's black ceiling tiles and the bathroom's bright green walls are covered with graffiti. "Keep Tulsa queer," reads one bathroom message. "This is my first time at a gay bar," reads another. "Call Paul for the best head of your life," reads a third.

We mingle with a crowd of all genders and sexualities. That night, we meet two women essential to the YBR community: Amanda, then the bar's manager, and Sarah, a former bartender and longtime regular. Amanda and Sarah have one thing in common that places them in the minority of people we've interviewed: They're both straight. Both are quick to convey another facet of their identity to us, though.

"I am an ally," Amanda tells us.

Sarah echoes the sentiment later in the night. "Well, I've been a lifetime ally," she says.

In our circles in New York, or in various left-leaning corners of the internet, one might be laughed at for sincerely self-identifying as an ally. Allyship is seen as the bare minimum, and therefore the label is often tossed around somewhat facetiously.

But in Tulsa, Oklahoma, the word *ally* holds more weight than we are accustomed to. In a predominantly red state—which as of 2025 has no state-level laws in place to protect LGBTQ+ people from discrimination—support of the LGBTQ+ community is by no means a given. So allyship is deeply valued and *ally* is a label claimed in earnest, reflective of a true commitment to respect and protect the LGBTQ+ community. Sarah and Amanda both started working at YBR around the same time, in 2014. They had to prove themselves as allies, demonstrating their commitment through their actions, not just their words.

"When I started working here, it was strictly a lesbian bar," Amanda asserts. Despite never having marketed itself as an exclusively lesbian space, YBR was claimed by the lesbian community as their own. Men were never turned away at the door, but Amanda says, "[Patrons] would just make [men] so uncomfortable that they would leave."

Sarah remembers vividly what it took to break into this world and earn the trust of the YBR regulars as a straight woman. One patron, Jaime, would post up at the bar just to give Sarah a hard time. "She would stand there and then yell at regulars on the other side of me to talk shit about the straight girl. Like not subtle at all," Sarah says, laughing.

Finally, one night Sarah asked Jaime what the constant cajoling was all about. Jaime confessed that Sarah's presence felt like a threat, and that she was worried Sarah would yell at her for using the wrong bathroom.

"They're one-holers," Sarah said to Jaime, describing YBR's toilets, "I don't care! I'm going to whichever one's open, I hope you are too." The two talked about it for a bit, and from that point on, they got along. The interaction was eye-opening for Sarah. "It hadn't occurred to me when I started [bartending] that just being very feminine presenting and straight would be a safety threat to them," she explains. This realization taught Sarah how she could be of service to the YBR community in a tangible way, beyond pouring drinks.

If patrons felt threatened by Sarah, who had the purest of intentions, what was it like when a different sort of person enters? As a bartender, Sarah made it her mission to help safeguard the space for the YBR community.

Like Jaime, the rest of the YBR patrons soon realized that Sarah was a friend and protector, not a threat. "I was just me. And that worked out over time," she states. Part of why allyship comes so naturally to Sarah is because she learned it from her mom.

"My mom was a PE teacher, so in all of that clichéd fashion, most of her friends were lesbians," Sarah says. Though her mom herself was straight, she felt more at home among her gay and lesbian friends. "Growing up in Oklahoma, there's an expectation of femininity and a sort of male privilege that I wasn't raised with. I just didn't get the memo, because that wasn't who my mom was."

Instead, Sarah grew up surrounded by the gay community, although no one explicitly labeled it as such. Eventually, Sarah figured it out for herself; "Wait a minute, Pam and Carmen aren't roommates!" she remembers exclaiming to her mom.

"You'll have to ask Pam," was all her mom would say.

Not because she was shying away from discussing the topic with her daughter, but out of respect for Pam. "You didn't out people. That didn't happen, because it was dangerous," Sarah reasons, and in many circumstances, it still is today. With her quiet acceptance, Sarah's mom instilled in her a fierce protectiveness, teaching her that "these are our friends, and we love them, and the world might not. So, we have to make sure to love them extra and to protect them from what won't love them."

When Sarah needed them most, her community at YBR was there to love her and protect her too. In 2015, her mom was diagnosed with brain cancer. "I have a very distinct memory of a friend in full drag, putting cold towels on my back out here while I cried. [. . .] This bar is kind of like a chrysalis. It just holds you while you turn to goo, until you're ready to grow your wings."

In November of 2015, Sarah's mom passed. "I was standing right there the night I got the call that she was dead," Sarah says, gesturing to a spot on the bar's patio. She was working that night and remembers walking in the back door after hanging up the phone. "My legs were going out from under me, like I couldn't stand. And at that moment, one of the other bartenders opened the door, just coming in [for a] drink, and saw me dropping and knew what happened. She caught me before I hit the ground, and they closed down the bar. I had to tell people to stop hugging me," Sarah remembers.

Her mom only ever visited YBR twice, but from those visits alone, she could see why it meant so much to Sarah and to the community. "[She] deeply encouraged me to buy it. [. . .] She said, 'This is your home. I get it,'" Sarah narrates. For several years, Sarah actually was in conversations about buying the bar. Back then, it was primarily owned by a man named Blake Ewing, whom Sarah suspects kept YBR mainly for tax purposes. Sarah thought the bar should be owned by someone who was truly invested in the community. "I tried for years to buy this place," she says. "I love this bar in a way that I can't quantify or qualify for anybody. This place has been a home for me, for my friends. [. . .] You can take the worst blow you've ever taken, and somebody will catch you before you fall here. It's not a replaceable feeling."

In 2018, though, after multiple attempts to purchase the bar fell through, Sarah left her bartending job at YBR. "We had some regulars here that had alcoholism. And at some point, I had to admit I was profiting off of killing my friends. And I couldn't live with that," Sarah admits. Yet, when we met her in 2021 she was still dreaming about buying the bar, hoping the opportunity might someday arise. And of course, she continued to visit as a patron. "It's always there when I need it," she says. "It's home and it's always gonna be home. The running joke amongst the bartenders is, it's [like] Hotel California. You can check out, but you can never leave."

In July of 2022, YBR suffered an accidental, though devastating, electrical fire. It was initially considered a total loss. But the YBR community—scrappy and resilient as ever—quickly rebuilt, and in June of the following year, the bar reopened.

YBR's interior is brighter and cleaner than its previous incarnation. Gone are the deep red walls and graffiti-covered ceiling, and smoking in the bar is no longer permitted, despite being legal in the state. But the biggest change is that now, YBR is almost entirely queer run. Val Binkley, a Tulsa native in her thirties, is the first lesbian to manage the bar in over a decade. Ownership has also changed. Today, Dr. Farshid Zandi owns the space, and although he's a straight man, Val says he's fairly hands-off when it comes to the day-to-day operations. "He's like, 'You're the lesbian, you run the lesbian bar.' He trusts me [. . .] and he's very appreciative of what me and my team have allowed YBR to become," Val explains.

Under queer management, YBR has blossomed. "Not to bring straight people down, but there's obviously things that are gonna be overlooked," Val says. This year, for example, Val set up a meeting with some members of the local trans community to better understand what they want and need from YBR. "I will never understand the trans experience, as I am not trans," Val acknowledges. "That meeting we had so we can all be educated and help our trans family members feel the most welcome possible." She's also made an effort to partner with local queer organizations. Inside the bar is a queer library, installed in partnership with QueerLit Collective, a local nonprofit with the mission to establish unrestricted access to queer literature for the 2SLGBTQIA+ community and its allies.

The bar has had just as much of an impact on Val as Val has had on the bar. It's only within the last five years that she has entirely embraced her identity. Her first relationship with a woman was an abusive one, and processing that experience complicated her ability to fully unearth her queerness.

"[In] my first relationship with a woman, I still struggled with even understanding that I was gay. 'Cause everybody in Oklahoma has religious trauma, whether they're gay or not," she says. It's only recently that Val has claimed the word *lesbian*. "I know I'm a lesbian, but I still struggled with being called a lesbian, until I started working at YBR," she explains. "I'd never been in a place where I was surrounded by so many queer women, just openly being their authentic self. Like loving women loving women."

Sarah's greatest wish for YBR, it seems, has been fulfilled, and she no longer thinks about buying the bar. "I was there to protect it when it needed protecting, but now the community is big enough and strong enough that they don't need my help that way," she says. "For me, the ability to step aside and know it's safe gives me a ton of hope. Even with all the terror of this administration, I can see that we're bigger and stronger than ever. Now if it was ever in jeopardy, I'd step back in in a heartbeat, but I honestly don't see that happening anytime soon."

Chapter Twenty-Six

ALIBI'S AND FRANKIE'S

OUT AND PROUD IN OKC

OKLAHOMA CITY, OK

To my surprise, Oklahoma City had *two* lesbian bars when we visited back in 2021. We began our one night in town at Alibi's, then headed over to Frankie's. At both bars, we heard stories about a historic Oklahoma City queer dance club that many hold near and dear: the Wreck Room.

The Wreck Room advertised itself as "the gay party place for all ages."[1] It was established in 1985 and sat on Thirty-Ninth Street, at the center of Oklahoma City's gayborhood. It was an alcohol-free venue, although former regulars remember being able to buy poppers—the recreational inhalant popular among gay men—before they were banned in the US in 1990.[2] In addition to serving as an after-hours dance club, staying open long past the city's 2 a.m. bar curfew, the space also acted as a safe haven for LGBTQ+ teens earlier in the evening. For nearly four decades, until its permanent closure in 2019, the Wreck Room was hugely influential in the lives of LGBTQ+ folks who grew up in the OKC area.

We first hear about the Wreck Room from Lisa Thomas, a pink-haired thirty-something-year-old bartender we meet at Alibi's. Lisa and her friends discovered the Wreck Room as teenagers. "It was the only club that you could go to at such a young age. It was the only thing we had," Lisa says. "It was the first time I'd been introduced to a drag show, a drag queen, a drag king, anybody that was trans. [. . .] That's what the Wreck Room was for a lot of us."

At first, going to the Wreck Room was mainly about getting out of her small town, Mustang, about twenty-five minutes outside of OKC. "It was the one place that we had that we didn't see anybody else that we knew. It was right here in the middle of the city, and it was just full of gay people! It was heaven," Lisa recalls.

Initially, Lisa identified as straight. "I was just going because my friends were gay and it was one of those things that we could do when we were fifteen, sixteen," she says. Soon, Lisa met a girl there. They started texting and calling, and Lisa remembers telling her, "Oh no, I'm just coming out with my friends, I'm not gay."

"And then you know what? I was. I still am," she tells us, laughing. Before long, Lisa and the girl from the Wreck Room were officially dating, and at sixteen, Lisa came out to her friends and her mom. She feels she was able to come out that young because of the sanctuary and community she had found at the Wreck Room.

The Wreck Room had this effect on many other people in the Oklahoma City queer community. At Frankie's later that night, we meet Raven, a drag queen who started performing at the Wreck Room more than thirty years ago, in the '90s.

Like Lisa, Raven was fifteen when she first discovered the Wreck Room. "It was during a time where you had to get there early and get in [and] out of drag there, or people would bash you or you could go to jail," Raven describes.

Despite the oppressive attitudes toward gay and gender-nonconforming people in the larger Oklahoma community back then, Raven was fortunate to have a solid support system. "I always had really good gay friends. [. . .] My family was always so open, so if you were a gay kid, you could come to my house and not be judged," Raven explains.

From the time Raven was six or seven, her family made an effort to introduce her to other gay people. "Because I think they kind of knew," Raven reflects, emotion creeping into her voice. Raven's dad was particularly supportive. "We have this thing called *The Gayly*, which has been around forever," Raven begins, referring to the Oklahoma City–based LGBTQ+ publication that was founded in 1983. Raven's dad would collect editions. "And then when nobody else was around, he would show them to me," Raven recounts. "That was the first time I had ever seen somebody in drag."

It was Raven's dad who first encouraged her to go to the Wreck Room. "My dad had a friend that he worked with who had a gay son in the military. [. . .] On the weekends [his son] would go to the Wreck Room because he still wasn't of age," Raven says. Upon her father's suggestion, Raven joined this friend at a Saturday night show.

She describes the Wreck Room as dark, filled with fog and flashing club lights, music pumping through the speakers. "Kind of what you see portrayed in any gay club movie from, like, the early '90s, but not as sketchy," Raven details. From that moment, she was home.

These early exposures to drag and to queer community were revolutionary experiences for Raven, who had been seeing a therapist to sort through her feelings about gender and sexuality. "Once I saw the drag queens, I was like, 'Oh, I can do that, and I can still be who I was born as,'" Raven explains.

A few visits later, Raven met the show host at the time, Desiree Turrelle. "Desiree was really good about helping new queens," Raven says. Desiree handed Raven a list of what she would need to get started in drag.

"Come next Saturday. You can do the late show. Bring what you have; I'll do the rest. And we'll see how you do," Desiree instructed Raven.

"Apparently, I followed the directions and impress[ed her], because I was booked on the late show for the next six months, every Saturday," Raven recalls with pride.

The late show was the coveted slot at the Wreck Room. There was an early show each night at 10 p.m. as well, but the earlier crowd always consisted of underage kids, who weren't coming with cash to tip their performers. Instead, they tipped with tokens, which the Wreck Room would hand out at the beginning of the night, and which performers could then redeem for sodas and snacks.

The late show, which started at 2:30 a.m., was the real moneymaker. "All the older people would come from the bars to sober up," Raven explains. "We were in tattered costumes and probably really bad Halloween wigs and whatever makeup we could figure out together. But the energy would be so crazy because [. . .] they're drunk, they're giving us all this money [. . .] and so to us, we're superstars. Like, we're rich," Raven recalls. "At sixteen years old, sometimes you're going home with like five to six hundred bucks in tips."

Today, Raven performs weekly at Frankie's. Here, she's found a community unlike anything she has previously experienced. "It's just so different that it's almost like you don't believe it's real. You know, we always say, as gay people, [that] we make our own family. And yes, I have done that through my life. But I didn't expect that at this point—at forty-three—to have a whole other family," Raven marvels.

It's a Tuesday night when we visit Frankie's, and there's no drag show for us to see. Instead, Tuesday at Frankie's just so happens to be "family night," the one night a week where performers, staff, and their closest friends come in for a night off. Walking in on this intimate evening, as out-of-towners with our microphones and headsets, feels a bit intimidating. Long tables are pushed together in the center of the room, and a group of about twenty regulars and staff members lounge around them, chatting energetically, sipping their drinks, and smoking.

We only have a moment to take it all in before Frankie's founder and owner, Tracey—in her sixties, butch, and sipping a Michelob Ultra—ushers us in, warmly introducing us to everyone. We are welcomed into the group with much enthusiasm, offered drink recommendations, and challenged to games of darts.

Tracey owns and runs Frankie's with her wife, Ann. A bit older than Raven or Lisa, she didn't have the Wreck Room to anchor her as a young queer person in OKC. In fact, she had a very different journey to the LGBTQ+ community and to her own identity. After high school, she played basketball for Oklahoma State University. "I was a college athlete, so I had to sign a morals clause to play sports," Tracey tells us. A morals clause prohibits certain behavior in one's personal life that is deemed immoral, and according to Tracey, at OSU in the late 1970s, this included homosexual behavior.

"You couldn't be gay," says Tracey. Or rather, you couldn't get *caught* being gay. "Coaches were not dumb," Tracey remarks. They knew they had gay players on their teams. They instructed Tracey not to wear anything that could identify her as an OSU athlete—such as her letter jacket—while doing anything that could violate the morals clause.

For her first few years at OSU, Tracey didn't give her coaches' advice much thought. She was entirely focused on playing basketball and altogether uninterested in dating. Then, the summer before her junior year, everything changed. "I remember the whole night vividly," Tracey tells us. "I was playing softball in the summer [. . .] and it was the last game." Afterward, some of Tracey's teammates invited her out to a bar in Oklahoma City. "I didn't realize I was in a gay bar 'til it got late. And then I'm like, 'Oh, there are girls making out by the bathroom!'" From that moment on, Tracey knew. "It was kind of a realization that that was my comfort place.

And then later, I looked back and there were lots of signs. I just didn't recognize them or act on them."

The next morning, one of Tracey's teammates called to check on her. "We're going back today. Do you want to go?" the friend asked.

"I do," said Tracey.

"And the rest is history. Here we are," Tracey tells us, sitting in the backyard at Frankie's. It would be many years, and a few careers, before Tracey could be truly out, never mind open a lesbian bar of her own. Following college, Tracey faced another morals clause as a teacher. "And being gay was immoral, and I could be fired," Tracey adds.

In 1988, Oklahoma City held its first ever Pride parade, but due to her teaching position, Tracey couldn't go. "There were [news] cameras," she clarifies. "I could go in the bar, but I couldn't go where I might be filmed because I would lose my job." Even going to the bars, she had to take precautions.

"You had to actually sign in at the bar, so that if [the government] ever wanted to check to see if you were eligible to vote or eligible to work with children [they could]," Tracey explains. Bars complied with this policy, but didn't cross-check signatures with IDs, so Tracey always gave a false one. She also always parked in the lot behind the bar, because if you parked on the street, the cops could identify you by your plate number.

Eventually, Tracey landed a job as a therapist at Red Rock Behavioral Health Services. For the first time in her life, she could be publicly out at work. There were no morals clauses in her contract, and what's more, her colleagues were accepting. Outside of work, she could finally go to Pride events and gay bars without fear of losing her job. One of her go-to spots became Partners and its sister bar Partners II, founded in 1996 by a woman named Kay Thomas.

Through the Partners' dart league, Tracey eventually met Ann. According to Ann, their romance kicked off at Pride in 2014.

"How do I get on your list, to date?" Ann inquired.

"For you? Just ask," replied Tracey.

"Well, I'm asking," said Ann.

"And I was the last one on her list," Ann laughs.

Tracey remembers it slightly differently. "It is not a list," she insists. "At the time, what I called it was 'play-dating.' I'm between relationships, I don't want to be in one." In Tracey's memory, Ann asked for one of these play-dates and Tracey gladly obliged.

Around this time, Ann and Tracey started to notice that business at Partners and Partners II was drastically slowing. "It used to be [that] those two lesbian bars, side by side, were packed every weekend," Ann remembers. "We could see that the bar was declining [. . .] and we didn't want to see it die," Ann adds. So, in 2017, when she and Tracey got a phone call from Kay, asking if they wanted to buy one of her two bars, they said yes.

Later that year, Tracy and Ann officially took over Partners II, renaming it Frankie's. The biggest change they made was making the space all-inclusive. The original Partners was exclusively for women. "They wanted a safe space for women, I totally understand that. A lot of the men's bars were the same way—they wanted a safe space for men," Tracey says. But this was never the way she imagined running her own place.

Today, while Frankie's is run by queer women and honors its history of catering to lesbians, Ann and Tracey are intentional about welcoming everyone. "We just wanted a place where all my friends could go at the same time, which has worked out really well for us," Tracey says.

This shift has been extremely good for business. To celebrate the opening of the new bar, Tracey and Ann invited a group of their friends, from all walks of life, to come paint and rebrand as Frankie's. "We had some trans men, we had some trans women, we had a bunch of lesbians, we had some gay men—they all came in and helped us just get open. We started out pretty successful for a brand-new bar because we already had those friends. And then they told their friends, and it was cool. It still is cool," Tracey recounts.

By spring of 2022, Tracey and Ann bought a larger space just a few blocks south of the original location. They gut-renovated the new building, which offers about eight hundred square feet of additional space, plus ample parking and a large front patio. "We were able to custom design where we wanted everything," Tracey tells us recently, over the phone. She held the needs and desires of their performers and patrons at the center of all their design decisions; one must-have was a large dressing room. "So many times [performers are] just crammed in a closet somewhere. They're expected to bring business to your bar, and you make money off them, but then they're not really catered to. And we wanted to cater to the performers."

It feels particularly important to protect drag artists at Frankie's these days, given the introduction of Oklahoma Senate Bill 550, which seeks to criminalize drag performances anywhere children might be present.[3] On paper, this bill wouldn't affect Frankie's operations, but Tracey worries about its implications for the community outside the walls of her bar. "[For] some of these performers, it takes them two or three hours to get their face on, [. . . so] they [get ready] at home," Tracey explains. "And what if they stop for gas or a soda on their way to Frankie's? Are they open to a fine and jail time because they have the drag face on?" Tracey questions. The bill could have dangerous consequences for the trans community, too. After all, who gets to decide whether someone is trans or whether someone is in drag?

"There's always a fear that when things get ugly, that people start hiding, staying at home and being afraid to go out," Tracey says. But fortunately, this isn't what she sees happening. Frankie's has seen a big influx of new, young drag artists in the past few years. "There's lots of kids performing in Oklahoma, which is odd 'cause it's such a red state, but they're all looking for safe places," Tracey asserts. "The political climate in Oklahoma is dangerously scary, you know? But they're not hiding."

Chapter Twenty-Seven

PEARL BAR

BECOMING HUMAN

HOUSTON, TX

Julie Mabry, owner and founder of Houston's Pearl Bar, has known she wanted to open a lesbian bar since she was a teenager. She can trace the desire back to the early '90s, when she first saw her older sibling, Sarah, in a gay bar. When Julie and Sarah were teenagers, their family relocated to San Antonio from Albuquerque, New Mexico. Sarah, visibly queer with a mohawk and shaved sides, had a hard time fitting in, while Julie, adaptable and social, adjusted with ease. Still, like most younger siblings, Julie longed to do everything her older sibling did. Their mother even suspected Julie's burgeoning queerness stemmed from her desire to be like Sarah. But Julie assures us that these feelings were her own. "I've known since I was really young," she says. "I always had crushes on my friends."

As a teenager, Julie also always had crushes on Sarah's friends, alluring and older. She would often tag along with the group, her first foray into the gay community. "We would go to this park called Olmos Park [. . .] and then we would go to the club," Julie details.

Sarah never minded having Julie tag along. But, outside of their social group, Sarah was struggling. "I hated high school," Sarah tells us. "There [were] probably like three gay people in my school and everybody else was into football and cheerleading and it was torture." All Sarah's classmates had to do was look at them to know they didn't fit in. "I dressed kind of punk rock. I wasn't a normal girl. I dressed like a boy. [. . .] I was called a dyke all the time, and I was bullied."

Sarah started skipping school—mainly, PE. "I hate[d] dressing up in the locker room with the other girls," Sarah explains. It wasn't just about their sexuality; Sarah was also experiencing gender dysphoria. "My body was more mature, was very much a woman['s], and I didn't identify with that," they say. At the time though, they didn't have the language to express any of this. "If I was fourteen today, I would transition. I didn't know [gender dysphoria was] what I was going through, and my mom didn't know, and she didn't understand. [. . .] Back then, it was a mental illness."

Outside of school, Sarah began seeking community in the gay bars. "I saw people that were like me, that were being who they were. And it just made me feel comfortable," Sarah remembers. When Julie was sixteen, she joined Sarah—then nineteen—for her first night out at a gay bar, The Bonham in San Antonio. For Julie, watching Sarah in this space was revolutionary. She saw Sarah's shoulders drop, watched them "become a human," as Julie puts it, "happy, dancing, socializing." This was the moment that changed everything for Julie, when she realized that "a bar in our community is a house, a home for people, and a family."

From that night on, Julie knew what she wanted to do with the rest of her life. "I became obsessed with wanting to open a lesbian bar," she says. She did a little bit of everything in her first years out of high school. She tried community college, worked in real estate, worked in the stock market. "But for the majority of the time, [I] was in the service industry. I was just a hustler from day one," Julie tells us.

At twenty-four, she moved to Houston. She was drawn to the vibrant queer community and the more open, liberal environment. She spent a lot of time in Houston's LGBTQ+ bars and clubs. Her go-to spot was a lesbian bar called Chances, which ran from 1994 to 2010. But Julie didn't go to party; she went to study. "I would just go in there and watch the customers, [. . .] whether they drink beer, what kind of liquor they drink, what music they listen to," Julie describes.

Then, in the early 2000s, Julie started working as a lesbian party promoter. She worked her way up into part ownership of local lesbian bar The Usual, which was right around the corner from an existing spot called Pearl Bar. The old Pearl Bar wasn't explicitly a gay bar, but it was known for being gay-friendly. Around the time Julie left The Usual, the original Pearl Bar was evicted, and Julie saw an opportunity, taking over the lease.

She decided to keep the Pearl Bar name. "It already had a great reputation in the gay community, and it's stuck," Julie explains. On October 12, 2013, Pearl Bar as we know it today opened its doors. When we visit on a Thursday night in 2021 on the heels of the pandemic, Pearl Bar is bustling. It's steak night, and Julie herself is the grill master. Her long, blonde hair pulled back into a messy bun, she is frantically preparing for the night ahead when we arrive at opening.

At first, we're not sure whether she'll have the time to talk to us, or whether she wants to, for that matter, but once the grill is lit and the steaks are served, she settles at a picnic table. Dusk has fallen and cicadas chirp loudly in trees above. The patio's bright string lights blink on. Steak night is a lot of work, Julie tells us. "But I like doing it," she says. "It's kind of like being able to dine with your friends, and I still get to interact with the customers. I don't drink. I'm going to be nine years' sober on November 7th. So, I don't typically come up here and drink and hang out and socialize like that. [Steak night]'s kind of my socializing time."

Julie's relationship with alcohol had gotten somewhat out of control during her years bartending and party promoting. "Probably why I had to quit drinking [is] because I started at sixteen," she says, reflecting on the shots she used to sneak when she went out with Sarah as a teenager.

"There is a lot of addiction in and among the queer community," Julie points out, and it's true. For so many queer people—like Sarah and Julie—it can be toxic when the only safe spaces available to you are so deeply associated with alcohol. As a sober bar owner, Julie works hard to foster a culture that doesn't entirely hinge on drinking. "There's a lot of people that come in and just have a Topo Chico or a Coke, and they'll sit here for two or three hours either by themselves or with their friends because this is still their safe place," Julie emphasizes.

Julie also acts as a resource for people in the community who are struggling with alcoholism and addiction. "I will talk to people, or they'll come talk to me about it if they need advice. And I've helped quite a few people get sober and they still come to Pearl," Julie says.

Sarah got sober soon after Julie did. "I struggled with addiction from the age of, like, eighteen," they confess. Their addiction was largely fueled by gender dysphoria: "I didn't feel comfortable in my body, and the first time drugs were offered to me, that was my escape. Boom. And I grabbed onto it."

"I would stop and start and stop and start," they recount. Then, the same month that Pearl Bar opened, Sarah lost their own business and decided it was time to get help. "Something just shifted and it worked. I attend Crystal Meth Anonymous meetings, and I have stayed sober through that and [by] also doing Refuge Recovery, which is a Buddhist-based recovery program," Sarah says.

Shortly after getting sober, Sarah's sponsor bought them their first chest binder. "The first time I put it on, I came out with tears in my eyes. [. . .] I didn't even know that those things existed. I just always wore sports bras that were like seven sizes too small, you know? Cutting off my circulation," they describe.

Today, Sarah works for the very agency that helped them get clean. They're a licensed chemical dependency counselor and a case manager at Angela House, an organization that helps women transition into society following incarceration.

More than three decades after their days of skipping PE class and sneaking out to the gay bars, Sarah still doesn't feel quite at home in their body. They're making plans to undergo top surgery. "I've lived this long," they explain, "I just want my body to look the way I want it to look. So, I'm planning on [getting the surgery] this year. [. . .] I do want to have these suckers off my chest."

Sarah has spent a lot of time thinking about what aspects of social and medical transition might be right for them. "I think I've come to the realization that I'm just a lesbian that wants to have my breasts cut off. [. . .] If I was like fifteen, and I was going to have to start my whole life over, absolutely. I would be a male," they say. But today, in their fifties, that feels out of reach. "I don't have the energy in me to fight that fight and do that explaining and change careers," they add. They would no longer be able to work at Angela House, as it's a female-only facility. So, their primary focus is on feeling more comfortable in their body: "This is not the body I'm supposed to be in. I don't identify with this body at all."

A few years after Pearl Bar opened, Sarah finally learned that they had personally inspired Julie's lifelong dream to run a lesbian bar. "I didn't know at the time that she was watching me struggle and it was affecting her too. [. . .] It's not something that she and I talked about," Sarah explains. Thinking back to that fateful evening at The Bonham back in San Antonio,

Sarah reflects: "I never knew that she saw it. [. . .] She saw me being who I was; she saw me being comfortable in my own skin in that environment."

"She was like a sponge," Sarah begins, describing teenage Julie that night, "and she was absorbing all that. And it was forming her to be the person that she is today." And today, Julie and Pearl Bar remain a safe place to land for countless other young queer people. Julie witnesses them walk into the bar and relax, just as teenage Sarah did all those years ago.

Chapter Twenty-Eight

SUE ELLEN'S

A QUEER BAR EMPIRE

DALLAS, TX

Kathy Jack had many career paths before she opened Dallas's lesbian bar Sue Ellen's in 1986. "I've been all over the map," she tells us. "I think that's why my name is Jack, because you know, 'jack of all trades, master of none.'" She initially wanted to be a horseback rider; she trained horses for equestrian competitions until she was injured and couldn't ride anymore. Then she went to beauty school to become a hairdresser, but dropped out when her then-girlfriend, also a hairdresser, grew jealous and competitive. She then embarked on her third, and most despised, career: working in an auto parts shop.

Through all her shifting jobs, the Dallas gay bar scene was a constant in Kathy's life. Back in the late 1970s, she frequented a spot called Boot Camp, where there was always a rowdy crowd. "One side of it was for women and the other side of it was for men," Kathy describes. When she was a teenager, she also began patronizing a club called the Conference Room. There, IDs were rarely checked, so while Kathy didn't have to worry about getting in trouble with the bouncer, she did need to worry about the police. And not just because she was underage.

"Back then, if the cops came in the bar and saw you sitting with someone [. . .] you're going to jail. If they caught you dancing, you're going to jail. Touching in any way, you're going to jail," Kathy says. The Conference Room had a clever system to warn patrons of impending raids. "When you walked in the door, there was a red light," Kathy recalls. If staff spotted police approaching the bar, they would turn the red light on, and patrons knew exactly what to do. If you were of age, you stopped dancing, kissing, holding hands, or touching in any way. And if you were underage, you ran.

"All the underage kids would go in the women's bathroom, and we had to climb out of the window," Kathy reminisces. "I never did get hurt or caught," she says, "but several of my friends did." Kathy remembers one particularly violent cop who had a penchant for picking on the gay kids in the bars. "They called him Red because his hair was red. He was a horrible man. I saw him kicking, beating several of my friends. [. . .] He'd beat the shit out of you and throw you down on the ground, put cuffs on you, and take you to jail. And that's just the way things were back then."

None of this deterred Kathy from making her first foray into the bar business herself in 1982. She hated her job at the auto parts shop, so she spent all her time after work drowning her sorrows at a tiny lesbian country-western bar called High Country, located in Oak Lawn, Dallas's burgeoning gayborhood. There, Kathy quickly befriended the owner, a man named Ray, who eventually offered her a manager job for a new business venture: a ladies' dance bar. "I didn't know how to bartend. I didn't know anything about running a bar. But he had faith in me that I could do it. And he gave me a job," Kathy recalls.

Later that year, Kathy opened The Unicorn, a women's bar with a dance floor in Oak Lawn. "[Ray] gave me the keys and got me started," Kathy recounts, "and sometimes I don't know whether to thank him or punch him in the face, but it's been a great ride."

In the mid-1980s, while Kathy was managing The Unicorn, the relationship between the Dallas LGBTQ+ community and the local police began to improve. This was largely due to the efforts of a man named Earl Newsome, a sergeant with the Dallas Police Department (DPD). While many officers begrudged working in the gayborhood, Newsome didn't mind "because a person's sexual preference or orientation had never been anything to worry about," he reasoned in a 1989 interview.[1]

The DPD wouldn't appoint an official LGBTQ+ liaison until the early 1990s,[2] after finally dissolving their policy barring homosexuals from being hired.[3] Yet, nearly a decade prior, Newsome became a de facto liaison. Just two weeks into his assignment in Oak Lawn, Newsome's captain sent him to talk with members of the Dallas Gay Alliance.[4] They were planning a rally in the park to coincide with the Republican National Convention happening in the city that summer.

"I'm going to come to the rally," Newsome told the group.[5] Due to the presence of the Republican convention, he was concerned about the safety of the rally goers, and since he didn't have an officer officially scheduled to work the event, he showed up himself. At the rally, he listened attentively to the speeches and connected with a number of gay leaders and activists, kicking off his long-standing relationship with the Dallas LGBTQ+ community.

Newsome made it his mission to ensure that all officers under his direction treated gay people in Oak Lawn fairly and respectfully. When asked if he ever got flak from his fellow officers, Newsome replied: "Lots of it. The majority of it is in fun. It is not unusual for me to be introduced as the Queer Sergeant."[6] Snide remarks aside, as a straight, white man, Newsome was largely tolerated in the Dallas Police Department. He was even able to restructure the Dallas Police Academy's cultural training as it related to the gay community, a significant change at a time when the department outright refused to bring in any LGBTQ+ people to do this work directly.

In the gay community, Newsome was largely revered for his efforts. He served as the grand marshal for both the 1987 Dallas Freedom Day Parade, a precursor to Dallas Pride, and the 1987 Texas Gay Rodeo.[7] A 1989 article in LGBTQ+ magazine *This Week in Texas* said: "Prior to Newsome's arrival in Oak Lawn, it was not uncommon—as recently as 1984—for gay bars to be raided and for gays and lesbians to be harassed by officers and gay bashers. Since Newsome's arrival on the gay turf, hostility and violence have subsided."[8]

Kathy Jack agreed. "He actually [. . .] had a meeting with everyone at one of our bars," she recalls.

"Things are gonna change. There's no reason for all this to be happening," Kathy remembers him saying, in reference to the frequent raids and harassment.

As a bar owner, Kathy never had to contend with the kind of police harassment she had witnessed as a teen—in large part thanks to Newsome's efforts. Her first lesbian bar, The Unicorn, ran smoothly for about four years, closing in January of 1986. The following April, she got a job at another gay bar in Oak Lawn, which was owned by a company called Caven Enterprises.

From the 1980s to now, Caven Enterprises has owned nearly all the gay bars in Oak Lawn. In 1986, all four Caven bars were boy bars—it was a male-dominated and somewhat misogynistic environment. So, despite her years of management experience, Kathy was hired to work the door.

But just three months later, the manager of another Caven-owned bar, Village Station, was fired. "They immediately put me in his spot," Kathy says, "and it was a shock for everyone." Of the twenty-something staff members who now reported to Kathy, only one was a woman, and she and Kathy were among only three women working for all of Caven Enterprises.

"There was a lot of pushback from the employees," Kathy recalls. "It was a tough first couple of months. They were used to the guys being the managers [who] kind of let them do whatever they wanted to do, and I don't manage that way. I'm getting a little easier to work for now because I'm getting older, but back then I was young and hungry."

Her staff made their dissatisfaction known: "I got 'bitch,' 'dyke,' they would call me names [. . .] under their breath," Kathy says. For the most part, she ignored them. "I figured the more they got to know me, the more, hopefully, they would respect me and like me, and that's exactly what happened," she reflects.

Village Station "was predominantly a men's dance club," Kathy says. "As I worked there, year after year, I got a lot of women that were coming in looking for a place because they didn't have a dance club anymore." So, Kathy pitched a women's bar to her bosses.

"Well, we don't know anything about lesbians," they countered.

"Well, I certainly do," Kathy told them.

Eventually, after many months of asking, Caven Enterprises said yes. "It took about a year and a half to get [the bar] off the ground," Kathy remembers, "and we opened up in January of 1989." They named it Sue Ellen's.

At the time, Sue Ellen's was shinier and fancier than any of the other bars on the strip. "They really went all out because they'd never done a bar for women before," Kathy explains. "They wanted to make it pretty. And it really was striking. And the guys got very jealous." But Kathy never made any attempt to keep the boys out. In fact, she wanted to see more commingling of the still staunchly divided gay and lesbian communities in Dallas.

At first, the men refused to enter the women's bar. "Some of my best customers that I had in the bar literally next door would walk right by me like they didn't even know me and wouldn't come in," Kathy says of her old regulars from Village Station. Finally, when a few men ventured into

Sue Ellen's one evening, Kathy reassured them they were welcome. "That's when things started changing," Kathy tells us.

In 2008, Sue Ellen's moved to their current, larger location: a two-story club on Throckmorton Street. Today, it's by far the biggest lesbian bar I have ever stepped foot in. It has two levels of outdoor patio seating, a stage, dressing rooms, three pool tables, a spacious dance floor, and three separate bars. The massive, rectangular downstairs bar alone can seat at least forty people.

The expansive space is warranted; particularly on the weekends, Sue Ellen's draws a crowd. "Sue Ellen's has *never* done this well," Kathy says, remarking on the spike in business they've seen following the pandemic.

In recent years, the bar has found a loyal base of supporters by way of a local social group called Lez Be Friends. Erica Sanders, a Sue Ellen's regular, founded the group in 2021 and it's since grown to over ten thousand Facebook members. "We try to have as many events as we can here," Erica explains. "We come every other Wednesday. [. . .] It's just the culture that we're trying to build here." Supporting their local lesbian bar, both by simply showing up and by cultivating a safe and welcoming environment there, is at the heart of Erica's mission with Lez Be Friends. That's "how we can save all of our bars," Erica says.

Sue Ellen's continues to maintain its identity as a lesbian bar, but draws an expansive, gender-diverse crowd. It's a far cry from the bars of Kathy's young adulthood, where the men and women stood on opposite sides of the room. "It's about forty percent men and sixty percent women on the weekends," Kathy remarks on Sue Ellen's typical demographics. "We [also] have a lot of straight people in the community. [. . .] They come down and they party at the gay bars, and they love it," Kathy adds.

In January of 2025, thirty-six years after opening Sue Ellen's, Kathy Jack retired. Hundreds of people showed up at Sue Ellen's to celebrate Kathy's long career. "I would do it over again, if my body allowed, two more times," she said in her retirement speech, to whoops and laughter from the crowd.[9]

While Kathy's chapter at Sue Ellen's is coming to a close, she feels confident that a long and healthy future lies ahead for the bar. As a large corporation, Caven Enterprises has always offered Sue Ellen's a great deal of security. "Them just going out of business one day [is] not gonna happen," Kathy asserts. "We're thankful that Sue Ellen's got open and it's still gonna be there for years and years to come."

Chapter Twenty-Nine

HERZ

HOW TO MAKE AN UNLIKELY ALLY

MOBILE, AL

Mobile, Alabama, may seem like an unlikely destination for one of the country's small handful of lesbian bars, but from 2019 to 2023 Herz stood proud. A 2025 study ranked the state as the seventh most dangerous in the country for LGBTQ+ people,[1] and it has no statewide policies protecting individuals from discrimination based on gender identity or sexual orientation.[2] Of course, none of this means that Alabama lacks a thriving LGTBQ+ community, particularly in cities such as Birmingham and Mobile. Mobile's official tourism website pronounces that the city "proudly embraces the LGBTQ+ community with open arms" and details the city's annual Pride parades, local LGBTQ+ support groups, LGBTQ+ Mardi Gras societies, and the handful of LGBTQ+ bars.[3]

To find a larger queer scene, Mobile-area folks often make the two-hour drive west to New Orleans. It was one of these pilgrimages that inspired Sheila and Rachel, wives and cofounders of Herz, to open their bar. They had gone to New Orleans for Pride in 2016, and one evening they stumbled into a local gay bar.

"We just strolled in, not having any idea about this bar," Sheila recounts, "and once the bartender noticed that we were in there, he got to yelling and flaming and carrying on." Unbeknownst to Sheila and Rachel, they had just walked into a space purportedly for gay men only. All of a sudden, the two women were being ushered out the door. "It was just horrible. I'm like, 'Well y'all don't have to talk to us like this. We had no idea. We apologize,'" Sheila recalls telling the bartender.

Even in nearby New Orleans, there were no spaces intentionally for LGBTQ+ women. Les Pierres, Charlene's, and Alice Brady's had long since closed their doors. Sheila began thinking about the need for a space in her own area that could center queer women. "I wanted a home for lesbians," she tells us. "I just wanted an atmosphere where lesbians could go and hang out with other lesbians, and [not] have to worry about being kicked out, or having to share it, or be uncomfortable."

Around this time, Sheila retired from a long career in law enforcement and criminal justice. "I did not want to just sit at home," Sheila stresses. "I got this idea in my head one day: maybe I should just open my own bar and be my own boss, and do something fun, something that I enjoy doing."

Rachel was on board. "We passed by this place for about a year, and it was for sale," Rachel tells us as she gestures around her to the building we're standing in on Highway 90 where Herz originally opened. "So finally, we said, 'Let's just buy it and open a bar.'"

Buying the building turned out to be more challenging than Sheila and Rachel had hoped. As two Black women, they faced immediate racial discrimination. When Sheila inquired with the realtor managing the sale of the space, the first words out of his mouth were: "Well, it's not for lease; it's for sale."

"I realize that," Sheila told him.

"Well, you have to put 25 percent down," he said.

"Okay, is there any way I can look at the bar, please?" Sheila asked.

"So, you're willing to pay 25 percent down?" the man prodded, his words tinged with disbelief that Sheila would be able to afford it.

Knowing when to walk away, Sheila told him to forget it. "Why am I doing this? Let me get with my realtor and see what she has to say," Sheila thought to herself. Her realtor came back with a list of potential properties, and of course, the empty bar on Highway 90 was among her top suggestions.

With an entirely women-led team behind them, Sheila and Rachel finally purchased and renovated the space. "I had a female realtor, I have a female loan officer, of course, and all the repairs that were done in the bar were done by females," Sheila emphasizes.

Sheila and Rachel weren't always the out, proud queer women they are today, assembling a badass team of women to open a lesbian bar. Sheila began to understand her own sexuality during her senior year of college, but she didn't tell anyone in her family that she was gay until after she had opened the bar.

"[My brother] knew that I was making an investment in a commercial building," Sheila says. She hoped he would ask her about her business plans, giving her an easy opening to a conversation about her gay identity, but he never did. So finally, she called him up to broach the subject. "He was excited about it," Sheila recalls, "and I could just see the smile on his face, although it was over the phone."

Unlike Sheila, Rachel never had to come out to her family. "My mother was a lesbian, and I've always had two moms. So, I understood what it was to love a woman," Rachel explains.

Whether she was bringing home boyfriends or girlfriends—over the years Rachel had both—she suspects her mom always knew she was gay. "She would always say, 'Rachel, you're more like me than any of my children,'" she recalls. "That was an indication right there. Stop wasting your time," Rachel says with a laugh, alluding to the many years she spent married to a man.

Even with lesbian parents, the pull of compulsory heterosexuality was strong, and Rachel ended up marrying a man—"a pastor," she adds laughing. "But the whole time I was married to [my ex-husband], he knew, and I knew, that I was gay," she reflects. He tried for many years to be understanding, but ultimately, Rachel's sexuality was beyond his comprehension—something that made him angry. Rachel stayed married for twenty-two years before finally leaving, not because of a sudden realization about her identity, but because the marriage itself wasn't working. "I left the marriage because it was a broken marriage. So, it was time to go."

When Sheila and Rachel first met, Rachel was still with her husband. "She was involved with someone, and I was involved with someone," Sheila explains. Still, they exchanged numbers and fell in and out of contact over the decades, "as friends, of course," Sheila clarifies, affirming that there wasn't an immediate, romantic connection.

Then, in 2014, their paths crossed again. "[Sheila] came to a church event that I was having, and that is when we rekindled," Rachel recalls.

"And it just happened from there," Sheila says with a smile, referring to their decade-plus-long relationship.

Despite having spent much of her life around the church—Rachel was married to a pastor, after all—she is no longer involved with any particular denomination or place of worship. "Rather than being a religious person, I'm more of a spiritual person," Rachel remarks. "I don't have anything against what anyone else believes. I've just developed my own systems of beliefs, and it doesn't require me to have a relationship with the church."

In January of 2021, Rachel and Sheila got married at Las Vegas's legendary Chapel of Crystals: not a traditional church, but the ceremony was undoubtedly meaningful and spiritual. Herz became a spiritual place for Rachel, too. "The energy in here is just so great. You walk in and you feel it, and I attribute that to [the bar] being spiritual," Rachel asserts.

We visited Herz on the evening of its two-year anniversary party, and I can feel what Rachel means. As the night goes on, the sky over the bar streaks with bright pink and purple, matching the neon lights of the bar's interior, which cast everything and everyone in a vibrant pink glow. A live band plays, drinks flow, and conversations and laughter overlap on the patio.

From outside, Herz is unassuming. It's about eight miles from downtown Mobile and sits across from a small shopping plaza and next door to the retro-looking Bama Motel. The bar itself is a squat brown-and-tan building with small, shaded windows.

To a passing stranger, the only indication that Herz is a gay bar is the classic white marquee on the side of the building, its interchangeable letters spelling out DRAG BRUNCH SUN OCT 3RD. The bar's most attention-grabbing feature is its large, glowing pylon sign, featuring the Herz name and logo: the silhouettes of two women in high heels, sipping drinks. To an in-the-know queer, the silhouettes of course read as hyper-femme lesbians. To straight strangers, they might be mistaken for strippers.

Between the sign and the discreteness of the building itself, it's not unusual for straight men to wander in thinking it's a strip club. But this is on purpose. "That's why I did it, you know? Sex sells," Rachel says matter-of-factly. "If I put that rainbow flag up there, [. . .] that [symbol] would have been a reason for people not to stop by. [. . .] They'll go to the strip club before a gay bar."

When straight men wandered into the bar looking for strippers, Rachel would tell them, "Oh yeah, they're in the bathroom. Have a seat, let me get you a beer."

They'd get to talking, and after a few minutes, the men would say to Rachel, "This is not a strip club, is it?"

"No, but you don't want to leave, do you?" Rachel would counter.

Time and time again, this exchange is how Herz began to build a patronage of unexpected allies. "This is how we got most of our straight clientele," Rachel explains, "and we have quite a large straight clientele. It's a nuthouse in here, they love it."

In April 2023, Herz closed its doors for good. After nearly four years at the heart of Mobile's queer community, Sheila and Rachel were ready to move on to their next chapter. Though the bar is gone, its legacy endures. In the comments of a Facebook post announcing the closure, patrons expressed heartfelt gratitude for the safety and comfort Herz provided. And scattered throughout the Gulf Coast are countless straight men who stumbled in looking for strippers, only to get a crash course in LGBTQ+ community instead, leaving with an open mind, a bit more empathy, and a story they're likely still telling today.

Chapter Thirty

MY SISTER'S ROOM

WHEN YOUR HEALTH INSURANCE FAILS, YOUR LESBIAN BAR SHOWS UP

ATLANTA, GA

My Sister's Room, or MSR for short, has gone through six different iterations in its thirty years of business. It's taken many shapes, but it has always offered safety and sanctuary for the queer community in Georgia.

The bar was born out of another spot in midtown Atlanta—the now-closed DuPree's—which one Yelp review describes as "a smoke-filled lesbian-heavy hipster haven."[1] In 1996, a DuPree's bartender named Susan Musselwhite, who had built up quite the lesbian following, opened a second spot next door: My Sister's Room.

After just a year in midtown Atlanta, MSR had outgrown its original space, and Susan moved the bar to Decatur, Georgia, a city just east of Atlanta. This is where current MSR owner Jen Maguire first discovered the bar. "It was a really cool venue," Jen describes. "It was actually like a horse barn, where people danced inside, and then it was mainly outdoors and had a big outdoor stage." Jen would often spend weekends performing on that stage as a drag king.

After ten years of business in Decatur, the barn was torn down for condos, and MSR moved to its third location, in East Atlanta. Jen will always remember this spot as the place she met her wife Jami in 2008.

Jen and Jami quickly became business partners in addition to romantic partners. "We collaborated as a team to start throwing these crazy parties at MSR," Jen says. "[Jami's] like the marketing, the flyers, the behind the scenes, more of the introvert, where[as] I'm the extrovert."

In 2011, Susan Musselwhite was ready to sell MSR and approached Jen and Jami, thinking they would be the ideal pair to lead the bar into the next era. "We never anticipated owning a bar," Jen insists. "I came from eighteen years [of] finance, real estate investment background. My wife, she flipped and built houses on the side." After a bit of prodding from Jami, they purchased MSR, and in 2014, they relocated to Midtown.

"We just wanted to get back to the gay Mecca. Midtown is where all the gays are, and lesbians," Jen explains. In 2018, they moved MSR a few doors down to its fifth location, a two-story, 5,200-square-foot, hundred-year-old building with a sprawling back patio. This is the spot we visited in October of 2021, during Atlanta Pride. We arrive in the late afternoon, and already, the patio is packed and the crowd on the basement dance floor is getting rowdy.

Working the door, we meet Jill, who has one of the most important jobs here at MSR: head of security. Jill first discovered MSR back at the Decatur location—the one in the big, open barn. "I was a twenty-year-old in college, and [I had just come] out of the closet, and I was surrounded by beautiful women. So yeah, it was great," she recalls. What was not great was Jill's quickly spiraling relationship with alcohol. "I just wanted to go out and get wasted. So that's what I did every weekend with my group of friends," Jill details. "I was getting angry all the time when I was drinking, punching random people in parking lots. It got to a very crazy point that was not good for my health or my well-being, and that's not the person that I wanted to be."

Everything changed when Jill ran into Jen Maguire at a Pink concert in 2011. "I saw her for the first time in a long time," Jill remembers, "and she came up to me and patted me on the arm." The pair had become friends years before through the drag king scene in Atlanta.

"You got some broad shoulders; you want to work security for me?" Jen asked.

She might have been joking, but Jill took the idea seriously. "I came in just on a whim, because I'd never done any sort of security before in my life—I am a PE teacher by day. I have not looked back since," Jill tells us.

A job at a bar isn't necessarily the best choice for someone struggling with their relationship with alcohol, but for Jill, it was exactly what she needed. By working security, Jill gets to be part of the community that she loves so much, and since she's not allowed to drink on the job, there's a clear boundary between her and alcohol. "Instead of going out and having party friends, I come here and work," Jill reflects, "and so, the regulars are kind of my friends now. And the people that work with me are obviously my friends and family."

Like Jill, many people have found so much more than a place to party at MSR. For Skyler Jay—a longtime MSR regular and a local celebrity due to his appearance on a 2015 episode of *Queer Eye*—the bar has been a central part of his journey to his trans identity.

Skyler first found MSR through Atlanta's drag scene. "I did drag for several years before I started transitioning medically," Skyler explains. "I was meeting so many trans people and queer people [at MSR], specifically; that really just helped me figure out a lot of my shit."

When *Queer Eye* came to Atlanta seeking an out trans man to feature in an episode, several local LGBTQ+ organizations gave them Skyler's name. He was already well known in the community, both as a drag performer and also as the director of operations for the nonprofit Aadya Rising, an organization with a mission to support at-risk and marginalized LGBTQ+ people.[2] He also happened to be raising funds for his top surgery, a process the episode of *Queer Eye* documented.

"I actually filmed a lot of the show in [MSR] because this bar helped me raise money for my top surgery," Skyler tells us. "Drag shows, bake sales, art sales: they let me use their space as an open forum to bring in anything that I could to raise money." The bar would pitch in too, donating a keg or giving Skyler the night's door sales.

"MSR actually often opens its doors on Sundays for day-party shows to help different trans people in the community raise funds like they did for me. So, this is not an uncommon practice," Skyler says. Many trans people in Atlanta have had to figure out how to fund their surgeries out-of-pocket because the state of Georgia does not require private health insurance companies to cover gender-affirming surgeries.[3]

Skyler, though, as a University of Georgia employee, had state health insurance, not private. While filming *Queer Eye*, in addition to fundraising, he was also in the process of suing the state for refusing to cover the procedure. "They had a specific exclusion for trans people to receive the health care, even though a double mastectomy for a cisgender person or a gynecomastia for a cisgender man was covered," Skyler highlights.

So, Skyler took the state to court. "My lawyers were actually trans people themselves that specialize in removing [transgender healthcare exclusion policies] throughout the nation," he says. This lawsuit was part of the reason he said yes to *Queer Eye*. "I knew that if I went on the show, and leveraged all the media attention, that would help me win my case," Skyler explains. And it worked. "In October of 2019, the case closed in my favor, and they removed the transgender healthcare exclusions for 160,000 state employees, the first Southern state to do so and only the eighth state in the nation to do so."

Unfortunately, at the time of writing this, Georgia Senate Bill 39 threatens to reverse the outcome of Skyler's lawsuit. The bill, which has passed the state senate but has yet to pass the house, would prohibit state health insurance plans from covering all gender-affirming medical care beginning in January of 2026.[4]

Still, nothing can undo the six years of access to necessary and life-saving care that Skyler and his team won for trans Georgians, nor can it diminish the lasting impact of trans folks like Skyler openly and visibly fighting for protections and living authentically. In fact, the opportunity to offer positive representation of trans people on television was another key reason Skyler said yes to *Queer Eye*. "Especially for trans people, like the people you see in the media until very recently, [. . .] it was the dead body on the side of the road or the hooker or the mentally unstable serial killer. Those were the trans tropes that were put in the media, that are fed to people," Skyler explains.

As Skyler grew up without any sort of positive, realistic trans representation in the media, it took meeting his first trans person in real life for him to realize that he had a shot at living an authentic, happy, healthy, successful life. And now, Skyler knows for a fact that his appearance on *Queer Eye* has had the same impact on others. Countless people have told him so, in real life and online. There's one post in particular that has stood out to him. It was from a young person, reflecting on the experience of watching Skyler's episode with their dad. Skyler reads it aloud to us:

"We're watching the new season of *Queer Eye*, and my dad is actually crying over the episode with the trans dude. Like he's talking about his top surgery, and my dad is in tears going, 'When you sculpt the marble, the sculpture is already inside. You're just getting rid of what isn't part of it. He's just getting rid of what isn't part of him.' So, from my old-ass seventy-year-old dad to all my trans people, y'all are marble sculptures and you're perfect."[5]

Just one month after we met Skyler at MSR, Jen and Jami were notified that they had a year to find a new home for the bar, as the current building was going to be torn down and replaced with condos.[6] But MSR isn't just a building; it's a community. Jen and Jami found an even bigger place to hold that community, still in Midtown, Atlanta, on Crescent Avenue. In July of 2022, they moved the bar for a sixth time. The neighborhood is sure to continue shifting, but so too will MSR, reshaping itself again and again to hold space for the people who depend on it.

Chapter Thirty-One

THE LIPSTICK LOUNGE

TAKE ME TO CHURCH

NASHVILLE, TN

The Lipstick Lounge—with its bright purple and hot pink exterior, larger-than-life lip-shaped bench on the sidewalk out front, and glowing neon sign—is impossible to miss. It's Nashville's only lesbian bar, and every night is karaoke night. But on Sundays, the bar transforms into a spiritual haven.

Co-owner and founder Jonda Valentine was raised in the Pentecostal Church in West Virginia, the daughter of a preacher. Now in her sixties, Jonda sports a platinum blonde-white pixie cut and dresses in smart, patterned suits and collared shirts, usually paired with a tie or bowtie. Despite knowing she was gay, at age eighteen she married a man and they soon moved to Nashville and joined Christ Church.[1] After nearly a decade of marriage, Jonda could no longer keep pretending. She came out, divorced her husband, and was kicked out of their congregation.

As the years went by, Jonda grew increasingly lonely and desperately missed the sense of community that the church had once provided. "You didn't just go to church for religion; you went there for fellowship," reflects Christa Suppan, who today co-owns Lipstick with Jonda. "There's something that happens to you when you're basically banished from all the people that you know," Christa voices, "and Lipstick Lounge was the way that Jonda circumvented that and said, 'Okay, well if I can't have my fellowship there, I'll create my own fellowship, with an all-encompassing love and acceptance here at the Lipstick Lounge.'"

In 2002, the Lipstick Lounge, or simply Lipstick, opened its doors to the Nashville community. Christa started out as a bartender. Now in her early fifties, she still has the same radiant smile and warm, nurturing personality that drew in customers all those years ago. "There was nothing like [Lipstick] in Nashville. I've lived here almost thirty years, and it was so nice to go to work and just feel like this is my home. This is my space. I don't have to keep on searching for a place to go and feel comfortable if I want to hold my partner's hand or dance with them," Christa reflects.

After a few months, it became apparent that, from a business perspective, the bar wasn't doing well. Not wanting to give up on the community, Christa came on as a partial owner. Around this time, Christa and Jonda also started dating. "Oh, it was awful," Christa says, as she thinks back on the four-year period. "I wouldn't recommend owning any business with your partner. [. . .] It was hard. Jonda calls [those years] the dark times."

When they broke up, Christa insists "it wasn't for lack of love. [. . .] It was just too much." To this day, they have remained incredibly close. Jonda often says that she and Christa are soulmates—just not in the romantic way people usually imagine. "We're soulmates in a different realm of friendship and kinship and sisterhood," Christa explains.

It only took a few weeks for them to recover from the breakup and find a way forward as friends and business partners. "I was like, here's a great time for us to show people compassion and forgiveness, [by] moving through this and building Lipstick even better," Christa declares.

As with Jonda, it was religion that first instilled in Christa the core values of compassion and forgiveness. "We were the Sunday morning, Sunday night, [and] Wednesday night folks. So, three times a week," Christa says, emphasizing how often her family attended church in her small town outside of Springfield, Illinois. These days, Christa hangs onto the values but could do without the organized religion part. "I feel like religion gets slapped around as far as [you're either] a good person if you go to church, or a bad person if you don't go to church, and I've never seen anything so untrue in my life," she reflects.

For those like Jonda and Christa who no longer feel at home in a more traditional church setting, the Lipstick Lounge has become a source of community, fellowship, and spirituality. "We've literally had church services down there on Sunday mornings, [and] we used to have a choir come in on Sundays during brunch. We've had several preachers do sermons at Lipstick," Christa says.

They've even joked about officially making the bar a church and changing the name to "Our Lady of Lipstick" so they could be exempt from paying taxes. While Lipstick remains legally registered as a bar, there is something undeniably spiritual about the place. "There's definitely some God, universe, whatever your word is, in there," Christa muses.

"One of the main reasons Lipstick is so important to me is that I feel like we give a home and a family to people who have been shunned from their church, from their family," Christa tells us. The staff and customers alike certainly appreciate it. On the night of our visit, we meet Lynn Hearn and his best friend BeBe McQueen. They're both burlesque performers and longtime regulars. Lynn also bartends at Lipstick.

"When your family and life fall apart, you can come to the Lipstick Lounge [to] find a new family," BeBe proclaims. As Lynn and BeBe both tell us, Christa and Jonda fall seamlessly into their roles as parental figures at the helm of this chosen family.

"When I text Christa or call Christa, I call her 'Mom.' [. . .] That is the role that she has taken on for herself," Lynn says.

"If it's muddy in your real life, it doesn't have to be muddy here. She's your mom. There's no question," adds BeBe.

"If you ever run into Jonda [. . .] Jonda's gonna corner you for at least forty-five minutes and tell you how much she loves you. That is the kind of place this is," Lynn details. "This place is about family, and parents build family, [. . .] and that's exactly what Christa and Jonda have done here."

For Christa herself, Lipstick hasn't just granted her a chosen family, it helped her repair her relationship with her own mom.

In 1992, Christa left her family behind in Illinois and moved to Nashville. "I came down here one weekend with one of my friends," she tells us. She remembers loving the way the city made her feel; something about it just fit. "I literally went back to Illinois the next week, packed up my things, and moved down [to Nashville] the following week," Christa says, laughing. "I needed to get out of that small town. It was a little bit too small for me, [. . .] not really where I saw my future at all."

A few years later, in 1996 at around twenty-one years old, Christa came out to her mom, Connie. "What did I do wrong?" was Connie's only response. Needless to say, their relationship grew strained. Then, in 2000, Christa's father unexpectedly passed away. Connie had multiple sclerosis and had used a wheelchair for most of Christa's life, depending on Christa's dad as a caregiver. With him gone, Christa stepped in, moving Connie in with her down in Nashville.

At first, perhaps Christa and Connie were able to skirt around Christa's gay identity, but by 2002, it became hard to avoid. The Lipstick Lounge had opened, and Christa's work and community were deeply grounded in queer identities. Christa would often invite her mom to come to work with her at Lipstick. For a while, the answer was always no.

And then one night, Connie declared: "I think I'd really like to go down there."

"It was so cool. I'm probably gonna cry," Christa says, reflecting on the memory. "When she came in there, it just felt so good to have a part of my family who could see what Lipstick was without having their imagination run amok on what they thought it might be."

Christa thinks that, at least at first, Connie's desire to go to Lipstick was born out of loneliness. "I'm sure she got tired of seeing my face all day long," she jokes. Connie had just lost her husband, had no other family left in Illinois, and many of her friends were older and had also passed away.

Soon, Connie—or "Miss Connie" as she was known there—was a regular. "They just embraced her, and she never thought another thing about it. It was really quite beautiful to see [the community] just love my mother," Christa says.

Eventually, Christa made the challenging decision to put her mom in a nursing home. "I just couldn't take care of her twenty-four hours a day anymore," Christa admits. But nothing could get in the way of Miss Connie's time at the Lipstick Lounge. "She would get on Access-A-Ride and come down on weekends," Christa recalls fondly.

In 2015, Miss Connie passed away. When Christa went to the funeral home to arrange a memorial service, they recommended their smaller chapel, seeing as Connie wasn't from Nashville.

"I'm pretty sure it's gonna be busy," Christa told them, settling instead on the larger chapel.

Of course, the Lipstick Lounge community packed the space. "It was so amazing to see all the people who touched my mom's life. She was able to feel so loved and so surrounded down here in Nashville after she lost my dad, so—pretty cool," Christa says tearfully.

"I hear so many stories of people who've come out to their family and who were discarded and basically just thrown away or kicked out. And it's so hard for me to wrap my mind around that because I know how fortunate I was. It could have been so different," Christa reflects.

This awareness of how close she came to never getting a relationship with her mom is a big part of what motivates Christa to keep the Lipstick Lounge open. So many queer people—particularly in the South—never get a second chance with their family or their church because they're never shown the kind of basic acceptance and understanding that Connie learned at Lipstick. Christa is taking what the space gave her and paying it forward, ensuring it's there to serve as a home, a family, or even a church for anyone who might need it.

Chapter Thirty-Two

BABE'S OF CARYTOWN

THE TALE OF TWO VICKIES

RICHMOND, VA

Babe's of Carytown is a wide brick building with bright-yellow awnings on the corner of South Auburn Avenue and West Cary Street in downtown Richmond. When owner Vicky Hester founded Babe's in 1979, gay bars were technically illegal under Virginia's discriminatory ABC (Alcoholic Beverage Control Authority) regulations.[1]

When Babe's first opened, Vicky had plenty of supporters, but she was also no stranger to ignorance and criticism. Most notably, according to local magazine *Style Weekly*, a fundraiser Babe's hosted for a local businessman who had been injured in a snowboarding accident prompted homophobic harassment.[2] One of the organizers, another local business owner, received an anonymous letter from someone claiming to be a "Richmond Physician," lambasting them for hosting the event in a gay bar. The writer alleged that a patient contacted them, concerned that she had been exposed to STDs at Babe's simply because she was around gay people.[3]

In response, Vicky offered her own statement in the *Style Weekly* article, discrediting the "physician's" claims: "You can do any kind of [public health] research, and [to] my knowledge, of all the things that go around bars, this singles' bar—of mostly women—would be the least likely place to catch anything."

Vicky spent the next forty-six years as a pillar of the Richmond LGBTQ+ community, up until her passing in September of 2025. As the outpouring of love and gratitude in the wake of her death made clear, she was fiercely protective, strong, and generous to a fault. She was notorious for pulling out her checkbook when local organizations were in need; thanks to her frequent donations, the Richmond Metropolitan Community Church even named its food pantry after her. Most of all, though, people remember her for how she made them feel: safe, welcome, and with a place to belong.

Her commitment to the community was evident in the way she ran Babe's: unafraid to stir up controversy in defense of the people she loved. At the height of the COVID-19 pandemic, the bar was embroiled in politically charged dissension surrounding the vaccine. Vicky had firmly instituted a vaccine policy at Babe's, and CBS 6 Richmond ran an article with the headline "Richmond Bar Owner: 'GET YOUR SHOT OR GO SOMEWHERE ELSE.'"[4] Both Vicky and the bar faced some intense backlash from the surrounding area's conservative demographic.

When we visit the bar in 2021, Vicky is altogether uninterested in speaking with us, and understandably so, given her past experiences with the media. We are strangers walking into the bar with a microphone and recorder in hand—not part of the close-knit Richmond LGBTQ+ community. Still, over the course of our two days in Richmond, we connect with a number of folks who are excited to share their stories.

Saturday afternoon, before the bar gets busy, we strike up a conversation with the bartender—a woman named Xtina, or X for short, who tells us she has been coming to Babe's since the '90s. One of her earliest memories of the bar is of "photographs of Melissa Etheridge all the way around the top of the bar marquee," she says. Particularly in the '90s, photos of Melissa Etheridge on the walls were a sure sign you were in a lesbian bar; Etheridge is a singer-songwriter known for her sapphic hits, who got her start playing in lesbian bars in the 1980s and rose to lesbian icon status after publicly coming out in 1993.

X also recalls lots of line dancing and lots of queer women, though she says that the bar has never felt exclusively lesbian. In the decades since X's first visit, Babe's has become more gender diverse. "But I mean, don't get me wrong, people still call it a lesbian bar," she clarifies.

Though Babe's has become increasingly inclusive along lines of gender and sexuality, the pace of change around racial diversity has been slower: something we began to understand more deeply when we met Kristen, a regular of nearly a decade.

"It's such different worlds," Kristen says, as she begins to detail the ways in which the Richmond Black lesbian community has their own spaces, implying that Babe's is seen by many as a white lesbian bar. "I guess I wasn't your typical Black lesbian. [. . .] I was the friend that came to Babe's when all of my other friends wanted to go to Godfrey's and Colours. Those were the African American clubs for lesbians and gays," Kristen details. "I don't want to just hear one type of music. I want to hear all the different types of music. So that's what brought me to Babe's. It's a really happy place."

Kristen also gives us a window into another vital part of Richmond's Black queer community: ballroom. Ball culture is a Black and Latinx LGBTQ+ subculture organized around gender-subversive performance, where participants compete in categories like voguing, femme queens, and best dressed. Ball communities exist all over the world and are made up of houses: chosen families who compete together, led by "house parents." Kristen first discovered the ballroom scene in Richmond as a teenager. "Most people who got into houses were looking [for] a family that they didn't already have," she explains. "My mom didn't support very much. So, I kind of had to find a family outside my family."

After running away from home at seventeen, Kristen moved in with her house mom, Jessica. They lived together on and off for about seven years. "Jessica and I were only a year apart, but she took me on as her daughter," Kristen says. Their ball house, the House of Amor, has since dissipated, but Kristen and Jessica are still family. "She treats me no different than the children she has now. [. . .] Her daughter calls me her big sister, her son calls me his big sister," Kristen adds.

A few months after our visit to Babe's, another Vickie walked into the bar: Vickie Keener—fifty-eight, with tatted arms and brown hair just past her shoulders. She hadn't set foot in Babe's in more than thirty years, but as she told X, who was behind the bar at the time, Babe's was hugely influential in her young adulthood. X texted me immediately. Because unlike owner Vicky Hester, this Vickie wanted to share her story.

Vickie stepped into Babe's for the first time in 1992. She was twenty-eight years old, and she had a husband and two kids back in Bedford, Virginia. But for a number of years, Vickie had been seeing a woman: Mary. They started off as close friends who simply liked to spend an inordinate amount of time together. Then, one afternoon in Mary's kitchen, Mary pinned Vickie against the counter and kissed her. "It was the beginning of my end as far as being a straight woman," Vickie recalls in her Southern lilt. "I knew at that moment, [that] this is what I want[ed]. [. . .] What I've had before, that ain't nothing compared to what I just felt. And that was just in a kiss."

There was no turning back after that. "I could literally have an orgasm without taking my clothes off. That's how much I felt when she would touch me. And she didn't necessarily have to touch me there, either. It was just, you know, a kiss, a hold, an embrace," Vickie reflects. "That was an exciting time for me, but it was also probably one of the darkest times for me." She was keeping this huge secret from her family, and she had no idea that there was any sort of gay community out there. Although she knew it wasn't a reality, she clung to the dream that one day she and Mary would leave their husbands and be together.

Then, in 1992, Vickie found herself alone in Richmond, attending a conference for work. She was still seeing Mary, but it had started to sink in that Mary was never going to leave her husband. That's when she heard about Babe's.

"It was the first time I saw gay people. At twenty-eight years old," Vickie exclaims. "I was brought up in this Southern Baptist home and I was married to this little country boy up in Bedford, Virginia. And I lived in the woods. [. . .] We didn't discuss these things. Gays didn't exist because nothing had ever been said about them."

Vickie remembers thinking, "I have to be the only person in the entire world who feels this way toward a person of the same sex." But when she walked into Babe's, seeing women in the arms of other women, she knew she'd been wrong: "Understanding suddenly [. . .] that there are people of the same sex who love each other, who are attracted to each other. It was the first time I ever realized that [queerness is] actually a thing. It existed other than in my mind."

At Babe's that night, Vickie met Karen. "She was pretty forward," Vickie recalls. Karen gave Vickie a crash course on lesbian culture. "It's almost like talking to a kindergartener about physics. Because that's how little I knew," says Vickie. After that first night, Karen began to pursue Vickie.

Once a week, Karen would intercept Vickie on her way to work. "I'd see her truck, it was a turquoise Ford Ranger, on the Blue Ridge Parkway," Vickie describes, "and she would [give] me a rose, a Mountain Dew, and a pack of Marlboros, which is my morning thing." After a few months of these weekly visits, Karen won Vickie over.

"[Karen] made me decide to leave my husband [and] talk to my kids. [. . . I also] let my mom know, which didn't go well," Vickie says. Vickie's mom convinced her to check herself into a psychiatric center, where Vickie spent a week. "That was horrible. [. . .] I went from being on nothing to suddenly lithium, and I was a zombie," she remembers.

Her husband's reaction was even worse. "He literally threatened to kill me," Vickie says. "I had to fight him off at one point and kind of run. I stayed away for about three days. And that's what he used in court as abandonment for my kids." Vickie's sons were eight and ten at the time, and Vickie couldn't imagine that the court would grant her husband custody in the separation. But she was wrong.

"Bedford County decided that the father, who worked nights and was asleep during the day, was a better parent than the mother who spent most of the time with them. Because I had been with a woman," Vickie says bitterly. Not to mention her husband's persistent abuse. However, even without formal custody, and with Karen's support, Vickie remained a primary caregiver to her boys. "I fed them, I did their homework, we got them to bed, we gave them baths. We did that every night of the week, and I had them on weekends. But I still couldn't get custody," Vickie details.

What's more, the court forced Vickie to pay child support to her ex-husband for the kids she was still raising. Eventually, Vickie's older son made the choice to move in with her full time. "It took me a year and a half after he moved in with me to get Bedford to reverse the child support, so for a year and a half I paid child support for a child that lived with me," Vickie stresses.

In 1999, Karen and Vickie split—though they remained good friends—and Vickie went to live with her mom, Judy. "Mom and I had a really strange relationship. I loved her dearly, but [I] couldn't stand her control," Vickie confesses.

On the surface, Judy simply couldn't accept Vickie's sexuality, and through Vickie's teenage years, Judy would often interrogate her about her close friendships with other girls. Strangely enough, though, Judy had an intensely close female friendship of her own. When Vickie's parents got divorced when she was ten years old, her mother's best friend—also recently divorced—moved in. "They lived together for fifty-two years," says Vickie.

The duo eventually bought property together out in the country. "[They got] two trailers so one could live in one, and one could live in the other. And they were right side by side," Vickie describes.

When Vickie needed somewhere to go after leaving Karen, Judy moved over into her friend's trailer, giving Vickie her own. "Which I know wasn't a problem," Vickie says with a knowing laugh. Judy and her companion lived together for half a century, until the day Judy passed—they did everything together and never dated other people. Vickie is confident they were more than friends. "I'll probably get a ghost visit tonight because of this conversation," she jokes.

Vickie attributes Judy's lifelong denial of her own sexual orientation to religion: "She was afraid of going to hell." Thankfully, Judy didn't manage to instill this fear in her daughter. In fact, watching the way Judy lived in secret only affirmed Vickie's desire to be out and proud. "It's really sad to me that she left this world and never got to acknowledge or say who she was," Vickie reflects. "My purpose in life is to not die like that. [To not] die denying who I am."

While it's been a hard road to get here, Vickie is living that purpose. "There's a whole decade of my life that I wish I could just erase. But if I had to go back and do it all again, I would, because of where I'm at now," she says. Vickie has a loving relationship with her two sons, now grown, and a beautiful marriage to her wife of more than two decades. In part, she owes it all to Babe's. She tells us, "That day I went to Babe's, back in the '90s, was the day I realized that I need to be who I am. [. . .] It was the day I realized that I'm not alone."

Chapter Thirty-Three

HERSHEE BAR

A THIRTY-FIVE-YEAR FIGHT FOR QUEER SPACE

NORFOLK, VA

In the late 1960s, at just eight years old, Annette Stone began daydreaming about opening a bar. At thirteen, while walking through Norfolk's Five Points neighborhood, she pointed to a particular spot and declared: "I'm going to open a bar on this corner one day." At fifteen, she visited her first gay bar. "I'll never forget it. I knew I was home. I just knew I had walked into my whole life, my whole future. It was the most beautiful feeling in the world," she recalls.

By early adulthood, after Annette realized she herself was gay, she was certain she wanted her future bar to be a lesbian bar, though not an exclusive one. "What I mean [by lesbian bar] is this is a safe space for anyone from any walk of life, but specifically if you are a lesbian, if you are coming out, if you are afraid, if you need a helping hand, [it's for you]," Annette explains.

This type of environment was essential in Norfolk and was missing from the other gay bars in town. At one spot where she used to DJ, Annette remembers facing homophobic physical violence from the neighbors. "The bar next door would come over and beat the crap out of us. We'd have to fist-fight in the parking lot to defend ourselves. It was harrowing to say the least," she says. Plus, the more time Annette spent in the existing gay bars, the more she came to realize that queer women weren't truly accepted there. "They didn't want us to have our own tables. They wouldn't seat us because women didn't tip as much as men. [. . .] They did not want the women to sit at the bar. They could order drinks, but they couldn't have a seat."

In 1983, barely old enough to buy a drink at a bar—let alone run one—Annette opened her own lesbian bar on the very corner she used to point to in Norfolk's Five Points neighborhood. "There was a huge dance floor and a stage. Four pool tables, [. . .] pinball machines," Annette describes. "It was like the warmest hug in the world, and we were very creative, so we had funky colors everywhere, [. . .] mannequins everywhere."

Annette named the space Hershee Bar—a playful pun on pronouns and the famous candy bar. The City of Norfolk was not a fan of the name. "They hated us right away for that," Annette asserts. But the city would have had a problem with the bar no matter what Annette decided to call it. "Most younger people don't understand what we had to go through. [. . .] In the state of Virginia, it was illegal to sell alcohol to a known homosexual, [. . .] so when I opened my bar, I was breaking the law," Annette explains.

Annette is referring to the Virginia ABC statute that said a bar's license could be suspended if "the bar has become a meeting place and rendezvous for users of narcotics, drunks, homosexuals, prostitutes, pimps, panderers, gamblers or habitual law violators." This statute also prohibited licensed bars from employing homosexuals.[1] The rule had been around since the 1930s and would remain on the books until 1991. Although it wasn't often enforced, it technically could be if authorities decided they didn't like a particular establishment,[2] and on Hershee Bar's opening night, local law enforcement came out in full force.

"Fourteen public officials came in full regalia: [. . .] the fire marshal, the police department, ABC, Vice and Narcotics, the health department," Annette lists. "They raided us opening night and arrested a couple of girls for using the men's room and beat up another girl pretty badly for no reason."

The raids only continued. "In my first year, in ninety days we had sixty-some-odd visits from Vice and Narcotics," Annette says. "We were not allowed to be dancing together or touching or kissing or any of that when Vice and Narcotics came in." Any evidence of homosexuality in the bar would be grounds to take away her liquor license.

It wasn't just the authorities that harassed Annette and Hershee Bar. A group of men from the bar across the street would often drunkenly stumble over to fight patrons in the parking lot. "Let's-beat-the-lesbian-up night," as

Annette calls it, "happened about once or twice a month." Never one to go down without a fight, Annette eventually decided to do something about it.

"The next time they come over, we're all going to grab a pool stick and beat them up," she told all the girls at Hershee.

"And we did, and they never came back. They had to go back to their little bar with everyone knowing that the lesbians across the street beat them half to death," Annette declares with satisfaction.

Annette was always determined to protect her community. "Our first Thanksgiving, we realized there were a lot of lonely hearts [at Hershee] that were kind of sad, [so] I started making food for everybody," Annette says, "and then we started a tradition where we were open every Thanksgiving and everything was free. You know, a full dinner." As we've seen before, lesbian bars tend to stay open for holidays like Thanksgiving and Christmas, offering gathering places for people seeking family and community.

Though Hershee was valued by the local queer community, local and state government continued to challenge Annette. A few years after opening, she applied for a full liquor license so she could sell more than just beer and wine. "ABC said they had never, ever, ever seen their little courtroom so packed, but it was not people supporting us. They were all in opposition of us. Just to get a liquor license, we had to fight," Annette says.

In 2018, after thirty-five years of business, Annette received some bad news. The city planned to buy the property on which Hershee sat.

"[The owners] made a deal with the City of Norfolk to sell the property," Annette explains. The deal first went to the Norfolk City Council in February of 2018, and the council voted to buy the property for $1.5 million, with the condition that all the buildings on the property would be demolished before the transfer of the land.

Looking back, Annette thinks the deal would never have gone through had her mom not been sick. "My mother was diagnosed with Alzheimer's," Annette states. Prior to her diagnosis, Annette had been heavily involved with the city council herself, and some things *had* changed in Norfolk since the 1980s, when she first opened her bar. There was a new city council person, Andria McClellan, who seemed to be supportive of the queer community, and public opinion toward LGBTQ+ folks had shifted some. "I think I would have been embraced as part of the community with the new council person," Annette speculates.

But with her mother's Alzheimer's diagnosis, Annette had to stop attending meetings, taking a step back from her involvement with the city. "They utilized that time to do some things to take my bar," Annette says.

Even in Annette's absence, Hershee wasn't going down without a fight. When word of the sale reached the Hershee community, they rallied behind their bar. "If you ever have an opportunity to watch what the community did when they fought for it at the council meetings—I think that's something that should make history because our community really came together and fought for their bar," Annette proclaims.

Between June and October of 2018, dozens of people showed up at various city council meetings to make the case for the preservation of Hershee. Many shared stories of what the bar meant to them personally.

"To me, and my family, Hershee Bar has been a safe haven. I can remember when I was first diagnosed with sarcoidosis and congestive heart failure, [the bar] put together a benefit show for me, to help me and to help my family," said one community member named Nina Blowe.[3]

"My family turned on me so fast with their Southern Baptist stuff. So, my family became Hershee," said another Hershee's regular, Cissy Elkins.[4]

"Throughout the country, lesbian bars and LGBTQ bars in general have been closing," said Cathleen Rhodes, who teaches queer studies at Old Dominion University. "It would be a real shame if Norfolk had the opportunity to keep one of these spaces [and didn't]—one that hasn't had to close its doors because no one showed up for beer on a Friday night, or because they couldn't afford to keep the lights on, but because the city wanted to raze the building and the community it housed for yet another parking lot."

At the end of the first June meeting, it seemed there was hope Hershee Bar could be saved. Councilmember Paul Riddick addressed the crowd, suggesting that they make an exception to leave Hershee standing to give the bar more time to find a new home. "When I first moved out there in 1985, they had the best bacon cheeseburgers in Norfolk," he said, to laughter from the crowd. "They're my neighbors, they're my friends. And so, I'm on their side. Whatever we can do to help them."[5]

But as the months wore on, it began to feel like the council wasn't listening. Still taking care of her mom, Annette watched the livestream of every single meeting from home. "I didn't expect the avalanche of emotion that I felt. I did not think I could cry that hard. You know, like the biggest scream you have on a roller coaster. [. . .] I never thought I could cry as much as I did and hurt as deeply as I hurt watching those—my kids, share their experience, to a city council that was not listening," Annette says.

At first it was just a feeling that the city council wasn't hearing the stories and pleas of the Hershee community. Then came some digital proof. On a Facebook post announcing the reelection of city council member Mamie B. Johnson, representative for Hershee Bar's neighborhood, someone had commented: "Congratulations. Now save a landmark in our community, The Hershee Lounge." Ms. Johnson's response? Three laugh-crying emojis.[6]

Screenshots of her comment quickly spread through the Hershee Bar community, becoming somewhat of a rallying cry. "At that point we felt targeted," recalls Jennifer Alomari, one of the leaders of the movement to save Hershee Bar.

On October 23, 2018, just eight days before Hershee was supposed to be shut down for good, thirty-nine people showed up to speak at one final meeting.[7]

"We've gotten up here week after week, we've brainstormed solutions," began one community member Hunter Noffsinger, "only to be completely ignored by members of city council. I've watched members of city council play on their phones as concerned citizens get up and voice their frustration."[8]

Another speaker, Dr. Kathleen Casey, a professor of history and gender studies at Virginia Wesleyan University, pointed out the risk that folks were taking by showing up to speak week after week. "For months, your LGBTQ constituents have been mustering up the courage to tell you—in a televised public meeting, where their names and home addresses will be published—that they feel left out of this process," she says. "They've been telling you how important Hershee is, and they've shared with you how often LGBT people are harassed, assaulted, and forced to create their own families out of thin air when they are disowned."[9]

Various individuals asked for an extension—for the city to hold off on the planned demolition of Hershee, giving the community more time to speak with council members and hopefully come up with a resolution. Mayor Alexander adjourned the session, sharing a story about how his own mother was gay. "Let me express to all of you that we hear you. We see you.

We listened since June. And we don't want anyone to leave here to think that we don't care," he said.[10]

But for many, this statement rang false. Nothing was going to change. Hershee was still set to close on October 31. "They'd already made their mind up, and that was it. It was a futile attempt to save a bar," Annette declares.

"It was such a sad state of affairs because the real estate transaction was so far gone at this point that we weren't in a position to make a change," city council member Andria McClellan explains to us. If anyone had been listening to the Hershee community, it was her. "I think it's our job to be respectful and to listen and to understand. And it's a shame that others didn't feel the same way," she says.

Still, she insisted that even among the less attentive council members, none of this was a targeted attack on Norfolk's LGBTQ+ community. "I truly don't believe that there was any sort of intentionality of getting rid of Hershee Bar," she says. "As horrible as it sounds, it was literally just a real estate transaction. And I think my other colleagues, they just wanted to move on, [. . .] and honestly, I want to be able to say when we screw up. I screwed up. We screwed this one up."

Not everyone on the city council agrees with Andria's assessment. In 2024, Sarah got a hold of Mamie B. Johnson on the phone to get her side of the story. Ms. Johnson didn't share Andria's regret over how the situation unfolded, nor did she seem to believe the real estate deal was too far gone to overturn. Instead, she felt that the real estate deal, and all of its implications, was in the best interest of the constituents of her ward—the people who lived in the neighborhood surrounding Hershee Bar.

She insisted that there were only a handful of people who cared about Hershee Bar. "There were about six people, I would say six to eight people, that came out over [those] months," she told Sarah.

"Oh, I actually have all of the records on it," Sarah quickly countered. "At the last meeting, I believe there were thirty-nine people that spoke about it."

Ms. Johnson doubled down—she was only counting constituents of her ward, not the voices of the larger Norfolk area LGBTQ+ community.

On October 31, Hershee Bar was forced to close its doors for good. Upward of three hundred people showed up for one final night in their home away from home. They scrawled messages on the walls: "My life began here,"[11] "I love my HB's family for life," "Lesbian spaces are sacred," "Our history lives inside of us, but it also lives here: in these walls that have witnessed our sorrows + our triumphs and our struggles."[12]

The city also made its position clear. "Much like the first night Hershee was open, the police came out in numbers," details Jennifer Alomari. All throughout the night, Jennifer estimates at least a dozen officers lined the fence along the parking lot. "Now, they were not there to protect nor were they to serve. [. . .] They didn't interact, they didn't come speak and be like 'Hey, we're just making sure everybody's safe'; they just sat there and watched us," Jennifer recalls. After the bar's early years of harassment, all those decades ago, it felt like a statement more than anything else, as if they were declaring "we won."

For months Hershee Bar sat vacant, until the city demolished it the following year. "It has been spellbindingly bad for all of us. We are dying without our bar," Annette asserts.

As if to rub salt in the wound, the property sat as an empty lot for three more years. In October of 2021, the city began developing the land into a park, and two years later, the park opened to the public. "It took five years for it to open. We could have been ushering in a new generation and helping people. We could have had a place to meet and have communion together for five more years, but we weren't able to do that," Annette emphasizes.

The city did offer Annette a reimbursement for up to $75,000[13] to assist with relocating, but finding a new space and keeping it open has proved challenging. Annette isn't giving up, though. Hershee Bar is always on her mind. "It's all I ever think about and all I ever dream about. [. . .] It takes a lot to knock me down because I have a lot of tenacity when it comes to our community. I put up with a lot to keep Hershee's open and it looks like I'm going to have to put up with a lot to reopen," she reflects.

In the meantime, Annette stays in touch with the Hershee community via Facebook, and she still hosts a Thanksgiving dinner each year, for anyone who wants or needs it. "That one person matters to me," Annette says. "There might be one little scared girl or trans kid that's coming out that might need us. That's why we stayed open on Christmas Day and Thanksgiving because [of] that one person."

Of one of the last Thanksgivings at Hershee, Annette tells us: "I remember very vividly being in the kitchen. [. . .] I was making a turkey, and I heard this little voice."

"I knew you would be here," said a young woman, through frightened tears.

"Whatever that day cost us, it was so well worth it to accommodate one person that needed us," reflects Annette. "So that's how our life here is. That's how I feel."

The Hershee Bar story serves as an important reminder that attempts by public officials to erase queer space are not a thing of the distant past. The image of police lined up outside of Hershee Bar on that final night—their intimidation bordering on harassment—seems like something out of the 1960s. But it was 2018. Still, while the Norfolk City Council may have succeeded in eradicating Hershee Bar in its physical form, they can never take away the way we show up and care for one another—bar or no bar.

Part Five

MASSACHUSETTS

COMING HOME

Chapter Thirty-Four

FEMME BAR

FOR DIANTÉ

WORCESTER, MA

Growing up in Acton, Massachusetts, located in the suburbs halfway between Worcester and Boston, even the best fake IDs wouldn't have gotten Sarah and me into a lesbian bar—there simply weren't any. Boston hadn't had a lesbian bar in decades. Worcester hadn't had any lesbian spaces at all since the Floating Dance Floor, a twice-monthly dance party that shut down in 2009.

So, when we heard about Femme Bar opening in Worcester, we were ecstatic. Sarah attended the soft opening in March of 2023 with her mom, Diane. Upon walking in, Sarah was surprised to find that owners Danielle Spring and Julie Toupin *recognized* her. Absolutely beaming, the pair greets Sarah: Julie, tall and femme, with cascading red-brown hair, and Danielle, a half-head shorter than Julie, masc, and sporting a sharp fade. "This whole journey started because of the podcast," Danielle confesses, to Sarah and Diane's utter disbelief.

"What?!" you can hear Diane exclaiming on the tape.

It had never occurred to Danielle and Julie that Massachusetts was lacking a lesbian bar. "To tell you the truth, we didn't know they even existed," Julie explains.

"It's your fault, actually," Danielle says to Sarah. "I started listening to your podcast, and I got super interested in the whole idea of lesbian bars, and why there aren't enough. [. . .] We traveled to Cubbyhole, because that was your first episode, and we fell absolutely in love."

"I did make Danielle stay 'til like four in the morning," Julie adds, reminiscing about their visit.

"On our ride home, we talked about how amazing that space was and how it felt like home. And we wanted to bring that back to Worcester," Danielle says.

While Danielle and Julie are co-owners of the space, Danielle first introduces herself as "wife to the owner." She's subverting an assumption people often have when walking into the bar, that she is the primary owner. In all fairness, Danielle is known in the industry, having previously owned and managed other bars in Worcester. But also, Danielle takes up a bit more space than Julie. She's more outgoing, whereas Julie, as she puts it, doesn't have the "loudest energy in the room." Plus, even within the queer community we can fall into patriarchal stereotypes, assuming that Danielle, as the more masc of the two, must be the owner.

"I want [Julie] to have her flowers. She did all this. I'm just here because I'm her wife. I support her," Danielle says.

"But we are co-owners," Julie clarifies.

The pair met more than a decade ago, on a blind date. "Through [. . .] friends of friends of friends," Julie explains. "I was the token lesbian in my friend group, and she was the token lesbian in her friend group. People that knew each other were like, 'Oh, I know a lesbian. You know a lesbian. Let's set 'em up.'"

After that first meeting, it took them a while to actually start dating. "You chased me for like seven months," Julie says to Danielle.

"Did you enjoy that?" Danielle teases.

"Yes," Julie affirms, laughing.

"It was the first time I ever had to chase somebody," Danielle reflects. "It did not feel good. It was well worth it, but I hated it."

Part of why it took them so long to get together was because Julie was newly out. "My family was still having a very hard time with [my identity], so it was very hard for me to come to terms with it," Julie explains. She had always been extremely close with her family, so it was particularly challenging to feel distanced from them. "We kind of were on the outs for like two years. They didn't really talk to me," Julie says.

Danielle, on the other hand, had been out for many years. "I'm quite a bit older than my amazing wife," she remarks, and she's never really been able to hide her gay identity. "I'm very much the definition of a tomboy, masc lesbian. And I live my life the way I want to live my life," Danielle explains. She made a solid attempt to date boys in high school and college, but there's one person who always knew the truth: Danielle's younger sister Dianté.

"I didn't ever have to come out to Dianté," Danielle says with a small smile.

Right before Danielle left for college, she was sort of seeing someone. A woman. Dianté told her, "I know what you're doing, and I don't mind it, but I understand why you're not telling nobody, and I love you."

"And that was the end of it. She's just been super supportive since she figured it out," Danielle reflects. When Danielle came out to the rest of her family, it was Dianté who pushed them toward acceptance. "She would come at things from a different perspective and make you understand that the love you have for that person didn't go anywhere just because they're not the way you thought they were."

When Danielle and Julie finally started dating, one of the first things Danielle did was introduce Julie and Dianté. "The only way that I can stay with someone is if Dianté liked them. So, if she didn't like them, I had to know pretty early on so I wouldn't waste my time," Danielle explains.

Fortunately for everyone involved—and for the Worcester-area lesbian community—Dianté and Julie became fast friends. "I did more stuff with Dianté than you at one point," Julie says to Danielle. "She was like my older sister, honestly. [. . .] I had so many first experiences with her. [. . .] She brought me out everywhere [. . .] I experienced my first strip club with Dianté and I was like, 'Why the fuck am I here? This is awesome!'"

When Danielle and Julie got engaged, Julie claimed Dianté for her own wedding party. In 2019, after seven years of dating, Danielle and Julie wed in a ceremony at the West Art Museum, Dianté by their sides. At close to midnight, they moved the party to a local whiskey bar called Bucks, where Danielle knew the owner from her early days in the bar business.

A few years later, following Julie and Danielle's transformative trip to Cubbyhole, Dianté began pushing them to open a lesbian bar in Worcester. Julie was sold on the idea, but Danielle required some convincing. "I didn't want anything to do with the bar business. I had a bar a long time ago, and I didn't love it," Danielle states.

But Dianté was spinning a different story. "[She] kept telling me how much Danielle really wanted to get back into the bar industry," Julie says, "and I was like 'I dunno, she keeps telling me she doesn't really want to do it.'" So, Dianté and Julie began scheming behind Danielle's back. "And the more I brought it up [to Danielle], the more she started actually being okay with the idea."

Given Dianté's vested interest in this potential lesbian bar, we had to wonder if she was queer herself, or just a passionate ally, sister, and friend. "You know, we don't know. . . . " is Danielle's answer.

"A little bit of both, I think," says Julie.

Tragically, this is a question that Danielle and Julie will never get the chance to ask Dianté directly, because she passed on March 18, 2022.

"It's really hard, 'cause it was super unexpected," says Danielle, her voice quavering. "She was poisoned."

Dianté died from fentanyl poisoning. She was thirty-six years old. A Worcester man has since been charged with manslaughter in connection to her death.[1] He had mistakenly provided Dianté and her boyfriend with a bag of fentanyl instead of cocaine.[2]

After Dianté's funeral, her family and friends gathered to celebrate her life at Bucks—the very same whiskey bar where Danielle and Julie had hosted their wedding after party. "[The owner] shut down the place and we all took over. [. . .] My sister knew a lot of people. So, a lot of people came down here with us," Danielle details.

While Danielle and Julie were reeling from the shock of Dianté's sudden death, the idea of opening a lesbian bar took a backseat. "It was just quiet for a few months," Julie says. "It took us a long time to actually even start talking about it again."

"Once we kind of started coming back to—I don't wanna say coming back to life, but that's really what it is, right? Grief is hard. And I think once [we] started coming full circle on the situation it was like, 'Okay, this happened. What are we gonna do?'" Julie recounts.

"How do we remember her?" adds Danielle softly.

It was actually Danielle who first resurfaced the idea to open their own bar. She was presented with an unexpected opportunity from the owner of Buck's. He was closing the bar where Danielle and Julie had celebrated their marriage, and where they had celebrated Dianté's life. The property was newly available.

"This is how we can do something really good for the community and remember Dianté," Danielle recalls thinking.

"She knew it was something that her sister wanted us to do," says Julie, "and I think it just kind of pushed us to actually—"

"Do it," Danielle cuts in.

With that, Femme Bar was born. The name came to Julie late one night in bed. "It doesn't mean it's only for femmes," Julie clarifies.

"I'll go to Femme to find a femme," Danielle jokes.

"At first people were asking us, like, 'What if butches don't come?'" says Julie, "and I was like, 'Everybody's gonna come. It's just a lesbian bar.'" She was right. "Our first weekend opening, it was crazy in here," she says.

"[There] was so much love," adds Danielle. "Even to this day, when people walk in the front door, they walk in with their heart open."

Dianté would have absolutely loved it. "She would have been here every day," Danielle says.

"Oh my God, she would've been the loudest part of this place," Julie says, laughing, "and everybody would have known her."

In a way, Dianté is at Femme every day. Not only in spirit, but in the form of a larger-than-life mural spanning the wall to the left of the bar. In it, Dianté is Medusa, with vibrant pink, purple, and green snakes for hair. She wears two gold necklaces: a Dianté nameplate, and one that reads Pride. She peers down at the patrons of Femme, an almost-smile dancing across her lips.

"That's like, the real look she would give. She would just look down on people and then just make you laugh," Julie declares.

"It shows a lot of her personality," adds Danielle.

The mural is a conversation starter, too, particularly among customers, staff, and new friends who didn't know Dianté or her story. "When you ask us, we get candid in talking about it," says Julie. But even folks who didn't know Dianté, and don't ask, fall in love with the mural.

"I appreciate all the people that take pictures with it, 'cause it means so much, [. . .] keeps her going. And her spirit is in all those pictures. It's amazing," Danielle marvels.

It's entirely fitting that Dianté's spirit is so central to the physical space of Femme. It was Dianté who so desperately wanted Julie and Danielle to open a lesbian bar, and it was the desire to honor her memory that finally made Femme a reality. Perhaps on some level, Dianté knew that this space was what her sister needed.

Today, Danielle couldn't be happier with her and Julie's decision to open Femme. "It's a blessing," says Danielle. "I know [. . .] that it helped me heal. We bring all these amazingly beautiful people together. It's the coolest thing we could have done."

CONCLUSION

In the period between me writing these words and you reading them, it's likely that new lesbian bars will have opened, and possible that some of the bars in this book may have closed. Bars have always been a business of very small margins, and as I've learned over the past five years, lesbian bars are even more susceptible to a myriad of additional challenges. There's the rapid gentrification of the previously "less desirable" neighborhoods where lesbian bars have been known to put down roots. There are local, political threats, like in the case of Hershee Bar. There are stereotypes that sometimes turn out to be true, like the fact that queer women are more likely to partner up and stop going out than our male counterparts, or that, on average, we simply drink less than men do.

Despite the odds, in the last few years even *more* new lesbian and lesbian-adjacent bars have continued to open. Dani's Queer Bar opened in Boston. Oklahoma City got two new sapphic spots, Indigo Lounge and the Secret Bar. Last Ditch bar opened in Western Massachusetts, and BOYFRIEND Co-op opened in Brooklyn. In Los Angeles, Honey's opened as a pop-up and seems to be here to stay. Not to mention the dozens of women's sports bars popping up around the country, many of which, like the Sports Bra, are queer-women owned and queer-women centric. The contemporary lesbian bar is gender expansive, trans inclusive, intersectional, and accessible. It has nonalcoholic options on the menu. It plays women's sports on the TVs. Perhaps we are ushering in a new wave of radical sapphic spaces and dyke dives, echoing the heyday of the 1980s, when more than two hundred lesbian bars dotted the country.

But this book is not about *why* lesbian bars close. Nor is it a rallying cry for more lesbian bars to open, although if they do, you certainly won't hear me complaining. This book is about how our community survives and thrives, and how it will continue to do so, no matter what. The disappearance of lesbian bars is not the tragedy I once thought it was. Their decline in numbers in the early 2000s is actually indicative of a more expansive queer culture and a more welcoming, open society as a whole. My wife and I don't *have* to go to a lesbian bar to hold hands or kiss in public. We don't even have to go to a lesbian bar to meet other lesbians or queer people. We can go to the park, the food co-op, the coffee shop, the gym, the bookstore, the library, the theater. And young queers no longer need to go to a lesbian bar to know they aren't alone, as was the case for women like Kevie in Oklahoma City or Vickie in Richmond. They can simply turn on the TV, scroll on TikTok, or open a book like this one. There are beautiful, vibrant, queer and lesbian cultures that exist out in the open now—not just rooted in dark bars or centered around alcohol as they once were.

No amount of legislature, or homophobia, or transphobia can make us disappear. The humans I've met in lesbian bars across the country have taught me this. Eve, Linda, Pat, Rikki, Nancy, Alice, Charlene, Leslie, and Juanita, just to name a few. Their stories of a time before—when the lesbian bar was one of the only safe spaces for queer community—serve as a reminder that we've always been here. We have a legacy of making and fighting for space for ourselves. And no one can take that from us.

ACKNOWLEDGMENTS

This book would not exist without the many, many people across the country who generously shared their stories, and their time, with *Cruising* podcast. Thank you for trusting us with your words.

Thank you to Eve Adams, Alice Brady, Charlene Schneider, Leslie Martinez, Mona Nystrom-Hood, Rikki Streicher, and Pat Ramseyer, with whom we never got to talk, but who paved the way for our very existence.

Thank you to Sarah Gabrielli for the expert interview skills, insightful notes, and collaboration.

Thank you to Jennifer McGinity for the never-ending love and support, and for the many hours in the driver's seat—both while lesbian barhopping around the country, and while I drafted many chapters of this book from the passenger seat.

Thank you to Michael Johnston at CAA for believing in this book and getting others to believe in it too, and for the endless support throughout this process.

Thank you to Catherine Tung, Rebecca Johnson, and everyone at Beacon Press for bringing this book to life.

Thank you to Ella Harris, Ines Maza, and Caroline Edwards for believing in our little independent podcast, *Cruising*.

Thank you to my mom and dad, for the encouragement and the many pep talks, but most of all for loving me and loving who I love wholeheartedly. Thank you to Sky and Sara, for making our family a queer space of its own.

And thank you to all the trailblazers, the history makers, the activists, and the bar owners—past, present, and future—who make space for queer community.

NOTES

Sarah Gabrielli conducted interviews with the following people, from which I quote widely throughout the book: Nina Alvarez (February 8, 2023, Riverside); Lisa Cannistraci (August 16–21, 2021, NYC); Barbara Kahn (October 17, 2022, Riverside); Jonathan Ned Katz (February 17, 2023, NYC); Lisa Menichino (April 8, 2021 and May 6, 2021, NYC; January 7, 2025, phone); Deb Greenberg (April 16, 2021, NYC); Shelia Frayne (July 13, 2022, New Jersey); Jack Jen Gieseking (August 1, 2021, Zoom); Ruthie Boirie (July 20, 2022, Brooklyn); Nikke Alleyne and Justine LaViolette (April 23, 2024, NYC); Macon Reed (April 28, 2024, Riverside); Sarah Hallonquist (April 16, 2024, Brooklyn); Rach "Coach" Pike and Jo McDaniel (July 17, 2021, DC; December 12, 2024, Riverside); Linda Barsaloux (November 14, 2022, Chicago); Barbara (August 21, 2023, Riverside); Tracy Baim (November 13, 2022, Chicago); Michele Jones (November 13, 2022, Chicago); Pat McCombs (November 14, 2022, Chicago); Shirley J (November 12, 2021, phone); Angela Barnes and Renauda Riddle (August 31, 2021, Zoom); Zoe Schor and Whitney LaMora (November 12, 2022, Chicago); Rainn Thomas (November 12, 2022, Chicago); Deb Gordon (September 14, 2021, Columbus, OH; October 16, 2021, Zoom); Marcia Riley (September 14, 2021, Columbus, OH; September 24, 2021, phone); Smoove Gardner (August 3, 2021, Zoom; November–December, 2021, phone; February 27, 2024, Riverside); Nicci B. (August 3, 2021, Zoom); Verna Vendetta (November 1, 2021, Zoom); Corvin Rose (November 13, 2021, Zoom); Becky Millar and Annie Calteaux (September 19, 2021, Zoom); Bet-z (September 17, 2021, Zoom); Beccah Schecter (January 13, 2025, Brooklyn); Jordan Feltner (January 12, 2025, Riverside); Jody Bouffard (August 12, 2021, Zoom); Beth Lemke (December 12, 2022, Pacifica, CA); Mandy Carter (December 8, 2022, February 2, 2022, Riverside); Jeanne Clark (December 12, 2022, San Francisco); Tom Frankel (December 12, 2022, San Francisco); Nancy Valverde (September

28, 2022, Los Angeles); Lillian Faderman (September 27, 2023, San Diego); Bryher Herak (December 4, 2021, Zoom); Ruth Pettis (January 2022, Zoom); Lamar Van Dyke (September 27, 2021, Zoom); Shelley Brothers and Martha Manning (September 24, 2021, Seattle, WA); Robin (February 28, 2023, Riverside); Olga Bichko (September 30, 2022, November 30, 2022, December 10, 2023, Riverside); Brandy Feit (December 6 and 13, 2023, Riverside); Anonymous Doc Marie's Former Staff Member (September 26, 2022, Riverside); Shane O'Neill (November 30, 2023, Riverside); Aundrenee (December 9, 2022, Portland, OR); Jenny Nguyen (December 10, 2022, Portland, OR); Thu Hoang (December 10, 2022, Portland, OR); Billie Hayes (January 13, 2022, phone); S.M. (October 7, 2021, Zoom); Moe Girton (August 5, 2021, Zoom); Lisa and Rudy Ramrod (October 1, 2021, San Diego; January 28, 2022, Zoom); Ellen Frayle (March 2024, phone); Frank Perez (March 31, 2023, New Orleans); Diane Dimicelli (March 28, 2023, Zoom); Randy Elwood (August 11, 2023, Riverside); Lois and Raleigh Winn (July 17, 2023, phone); Bobby Fieseler (April 1, 2023, New Orleans); Linda Tucker (April 3, 2023, New Orleans); Juanita Pierre, Michael Pierre, Imelda Sterling, and Kewanya Pierre (April 2, 2023, New Orleans); Audrey Corley (September 21, 2021, Zoom; February 16, 2022, phone); Nicole Ennis (October 2, 2021, Phoenix, AZ); Kevie Smith (October 27, 2021, phone); Amanda Sternke (October 4, 2021, Tulsa, OK); Sarah Kyndal (October 4, 2021, Tulsa, OK); Val Binkley (April 15, 2021, phone); Lisa Thomas (October 5, 2021, Oklahoma City, OK); Raven Delray (October 5, 2021, Oklahoma City, OK); Tracey (October 5, 2021, Oklahoma City, OK); Ann (October 5, 2021, Oklahoma City, OK); Julie Mabry (October 7, 2021, Houston, TX); Sarah Mabry (May 1, 2021, April 24, 2025, phone); Kathy Jack (September 20, 2021, Zoom; April 21, 2025, phone); Erica Sanders (October 6, 2021, Dallas, TX); Sheila and Rachel Smallman (October 9, 2021, Mobile, AL); Jen and Jami Maguire (October 5, 2021, Zoom); Jill Bennett (October 10, 2021, Atlanta, GA); Skyler Jay (October 10, 2021, Atlanta, GA); Christa Suppan (October 1, 2021, Zoom); Lynn Hearn (October 11, 2021, Nashville, TN); BeBe McQueen (October 11, 2021, Nashville, TN); Xtina Suzanne Hamilton (July 18, 2021, Richmond, VA); Kristen (July 18, 2021, Richmond, VA); Vickie Keener (May 17, 2022, Zoom); Annette Stone (August 4, 2021, Zoom; April 2, 2024, Riverside); Jennifer Alomari (April 8, 2024, Riverside); Mamie B. Johnson (April 15, 2024, phone); Danielle Spring and Julie Toupin (May 3, 2023, Worcester, MA).

PREFACE

1. Lena Wilson, "Where Did All the Lesbian Bars Go?" *New York Times*, May 7, 2020, updated April 15, 2021, https://www.nytimes.com/2020/05/07/arts/television/lesbian-bars-vida-l-word-batwoman.html.

2. Dorothy Hastings, Joshua Barajas, Chloe Jones, and Bella Isaacs-Thomas, "21 Lesbian Bars Remain in America. Owners Share Why They Must Be Protected," PBS NewsHour, June 10, 2021, https://www.pbs.org/newshour/arts/21-lesbian-bars-remain-in-the-america-owners-share-why-they-must-be-protected.

CHAPTER ONE: EVE'S HANGOUT

1. Bonhams, "Only Known Copy of the Only Book by the Remarkable Eve Adams," https://www.bonhams.com/auction/29312/lot/3, accessed on May 1, 2025.

2. Evelyn Addams [Eve Adams; Eva Kotchever, pseud.], *Lesbian Love* (New York: Privately printed, 1925).

3. Addams, *Lesbian Love*.

4. Barbara Kahn, interview, October 17, 2022.

5. Addams, *Lesbian Love*, 14.

6. NYC LGBT Historic Sites Project, "Eve's Hangout," https://www.nyclgbtsites.org/site/eve-addams-tearoom/.

7. Addams, *Lesbian Love*.

8. Addams, *Lesbian Love*.

9. "1891, June 15 (Julian Calendar): Birth Certificate of Chawa Zloczewer," Eve Adams: Documents, by Jonathan Ned Katz, OutHistory, https://outhistory.org/exhibits/show/evad/birth, accessed August 21, 2025.

10. "1912, May 25–June 4: Eve's Departure & Arrival Document," Eve Adams: Documents, by Jonathan Ned Katz, OutHistory, https://outhistory.org/exhibits/show/evad/depar, accessed August 21, 2025.

11. Jonathan Ned Katz, *The Daring Life and Dangerous Times of Eve Adams* (Chicago: Chicago Review Press, 2021).

12. *American Experience*, "Mother Earth First Volume," PBS, https://www.pbs.org/wgbh/americanexperience/features/goldman-mother-earth-first-volume/, accessed August 21, 2025.

13. Emma Goldman, *Mother Earth* 7, no. 4, June 1912 (New York: Greenwood Reprint Corporation, 1968), 118, HathiTrust, https://babel.hathitrust.org/cgi/pt?id=mdp.39015037030171&seq=118.

14. Goldman, *Mother Earth*, 118.

15. *American Experience*, "Emma Goldman (1869–1940)," PBS, https://www.pbs.org/wgbh/americanexperience/features/goldman-1869-1940/, accessed August 21, 2025.

16. Katz, *The Daring Life and Dangerous Times of Eve Adams*.

17. Warren W. Grimes, "Eva Adams: I. W. W. Organizer," Department of Justice, Washington, DC, July 14, 1919, Eve Adams: Documents, by Jonathan Ned Katz, OutHistory, https://outhistory.org/exhibits/show/evad/boi/grimes.

18. Addams, *Lesbian Love*.

19. Declaration of Intent for Eve Adams, September 11, 1923, Supreme Court of New York County, New York, New York, Eve Adams: Documents, by Jonathan Ned Katz, OutHistory, https://outhistory.org/exhibits/show/evad/item/4907.

20. Katz, *The Daring Life and Dangerous Times of Eve Adams.*

21. *Record of Hearing in the Case of Chawa (Eve) Zlotchever, alias Eve Adams or Evelyn Adams*, deportation hearing transcript, Women's Workhouse, Welfare Island, New York, November 30, 1926, US National Archives, Washington, DC; copy provided by Barbara Kahn.

22. *Record of Hearing in the Case of Chawa (Eve) Zlotchever.*

23. New York Penal Law § 1141 (1920).

24. *Record of Hearing in the Case of Chawa (Eve) Zlotchever.*

25. Robert Edwards, ed., *The Quill* 18, no. 6 (June 1926): 28, https://babel.hathitrust.org/cgi/pt?id=uc1.b5182164&view=1up&seq=108&q1=eve%27s+hangout, accessed April 30, 2025.

26. Robert Edwards, ed., *The Quill* 10, no. 4 (April 1922), 9, https://babel.hathitrust.org/cgi/pt?id=uc1.b5182154&view=1up&seq=13&q1=i+hate+women, accessed April 30, 2025.

27. "Evelyn Addams, 1 Yr. and Deportation," *Variety*, July 7, 1926, 33, https://archive.org/details/variety83-1926-07/page/n31/mode/2up, accessed April 30, 2025.

28. "Eve Addams' Ring of Rich Cultists," *Variety*, July 28, 1926, 37, https://archive.org/details/variety83-1926-07/page/n205/mode/2up, accessed April 30, 2025.

29. Thomas R. Minnick to Benjamin M. Day, Commissioner of Immigration, October 4, 1926, accessed at OutHistory, "Eve Adams: Documents, by Jonathan Ned Katz," https://outhistory.org/exhibits/show/evad/dep/con.

30. Immigration Act of 1917, Pub. L. No. 64-301, 39 Stat. 874 (1917).

31. Katz, *The Daring Life and Dangerous Times of Eve Adams*, 55–56.

32. *Record of Hearing in the Case of Chawa (Eve) Zlotchever.*

33. Addams, *Lesbian Love.*

34. *Record of Hearing in the Case of Chawa (Eve) Zlotchever.*

35. *Record of Hearing in the Case of Chawa (Eve) Zlotchever.*

36. Warrant of Deportation for Chawa Eva Zlotczewer, December 7, 1927, accessed at OutHistory, "Eve Adams: Documents, by Jonathan Ned Katz," https://outhistory.org/exhibits/show/evad/dep/war.

37. Eve Adams, Warsaw, to Ben, Anna, and Brutus Reitman, February 15, 1929, accessed at OutHistory, "Eve Adams: Documents, by Jonathan Ned Katz," https://outhistory.org/exhibits/show/evad/evc/ben1a.

38. Eve Adams to Ben Reitman, August 15, 1934, accessed at OutHistory, "Eve Adams: Documents, by Jonathan Ned Katz," https://outhistory.org/exhibits/show/evad/evc/aug15.

39. Eve Adams to Ben Reitman, September 1, 1941, accessed at OutHistory, "Eve Adams: Documents, by Jonathan Ned Katz," https://outhistory.org/exhibits/show/evad/evc/19410901.

40. "Eva Chawa Zloczower," internment card, Drancy camp, December 7, 1943, accessed at OutHistory, "Eve Adams: Documents, by Jonathan Ned Katz," https://outhistory.org/exhibits/show/evad/eaic; "Hella Soldner nee Olstein," internment card, Drancy camp, December 14, 1943, accessed at OutHistory, "Eve Adams: Documents, by Jonathan Ned Katz," https://outhistory.org/exhibits/show/evad/hosd.

41. Yad Vashem, "Transport 63 from Drancy, Camp, France to Auschwitz Birkenau, Extermination Camp, Poland on 17/12/1943," https://collections.yadvashem.org/en/deportations/5092635.

42. Yad Vashem, "Eva Zloczower," https://collections.yadvashem.org/en/names/3233042; Yad Vashem, "Hella Soldaner," https://collections.yadvashem.org/en/names/3220405.

CHAPTER TWO: HENRIETTA HUDSON

1. Centers for Disease Control and Prevention (CDC), "HIV/AIDS and HIV Infection: United States, 1981–1990," *Morbidity and Mortality Weekly Report* 40, no. 53 (1992): 1–13, https://www.cdc.gov/mmwr/preview/mmwrhtml/00001880.htm.

2. John Paul Brammer, "Meet the 'Quiet Heroes' Who Cared for AIDS Patients in the '80s," *Them*, August 23, 2018, https://www.them.us/story/quiet-heroes-doc.

3. *Cruising*, podcast (@cruisingpod), Instagram video, Diane "Cubby" Johnson, October 21, 2024, https://www.instagram.com/reel/DBZ5nzpNEqh/. On Cape Cod Hospital, see letter from the Provincetown AIDS Support Group to Philip Johnston, regional director of Health and Human Services, Boston, August 9, 1995, and Paula Peters Maher, "Woman Charges Hospital Guards," *Cape Cod Times*, July 14, 1995; both available at https://provincetownhistoryproject.org/PDF/asg_000_008-letter-from-dept-health-human-services-to-cape-cod-hospital.pdf.

4. Women's Museum of California, "The Blood Sisters of San Diego," *Women's Museum of California* (blog), April 10, 2019, https://womensmuseum.wordpress.com/2019/04/10/the-blood-sisters-of-san-diego/.

5. Philip Boffey, "Reagan Defends Financing for AIDS," *New York Times*, September 18, 1985, https://www.nytimes.com/1985/09/18/us/reagan-defends-financing-for-aids.html.

6. US Department of Health and Human Services, "A Timeline of HIV and AIDS," 2024, https://www.hiv.gov/hiv-basics/overview/history/hiv-and-aids-timeline.

7. ACT UP, "ACT UP Capsule History 1987," https://actupny.org/documents/cron-87.html, accessed May 25, 2025.

8. Devin-Norelle, "How Henrietta Hudson's Owner Plans to Keep Her Iconic NYC Lesbian Bar Alive," *Them*, May 19, 2020, https://www.them.us/story/henrietta-hudsons-owner-plans-to-keep-her-iconic-nyc-lesbian-bar-alive.

9. Comments by @holagemeny and @b_takes_brooklyn on Instagram post by @henriettahudson, "The Evolution," Instagram, https://www.instagram.com/p/CNap17fpvWu/.

CHAPTER FOUR: GINGER'S

1. "Julie's Place," *Lost Womyn's Space* (blog), December 10, 2014, https://lostwomynsspace.blogspot.com/2014/12/julies-lounge.html.

2. NYC LGBT Historic Sites Project, "La Papaya," https://www.nyclgbtsites.org/site/la-papaya/, accessed May 3, 2025.

3. NYC LGBTQ Historic Sites Project, "Lesbian Herstory Archives," https://www.nyclgbtsites.org/site/lesbian-herstory-archives/, accessed May 3, 2025.

4. NYC LGBT Historic Sites Project, "Rising Cafe," https://www.nyclgbtsites.org/site/rising-cafe/, accessed May 3, 2025.

5. Constance Curtis, "Jim Crow School Kids as Mentally Unfit," *New York Amsterdam News*, May 25, 1946, New York Civil Rights History Project, accessed at https://nyccivilrightshistory.org/gallery/jim-crow-school-kids/.

CHAPTER FIVE: THE BUSH

1. Alex Bollinger, "Trinidad & Tobago Bans Homosexuality . . . Again," *LGBTQ Nation*, March 28, 2025, https://www.lgbtqnation.com/2025/03/trinidad-tobago-bans-homosexuality-again/.

2. Alison Bechdel, *Dykes to Watch Out For*, comic strip, originally published 1983–2008; reprinted in *The Essential Dykes to Watch Out For* (New York: Houghton Mifflin, 2008).

3. NYC LGBTQ Historic Sites Project, "Ramrod," https://www.nyclgbtsites.org/site/ramrod/, accessed May 3, 2025.

CHAPTER SIX: A LEAGUE OF HER OWN AND AS YOU ARE

1. Michael K. Lavers, "Sale of Phase 1 Ends 45-Year Run as Lesbian Bar," *Washington Blade*, April 6, 2017, https://www.washingtonblade.com/2017/04/06/sale-phase-1-ends-45-year-run-lesbian-bar/.

2. Council of the District of Columbia, DC Law 23–51, Community Safety and Health Amendment Act of 2019, https://code.dccouncil.gov/us/dc/council/laws/23-51, accessed May 3, 2025.

3. TheHillisHome (@theHillisHome), "Email from Pope Barrow to ANC Commissioners [Screenshot]," Twitter, January 6, 2022, 11:33 a.m. https://x.com/theHillisHome/status/1479189892211093511.

4. TheHillisHome (@theHillisHome), "Email from Pope Barrow to ANC Commissioners."

5. Capitol Hill Advisory Neighborhood Commission 6B, *Special Meeting*, January 25, 2022, Webex video recording, https://dcnet.webex.com/recordingservice/sites/dcnet/recording/c38659d6606d103abe7f00505681a6ea/playback, accessed May 3, 2025.

6. Advisory Neighborhood Commission 6B, *Special Meeting*, January 25, 2022.

CHAPTER SEVEN: LOST & FOUND AND EXECUTIVE SWEET

1. Jacqueline Serrato, Charmaine Runes, and Pat Sier, "Mapping Chicago's Racial Segregation," *South Side Weekly*, February 24, 2022, https://southsideweekly.com/mapping-chicagos-racial-segregation/.

2. Adam M. Rhodes, "'We're Not Asking for Any More Than What We Are Already Deserved,'" *Chicago Reader*, November 25, 2020, https://chicagoreader.com/news/were-not-asking-for-any-more-than-what-we-are-already-deserved/.

3. Maggie Sivit and Ari Mejia, "Traveling Parties Are Part of a Queer Chicago Culture of Partying as Resistance," WBEZ, July 1, 2022, https://www.wbez.org/curious-city/2022/07/01/the-history-of-executive-sweet-parties-in-chicago.

4. Windy City Staff, "Executive Sweet Celebrates 25 Years," *Windy City Times*, December 20, 2006, https://windycitytimes.com/2006/12/20/executive-sweet-celebrates-25-years/.

5. Sivit and Mejia, "Traveling Parties Are Part of a Queer Chicago Culture of Partying as Resistance."

6. Tracy Baim, photo of Pat McCombs, "Executive Sweet Hosts Reunion," *Windy City Times*, July 14, 2013, https://windycitytimes.com/2013/07/14/executive-sweet-hosts-reunion/.

CHAPTER EIGHT: NOBODY'S DARLING

1. NYC LGBTQ Historic Sites, "David Mancuso Residence/The Loft," https://www.nyclgbtsites.org/site/david-mancuso-residence-the-loft/; Piotr Orlov, "Still Saving the

Day: The Most Influential Dance Party in History," NPR, February 19, 2020, https://www.npr.org/2020/02/19/807333757/.

2. Orlov, "Still Saving the Day."

3. Melody Mercado, "The Warehouse, Birthplace of House Music, Takes Key Step Toward Becoming a Chicago Landmark," *Book Club Chicago*, April 13, 2023, https://blockclubchicago.org/2023/04/13/the-warehouse-birthplace-of-house-music-takes-first-key-step-toward-becoming-a-chicago-landmark/.

CHAPTER NINE: DOROTHY

1. James Roman, letter to the editor, *Los Angeles Times*, September 8, 2001, https://www.latimes.com/archives/la-xpm-2001-sep-08-me-43587-story.html.

CHAPTER TWELVE: WALKER'S PINT

1. State of Wisconsin v. Sharon A. Dixon, No. 01-0261-CR (Wis. Ct. App. Oct. 16, 2001), https://www.wicourts.gov/ca/opinion/DisplayDocument.html?content=html&seqNo=3555.

2. Dish Grand Opening (flyer), 1997, Wisconsin LGBT History Project Archive, https://archive.wislgbthistory.com/business/bars/d-bars/dish/dish_9710-ISv14-21.jpg.

3. BizTimes Staff, "Walker's Point Emerges as One of Milwaukee's Hottest Neighborhoods," *BizTimes Milwaukee*, October 14, 2013, https://biztimes.com/walkers-point-emerges-as-one-of-milwaukees-hottest-neighborhoods/.

CHAPTER THIRTEEN: BLUSH & BLU

1. Complaint and Jury Demand, Feltner et al. v. Dragonfly Entertainment Group LLC et al., No. 21-cv-03052 (D. Colo. Nov. 12, 2021), https://towardsjustice.org/wp-content/uploads/2021/11/2021.11.12-Filed-Blush-Complaint.pdf.

2. Complaint and Jury Demand, *Feltner et al. v. Dragonfly Entertainment Group.*

3. Complaint and Jury Demand, *Feltner et al. v. Dragonfly Entertainment Group.*

4. Complaint and Jury Demand, *Feltner et al. v. Dragonfly Entertainment Group.*

5. Complaint and Jury Demand, *Feltner et al. v. Dragonfly Entertainment Group.*

6. Complaint and Jury Demand, *Feltner et al. v. Dragonfly Entertainment Group.*

7. *Settlement Agreement Between the City and County of Denver Auditor's Office and Dragonfly Entertainment Group LLC d/b/a Blush & Blu and Jody Bouffard*, October 2024, provided to Sarah Gabrielli by Beccah Schecter and subsequently shared with the author.

8. Sarah Scoles, "Inside Colorado's Last Lesbian Bar," *5280*, December 2021, https://www.5280.com/inside-colorados-last-lesbian-bar/.

9. Tiney Ricciardi, "Denver Is Home to One of Just 21 Lesbian Bars in the U.S.," *Denver Post*, June 24, 2021, https://www.denverpost.com/2021/06/24/blush-blu-denver-lesbian-bars/.

CHAPTER FOURTEEN: MONA'S

1. Mona Hood, Reba Hudson, and Rikki Streicher interview by Nan Alamilla Boyd, July 25, 1992, Wide Open Town History Project Records 2003–05, GLBT Historical Society, San Francisco, CA.

2. Hood, Hudson, and Streicher interview.

3. "Savage Maidens—Mona Sargent and Phyllis St. Claire," *San Francisco Examiner*, February 7, 1937, https://www.newspapers.com/image/457671630; "Heroine—Mona

Sargent," *San Francisco Examiner*, August 23, 1936, https://www.newspapers.com/image/457798907; "Costly Drink—Before Judge Dunn . . . Mona Sargent," *San Francisco Examiner*, March 17, 1938, https://www.newspapers.com/image/457510907/.

4. Hood, Hudson, and Streicher interview.

5. Hood, Hudson, and Streicher interview.

6. Harvey Smith, "The New Deal Artists of the Monkey Block," *Living New Deal* (blog), March 30, 2021, https://livingnewdeal.org/the-new-deal-artists-of-the-monkey-block/.

7. All information and quotes about Mona's life at the Monkey Block and later opening Mona's, Mona's Barrelhouse, and Mona's 440 club are from Hood, Hudson, and Streicher interview.

8. *Beverly Shaw Performs at Mona's 440*, circa 1940s, Wide Open Town History Project Records, GLBT Historical Society, Collection #2003–05, https://www.glbthistory.org/wide-open-town-records.

9. Advertisement for Gladys Bentley's performances, circa 1940s, Wide Open Town History Project Records, GLBT Historical Society, Collection #2003–05, https://www.glbthistory.org/wide-open-town-records.

10. Dick Boyd, "Before the Castro: North Beach, a Gay Mecca," *FoundSF* (blog), 2010, https://www.foundsf.org/Before_the_Castro:_North_Beach,_a_Gay_Mecca.

11. Hood, Hudson, and Streicher interview.

12. Hood, Hudson, and Streicher interview.

13. Hood, Hudson, and Streicher interview. During the interview, Mona reads aloud from an unnamed article.

14. Hood, Hudson, and Streicher interview.

15. "'Mona' Beaten by Mate," *San Francisco Examiner*, June 6, 1949, https://www.newspapers.com/image/457306256/.

16. "'Mona' Freed in Drunk Case," *San Francisco Examiner*, June 7, 1949, https://www.newspapers.com/image/457307294/.

17. Hood, Hudson, and Streicher interview.

18. Hood, Hudson, and Streicher interview.

19. "Ramona Hood," obituary, Legacy.com, https://www.legacy.com/obituaries/name/ramona-hood-obituary?pid=104582.

20. Hood, Hudson, and Streicher interview.

CHAPTER FIFTEEN: MAUD'S

1. *Last Call at Maud's*, directed by Paris Poirier (San Francisco, CA: Frameline, 1993), film.

2. Mona Hood, Reba Hudson, and Rikki Streicher interview by Nan Alamilla Boyd, July 25, 1992, Wide Open Town History Project Records #2003–05, GLBT Historical Society, San Francisco, CA.

3. Rikki Streicher interview by Nan Alamilla Boyd, January 22, 1992, Wide Open Town History Project Records #2003–05, GLBT Historical Society, San Francisco, CA.

4. *Last Call at Maud's*.

5. Streicher interview.

6. Streicher interview.

7. Streicher interview.

8. Streicher interview.

9. Streicher interview.
10. Streicher interview.
11. *Last Call at Maud's.*
12. Streicher interview.
13. Streicher interview.
14. Streicher interview.
15. Streicher interview.
16. Streicher interview.
17. Streicher interview.
18. Streicher interview.
19. Rich Manning, "How a Topless Bar Helped End California's Ban on Women Bartending," *VinePair*, November 22, 2023, https://vinepair.com/articles/california-women-bartender-ban-history/.
20. Streicher interview.
21. Streicher interview.
22. New Group NYC, "About," https://newgroupnyc.com/about, accessed May 30, 2025.
23. Streicher interview.
24. Associated Press, "Rikki Streicher, 68, Gay Rights Leader," *New York Times*, August 24, 1994, https://www.nytimes.com/1994/08/24/us/rikki-streicher-68-gay-rights-leader.html.

CHAPTER SEVENTEEN: GOSSIP GRILL

1. The Sisters of Perpetual Indulgence, https://www.thesisters.org/, accessed August 21, 2025.
2. The Sisters of Perpetual Indulgence.
3. The Sisters of Perpetual Indulgence Archive, "The Founding of The Sisters of Perpetual Indulgence: 1979–1982," https://spiarchive.omeka.net/s/the-sisters-of-perpetual-indulgence-archive/page/founding_timeline, accessed August 21, 2025.
4. Centers for Disease Control and Prevention, "A Cluster of Kaposi's Sarcoma and Pneumocystis Carinii Pneumonia Among Homosexual Male Residents of Los Angeles and Orange Counties, California," *Morbidity and Mortality Weekly Report* 31, no. 23 (June 18, 1982): 305–7, https://www.cdc.gov/mmwr/preview/mmwrhtml/00001114.htm.
5. The Sisters of Perpetual Indulgence, *Play Fair*, 1982, AIDS History Project Ephemera Collection, MSS 2000–31, UC San Francisco Library, Special Collections, https://calisphere.org/item/5cafc7e3-63d2-4e35-be05-1cab00b065c0/.
6. The Sisters of Perpetual Indulgence, *Play Fair.*
7. The Sisters of Perpetual Indulgence, "World Orders," https://www.thesisters.org/world-orders, accessed August 21, 2025.
8. Jennifer Medina, "Human Error Investigated in California Blackout's Spread to Six Million," *New York Times*, September 9, 2011, https://www.nytimes.com/2011/09/10/us/10power.html?scp=1&sq=blackout&st=cse.

CHAPTER EIGHTEEN: REDZ

1. Nancy Valverde interviews by Lillian Faderman, October–November 2004, June L. Mazer Lesbian Archives, West Hollywood, California.
2. Valverde interviews.

3. Allyson Vergara, "A Street Corner in Downtown L.A. Honors LGBTQ Community and Civil Rights Pioneers," *Los Angeles Daily News*, June 24, 2023, https://www.dailynews.com/2023/06/24/a-street-corner-in-downtown-l-a-honors-lgbtq-community-and-civil-rights-pioneers/.

4. Vergara, "A Street Corner in Downtown L.A. Honors LGBTQ Community and Civil Rights Pioneers."

CHAPTER NINETEEN: THE WILDROSE

1. US House of Representatives, "Abzug, Bella Savitzky," History, Art & Archives, https://history.house.gov/People/Detail/8276, accessed May 26, 2025.

2. Schuster v. Schuster, 90 Wn.2d 626, 585 P.2d 130 (Wash. 1978), https://law.justia.com/cases/washington/supreme-court/1978/44433-1.html.

3. Visit Seattle, "Capitol Hill," https://visitseattle.org/neighborhoods/capitol-hill/, accessed August 21, 2025.

CHAPTER TWENTY: THE SPORTS BRA

1. Jo Yurcaba and Brooke Sopelsa, "Women's Sports Bars Quadruple in the U.S. by 2025," NBC News, March 21, 2025, https://www.nbcnews.com/nbc-out/out-life-and-style/womens-sports-bars-quadruple-us-2025-rcna196763.

CHAPTER TWENTY-ONE: DOC MARIE'S

1. Brandon Tensley, "How the Memory of Stonewall Lives On in a Meme," *The Atlantic*, July 1, 2019, https://www.theatlantic.com/entertainment/archive/2019/07/who-threw-first-brick-stonewall-meme/592999/.

2. Ellena Rosenthal, "Who Crushed the Lesbian Bars? A New Minefield of Sexual Politics," *Willamette Week*, November 30, 2016, https://www.wweek.com/culture/2016/11/30/who-crushed-the-lesbian-bars-a-new-minefield-of-sexual-politics/.

3. Email from the Marie Equi Worker's Collective to Olga and Dmitri Bichko, July 3, 2022, provided to author by Olga Bichko, December 10, 2022.

4. All references to Instagram content originally posted on July 4, 2022, from @marie_equi_workers_collective, account and post since deleted. Screenshot in author's possession.

5. OSHA complaint shared by Doc Marie's, dated July 8, 2022, personal communication with author, December 10, 2022.

6. Katie Herzog and Jesse Singal, "Enjoy Your Death Trap, Ladies!" *Blocked and Reported*, podcast audio, episode 122, July 9, 2022, https://www.blockedandreported.org/p/episode-122-enjoy-your-death-trap.

7. Herzog and Singal, "Enjoy Your Death Trap, Ladies!"

8. Anti-Defamation League, "Online Amplifiers of Anti-LGBTQ+ Extremism," January 24, 2023, https://www.adl.org/resources/article/online-amplifiers-anti-lgbtq-extremism.

9. *Libs of TikTok*, "Lesbian Bar Shuts Down One Week After Opening Because They Weren't Woke Enough," Substack, July 19, 2022, https://www.libsoftiktok.com/p/lesbian-bar-shuts-down-one-week-after.

CHAPTER TWENTY-TWO: ALICE BRADY'S AND CHARLENE'S

1. "Alice Lee Brady," obituary from *Times-Picayune*, March 17–18, 2012, Legacy.com, https://www.legacy.com/us/obituaries/nola/name/alice-brady-obituary?id=8881949, accessed May 26, 2025.

2. “Alice Lee Brady,” obituary.

3. “Alice Lee Brady, obituary.

4. “Dorothea ‘Torchy’ Wilde,” Find a Grave, memorial ID 90067591, https://www.findagrave.com/memorial/90067591/dorothea-wilde, accessed July 30, 2025; “Stacy ‘Stormy’ Lawrence,” Find a Grave, memorial ID 246263332, https://www.findagrave.com/memorial/246263332/stacy-lawrence, accessed July 30, 2025.

5. Dave Doyle, “Miss Dixie: A Gay Icon’s Almost-Forgotten Music Career,” *Syncopated Times*, June 30, 2020, https://syncopatedtimes.com/miss-dixie-a-gay-icons-almost-forgotten-music-career/.

6. Diane Anderson-Minshall, “Legendary Lesbian Bar Owner Miss Dixie Dies at 101,” *The Advocate*, November 19, 2011, https://www.advocate.com/news/daily-news/2011/11/19/legendary-lesbian-bar-owner-miss-dixie-dies-101.

7. “Alice Lee Brady,” obituary.

8. Frank Perez, “Tom Caplinger and How Lafitte’s Went into Exile,” *Ambush Magazine*, March 6, 2024, https://www.ambushmag.com/tom-caplinger-and-how-lafittes-went-into-exile/.

9. Frank Perez, “LGBT+ History: A Local Timeline,” *Ambush Magazine*, November 9, 2023, https://www.ambushmag.com/lgbt-history-a-local-timeline/.

10. Rich Magill, *Exposing Hatred* (New Orleans: LAGPAC, 1989), Newcomb Archives, Newcomb Institute, Tulane University.

CHAPTER TWENTY-THREE: LES PIERRES

1. Elizabeth Fussell, “Constructing New Orleans, Constructing Race: A Population History of New Orleans,” *Journal of American History* 94 (December 2007): 846–55, https://archive.oah.org/special-issues/katrina/Fussell.html.

CHAPTER TWENTY-SIX: ALIBI’S, FRANKIE’S, AND THE WRECK ROOM

1. Advertisement for the Wreck Room, *The Gayly*, July 1985, 14, https://www.gayly.com/archives?field_arc_year_tid_selective=20751.

2. Melissa Wolf and Joseph Johnson, comments on Facebook post by Sarah Gabrielli in *The Wreck Room OKC*, Facebook group, May 22, 2022, https://www.facebook.com/share/p/1EL3hLT2rN/.

3. Barbara Hoberock, “Oklahoma Bill Barring Drag Performances Harmful to Minors Advances out of Committee,” *Oklahoma Voice*, February 11, 2025, https://oklahomavoice.com/2025/02/11/oklahoma-bill-bars-drag-performances-harmful-to-minors/.

CHAPTER TWENTY-EIGHT: SUE ELLEN’S

1. “White Knight: Interview with Sgt. Earl Newsome, Dallas Police Force,” Rodeo, 1992, Linda Jebavy Mitchell Collection (The Dallas Way) (AR0881), University of North Texas Special Collections, https://texashistory.unt.edu/ark:/67531/metadc1584419/?q=earl%20newsom. In some sources he is referred to as Newsom without the *e*.

2. Dallas Police Department, “LGBTQ+ Liaison Officer,” https://dallaspolice.net/communitys/glbtliaisonofficer, accessed August 21, 2025.

3. Associated Press, “Judge Overturns Ban on Gay Police,” *New York Times*, February 5, 1992, https://www.nytimes.com/1992/02/05/us/judge-overturns-ban-on-gay-police.html.

4. “White Knight: Interview with Sgt. Earl Newsome.”

5. “White Knight: Interview with Sgt. Earl Newsome.”

6. "White Knight: Interview with Sgt. Earl Newsome."
7. "White Knight: Interview with Sgt. Earl Newsome."
8. "White Knight: Interview with Sgt. Earl Newsome."
9. The legendary Kathy Jack giving her retirement speech, Facebook video, posted on Sue Ellen's business page, January 19, 2025, https://www.facebook.com/watch/?v=1837293667007507.

CHAPTER TWENTY-NINE: HERZ

1. Rob Gabriele, "2025 LGBTQ+ State Safety Report Cards," SafeHome.org, May 23, 2025, https://www.safehome.org/data-lgbtq-state-safety-rankings/#lgbtq-safety-grades-by-state.
2. Movement Advancement Project, "Alabama's Equality Profile," https://www.lgbtmap.org/equality-maps/profile_state/AL, accessed May 26, 2025.
3. Visit Mobile, "Love Lives Here," official website of Mobile, AL, https://www.mobile.org/plan-your-visit/trip-ideas/lgbtq/, accessed August 5, 2025.

CHAPTER THIRTY: MY SISTER'S ROOM

1. Ivan S., Yelp review of the Independent, March 13, 2009, https://www.yelp.com/biz/the-independent-atlanta?hrid=iIIYiwETWk7nAIsLKVGg1Q&utm_campaign=www_review_share_popup&utm_medium=copy_link&utm_source=(direct).
2. Aadya Rising, https://www.aadyarising.net/, accessed August 21, 2025.
3. Movement Advancement Project, "Equality Maps: Healthcare Laws and Policies," https://www.lgbtmap.org/equality-maps/healthcare_laws_and_policies, accessed May 26, 2025.
4. Georgia Senate Bill 39, 2025–2026 Regular Session, https://www.billtrack50.com/billdetail/1808035.
5. against-stars, "we're watching the new season of queer eye. . . .," Tumblr, January 29, 2019, https://kendermouse.tumblr.com/post/182394014629.
6. Beth McKibben, "Longtime Midtown Lesbian Bar Is Relocating to Crescent Avenue July 7," *Atlanta Eater*, June 27, 2022, https://atlanta.eater.com/2022/6/27/23184618/lesbian-bar-my-sisters-room-relocating-publico-atlanta-crescent-avenue.

CHAPTER THIRTY-ONE: THE LIPSTICK LOUNGE

1. Kathryn Post, "God's Bar: Nashville's Lesbian-Owned Lipstick Lounge Storied for Its Radical Hospitality," Religion News Service, January 23, 2023, https://religionnews.com/2023/01/23/gods-bar-nashvilles-lesbian-owned-lipstick-lounge-storied-for-its-radical-hospitality/.

CHAPTER THIRTY-TWO: BABE'S OF CARYTOWN

1. John F. Harris, "Va. to Drop Its Ban on Gay Bars: State Admits Law Is Unconstitutional," *Washington Post*, October 18, 1991, https://www.washingtonpost.com/archive/local/1991/10/19/va-to-drop-its-ban-on-gay-bars/827fa71c-37db-406f-9c12-29fcf9d5e6c5/.
2. Brandon Walters, "Spreading Fear," *Style Weekly*, January 1, 1980, https://www.styleweekly.com/a-fund-raiser-held-at-babes-prompts-a-curious-response-from-an-anonymous-letter-writer/.
3. Walters, "Spreading Fear."

4. WTVR CBS, "Richmond Bar Owner: 'Get Your Shot or Go Somewhere Else,'" posted June 13, 2021, on YouTube, https://www.youtube.com/watch?v=q-r_5BnOAtEJ.

CHAPTER THIRTY-THREE: HERSHEE BAR

1. Cindy Bray, "ABC Regulations Challenged in Court," Rainbow Richmond: LGBTQ History of Richmond, VA, 1625–2010, OutHistory, https://outhistory.org/exhibits/show/rainbow-richmond/the-fight-continues/abc-regulations.

2. John F. Harris, "Va. to Drop Its Ban on Gay Bars: State Admits Law Is Unconstitutional," *Washington Post*, October 18, 1991, https://www.washingtonpost.com/archive/local/1991/10/19/va-to-drop-its-ban-on-gay-bars/827fa71c-37db-406f-9c12-29fcf9d5e6c5/.

3. NorfolkTV, *Formal Session—Norfolk City Council 6/26/18*, YouTube video, 1:48:33, June 27, 2018, https://www.youtube.com/watch?v=WinPRy8UeQ0&t=6157s.

4. NorfolkTV, *Formal Session—Norfolk City Council 6/26/18.*

5. NorfolkTV, *Formal Session—Norfolk City Council 6/26/18.*

6. Screenshot of Facebook post by Mamie B. Johnson with comments by Mamie B. Johnson and Alma Kesling, originally posted July 5, 2018, shared with Sarah Gabrielli by Jennifer Alomari.

7. NorfolkTV, *Formal Session—Norfolk City Council 10/23/18*, YouTube video, 2:26:20, October 23, 2018, https://www.youtube.com/watch?v=W1YDMwXdWEM&t=7878s.

8. NorfolkTV, *Formal Session—Norfolk City Council 10/23/18.*

9. NorfolkTV, *Formal Session—Norfolk City Council 10/23/18.*

10. NorfolkTV, *Formal Session—Norfolk City Council 10/23/18.*

11. Virginian-Pilot, *Hershee Bar Closes Its Doors*, YouTube video, 1:49, November 1, 2018, https://www.youtube.com/watch?v=63ohpU7zLU4.

12. Curate U, "Kira Kindley: Our Own Podcast," aired October 25, 2021, 5:35, PBS, https://www.pbs.org/video/kira-kindley-our-own-podcast-6pyken/.

13. Annette Stone, text messages to Sarah Gabrielli, April 7–8, 2024, shared with the author.

CHAPTER THIRTY-FOUR: FEMME BAR

1. Worcester County District Attorney's Office, "Worcester Man Charged with Manslaughter in Connection with Overdose Death of Woman," September 2, 2022, https://worcesterda.com/worcester-man-charged-with-manslaughter-in-connection-with-overdose-death-of-woman/.

2. Worcester Police Department, *Incident Report/Warrant Request*, incident no. 2022000027426 (August 7, 2023).

INDEX

NOTE: Many of the people in this book are identified only by their given names or nicknames, while for others, surnames are given as well. To help make everyone identifiable, bar affiliation is shown in parentheses.